Essays on Levinas and Law

Essays on Levinas and Law

A Mosaic

Edited by

Desmond Manderson

Canada Research Chair in Law and Discourse,
Faculty of Law, McGill University

palgrave
macmillan

First published 2009 by
PALGRAVE MACMILLAN

Palgrave Macmillan in the UK is an imprint of Macmillan Publishers Limited, registered in England, company number 785998, of Houndmills, Basingstoke, Hampshire RG21 6XS.

Palgrave Macmillan in the US is a division of St Martin's Press LLC, 175 Fifth Avenue, New York, NY 10010.

Palgrave Macmillan is the global academic imprint of the above companies and has companies and representatives throughout the world.

Palgrave® and Macmillan® are registered trademarks in the United States, the United Kingdom, Europe and other countries.

ISBN-13: 978–0–230–20237–5 hardback
ISBN-10: 0–230–20237–3 hardback

This book is printed on paper suitable for recycling and made from fully managed and sustained forest sources. Logging, pulping and manufacturing processes are expected to conform to the environmental regulations of the country of origin.

A catalogue record for this book is available from the British Library.

Library of Congress Cataloging-in-Publication Data
Essays on Levinas and law : a mosaic / [edited by] Desmond Manderson.
p. cm.
Includes bibliographical references and index.
ISBN-13: 978–0–230–20237–5 (hardback : alk. paper)
ISBN-10: 0–230–20237–3 (hardback : alk. paper)
1. Levinas, Emmanuel. 2. Ethics. 3. Law—Philosophy.
I. Manderson, Desmond.
B2430.L484E76 2008
170.92—dc22 2008029949

10 9 8 7 6 5 4 3 2 1
18 17 16 15 14 13 12 11 10 09

Printed and bound in Great Britain by
CPI Antony Rowe, Chippenham and Eastbourne

To Laurence Grace
Hello

Contents

Acknowledgements

I must begin by extending my heartfelt thanks to the 100 scholars who participated in the *Centennial Conference on Levinas and Law*, held at McGill University in September 2006, and to all those who made it possible. The seed for the idea was sown, and tended assiduously, by Lawrence Knoll, from the Levinas Legacy Foundation; and continual support for the project was provided by Simon Critchley and Peter Goodrich. Thank you for your confidence. The Conference itself relied on the energy and goodwill of a large number of graduate and other students in the Faculty of Law. I have in mind Ryan Fritsch and James Parker, who were the conference administrators, Karen Crawley, just for her calming presence, Tom McMorrow, Lindsay Cheong, Tara Bognor, and many others who always operated unstintingly and without complaint. In addition, I want to extend a special thanks to Dr Sandy Buckley and Lorraine Oades, who together and on short notice, curated an astonishing exhibition of contemporary artworks specifically to coincide with the Conference. The ambience and the interdisciplinary synergy thus created were crucial elements to the event's success. But above all, I wish to thank each and every participant at the Conference, most of whom, of course, are not to be found within the pages of this collection. Yet the community thus forged and the relationships inaugurated during those few days have been tremendously important to me and many others since then, and I hope that some at least of their spirit has found its way between these covers. Thank you.

The Conference provided the initial impetus for this volume, where I listened to many of the papers collected here, and met many of the contributors for the first time. But the work of putting together this book did not, of course, end when the Conference did; on the contrary, it had barely begun. The work could not have grown without the steadying hand of Julie Fontaine in the Faculty of Law at McGill University, and without that institution's continuing support for my research. It could not have flowered without the marvellous help of Rosa Morgan Grahame, whose research assistance while I was on sabbatical at the Australian National University College of Law was crucial, nor without the generous resources and the hospitable environment that the ANU offered me, as it so often kindly does. And, finally, it could not have come to fruition without the able professionalism of the editors at

Palgrave Macmillan for whose commitment and care I am immensely grateful.

Much of the material in the current collection brings together seminal work on Levinas and law which has been written over the past several years, although the preparation of this book has involved the authors in a substantial process of dialogue through which their essays have been modified, developed, refined, or revised. Diane Perpich's essay, 'Getting Down to Cases: Can a Levinasian Ethics Generate Norms?' is adapted from *The Ethics of Emmanuel Levinas* © 2008 by the Board of Trustees of the Leland Stanford Jr. University, all rights reserved. Some aspects of Jonathan Crowe, 'Levinasian Ethics and the Concept of Law' originally appeared in (2006) 19 *Ratio Juris* 421–433. Certain parts of Jill Stauffer 'Productive Ambivalence: Levinasian Subjectivity, Justice, and the Rule of Law' appeared in *Journal of Law, Culture and the Humanities* 3 (2007) 225–243 and are forthcoming in Richard Cohen (ed.), *Levinas and Liberal Democracy* (Albany: SUNY Press, 2008), though in much earlier versions, and animated by a different constellation of thinkers. A substantially different version of Robert Gibbs, 'Verdict and Sentence' was originally published in 14 *Journal of Jewish Thought and Philosophy* 72–89. Desmond Manderson, 'Current Legal Maxims in Which the Word Neighbour Occurs: Levinas and the Law of Torts' draws on material which appeared in *Proximity, Levinas and the Soul of Law* (Montreal: McGill-Queen's University Press, 2006) pp. 51–72; 175–204; and parts of it were also published in (2006) 14 *Tort Law Review* 33, published by the Law Book Co, part of Thomson Legal & Regulatory Limited. A much earlier discussion of the *Bland* case by Marinos Diamantides was published in (1995) 6 *Law and Critique* 2. An earlier and extended version of Sébastien Jodoin 'Subjecthood and Alterity in International Law' was published in (2008) 21 *Leiden Journal of International Law* 1–28. The paper which Simon Critchley presented at the Centenary Conference on Levinas and Law and which appears as 'Anarchic Law' in this volume was also published in (2007) 1 *Law & Humanities* 248–255. An earlier version of Sarah Roberts-Cady, 'Rethinking Justice with Levinas' appeared in (2000) 7 *Philosophy and the Contemporary World* 1–12. In all cases the permission of the publishers to reproduce this material for this collection is gratefully acknowledged. In particular I wish to acknowledge the vital role of journals such as these in the inauguration, articulation, and circulation of ideas.

Above all, and in ways that are hardly capable of definition, thanks is due to those closest to me throughout this process. To Jackie, who gives me the balance and confidence to carry on; and to Laurence, a wellspring of energy and a source of wonder.

Like responsibility itself, then, the present collection is the product of many minds and many hands, who have made it what it is. As the editor, I take full responsibility for *Essays on Levinas and Law: A Mosaic* though I deserve none of the credit. As for the others, as Levinas says, that's *their* business.

Australian National University
Canberra, ACT

12 April 2008

Notes on the Contributors

Simon Critchley is Professor and Chair of Philosophy at the New School for Social Research, New York. He is author of many books, most recently *Infinitely Demanding* (Verso, 2007). *On Heidegger's Being and Time* (Routledge) and *The Book of Dead Philosophers* (Granta/Vintage) will be published in 2008.

Jonathan Crowe is a Lecturer in the T. C. Beirne School of Law and a Fellow of the Centre for Public, International and Comparative Law at the University of Queensland in Brisbane, Australia. His research centres on the theoretical relationship between law and ethics. His work has appeared in leading Australian and international journals, including the *Oxford Journal of Legal Studies, Ratio Juris,* and the *Australian Journal of Legal Philosophy.*

Marinos Diamantides LLB (Athens), LLM (Lancaster), PhD (London) is a Reader in Law at Birkbeck College, University of London. He teaches Constitutional legal theory, medical law, and ethics at undergraduate and postgraduate levels. He is currently writing on monotheism, Islam, and law. He has published extensively and internationally on the intersection of Levinasian philosophy and law and is frequently quoted. His most recent book is *Levinas, Law, Politics* (2007).

Marie A. Failinger is a Professor of Law and has served as Associate Dean for Academic Affairs at Hamline University School of Law, Minnesota, US. She is the editor of the internationally recognized *Journal of Law and Religion,* and teaches and writes in the areas of American constitutional law, civil rights, law and religion, and professional ethics. She formerly worked as a Legal Aid attorney, and is a graduate of Valparaiso University School of Law (JD) and Yale Law School (LLM)

Robert Gibbs is a Professor of Philosophy at the University of Toronto. He is also the inaugural director of the Jackman Humanities Institute. He has published widely on Continental Philosophy and Modern Jewish Philosophy, including *Correlations in Rosenzweig and Levinas* (1992), and *Why Ethics? Signs of Responsibilities* (2000). His current project explores the relation of Law and Ethics.

Dorota Glowacka teaches critical theory and Holocaust studies in the Contemporary Studies Programme at the University of King's College in Halifax, Canada. She is a co-editor of *Between Ethics and Aesthetics* (2002) and of *Imaginary Neighbors: Mediating Polish-Jewish Relations After the Holocaust* (2007), and editor of the special issue of *Culture Machine* entitled 'Community'. She is currently working on the project 'Jewish Memory in Today's Poland and the Polish National Narrative' and completing a book manuscript on representations of the Holocaust between ethics and aesthetics.

Sébastien Jodoin is currently an IBA Fellow in the Appeals Chamber of the United Nations International Criminal Tribunal for the former Yugoslavia as well as a Legal Research Fellow at the Centre for International Sustainable Development Law. He was formerly an Associate Legal Officer in the Trial Chambers of the United Nations International Criminal Tribunal for Rwanda. He holds an LLB and a BCL from McGill University and an LLM in public international law from the London School of Economics and has studied at the Université Libre de Bruxelles. His research interests include international law, legal theory, and international relations.

Desmond Manderson holds the Canada Research Chair in Law and Discourse at McGill University Faculty of Law, Montreal where his teaching and research attempts to connect interdisciplinary scholarship in law, literature, philosophy, and cultural studies with contemporary issues of legal and ethical significance. Recent books include *Songs without Music: Aesthetic Dimensions of Law and Justice, Legal Spaces,* and *Proximity, Levinas, and the Soul of Law.* Current research includes a book on the Shakespeare Moot Project; literature and justice in the work of D. H. Lawrence; and images and visions of the rule of law.

Diane Perpich is Assistant Professor in the Department of Philosophy and Religion at Clemson University. She is the author of *The Ethics of Emmanuel Levinas* (2008) and co-editor of the *Journal of French Philosophy*. She has published essays on continental philosophy, French feminism, and ethics.

Sarah E. Roberts-Cady is an Associate Professor of Philosophy at Fort Lewis College in Durango, Colorado. She teaches courses in ethical theory, applied ethics, feminist philosophies, and history of philosophy.

Her research and publications are focused on ethics, with an emphasis on issues of social justice.

Jesse Sims is a Doctoral Candidate at The New School for Social Research in New York City. He is currently completing a dissertation on subjectivity and transcendence in the early ontology of Levinas. Besides Levinas, his research interests include psychoanalysis, the theory of sovereignty, Derrida, and Nietzsche.

Nick Smith is an Associate Professor of Philosophy at the University of New Hampshire. In 2007 he completed a book titled *I Was Wrong: The Meanings of Apologies* (2007). He is currently working on the sequel to this book, also with Cambridge University Press, applying his framework for apologetic meaning to legal disputes.

Jill Stauffer is Assistant Professor of Philosophy at John Jay College/CUNY in New York City. Her latest publication is an edited volume, with Bettina Bergo, titled *After the Death of a Certain God: Nietzsche and Levinas* (2008). She works on the intersection of continental philosophy with legal and political ethics, interviews philosophers for *The Believer*, and has published in various academic journals.

Part I
Genesis

Introduction

Desmond Manderson

בראשית ברא אלהים as the Torah has it – 'In the beginning God created the heavens and the earth.' But 'in the beginning was the Word' says the Gospel according to John.[1] It is a legalistic revision of the story of origins which found favour with those engaged in the development of Christian institutions, and sought to give them an empirical and unchallengeable foundation. 'In the beginning God created the heavens and the earth.' This is all very well. But an institution, whether a legal system or a church, even if inspired by some transcendental insight, would rather that such a force did not continually destabilize or undermine its authority. God has a tendency to come between commanders and subjects. Law and religion would both rather we just read the Words and do as we're told.

Emmanuel Levinas (1906–1995) thought otherwise. He was a Jewish theologian and philosopher and not a Christian. For him, ethics is the *primum movens* that comes before words and makes them possible. Ethics is an optics, a way of seeing, and in his two major works in particular, *Totality and Infinity (Totalité et infini: essai sur l'extériorité),* first published in 1961, and *Otherwise Than Being (Autrement qu'être ou au-delà de l'essence),* ten years later, he tries to show us how the radical and irenic ethics he there expounds has the power to transform our relation to others.[2] But despite his overwhelming importance as a writer on ethics in the post-war world, and despite its implications for society and justice, little has been written that attempts to explore the relationship of Levinasian ethics to law: of creation to the word.

There are four reasons for that omission. Levinas' writing is poetic and moving, yet it can also be blisteringly obscure, and requires of any reader a considerable investment in time and effort if it is to be appreciated. His work belongs, and is indeed of great importance, to the post-structuralist current of continental philosophy[3] which has to date found only a limited audience within the pragmatic and result-oriented world of legal scholarship. Levinas' writing on law, while suggestive, is fragmentary and at times suffers, I think it is fair to say, from a simplistic understanding. Finally, where Levinas does write about law and about justice, we find a deep and irreparable schism between the ethical relation, intimate, personal, absolute, and singular; and the legal relation, which is none of these things. Law, Levinas himself concludes, is all about 'comparison, co-existence, contemporaneousness, assembling, order, thematization ... the intelligibility of a system. The saying is fixed in a said, is written, becomes a book, law and science'.[4] There are many within the legal profession who rather suppose that law and ethics are contradictions in terms. Ironically, for all the importance that Levinas attaches to our ethical relations with the Other, he might well be disposed to agree.

The genesis of this book lay in a desire to make good that omission, correct those impressions, and address these difficulties. More particularly, the Genesis of this book was an event, or rather two events 100 years apart. The first, the birth of Emmanuel Levinas in Kaunas, Lithuania in 1906 (or 1907, depending on the calendar you use; with Levinas, nothing is entirely certain). The second, to mark it a Centennial Conference on Levinas and Law was held at McGill University in 2006 (of that we can be sure). Over 100 scholars gathered on that occasion to explore the why and the how of Levinas' relevance to law. In the process of sharing their knowledge and, just as importantly, their perplexities, a community was forged. This book arose from that conference, at which I met many of the present authors for the first time, and at which many of the chapters in this collection were presented. But the community extends well beyond the select few found herein, and I take this opportunity to warmly embrace all those who participated with such enthusiasm in the Centennial Conference.

The present collection brings together essays specially commissioned from that conference together with a selection of other work which, over the last few years, have become milestones in our effort to think through the implications of Levinas for law. Not for politics. Not for justice. For law. This has involved these authors in two kinds of inquiries. The first, of a more general character, asks about the relationship of the realms of ethics and law. These questions bring us to the heart of the problematic relationship between something as singular and unpredictable as ethics, and something as general and as committed to predictability as law; between something as protean as ethics and something as rigid as law. Above all, what does it mean to 'apply' Levinas to the concrete world of law? When Levinas asks so much of our responsibility to the Other, and law typically requires so little, can we – indeed, should we – even attempt to bring one to bear on the other? Is 'infinite responsibility', and the theological resonances which Levinas imparts to the domain of ethics, even a good idea? Secondly, however, this collection very expressly goes beyond *whether* we can or should apply Levinas to law, to the more direct question of *how* we might go about it. Many of the chapters in this collection attempt to work elements of Levinas' teachings about our relationships with others and our responsibilities to them, into or against the grain of specific legal institutions, and specific areas of law. How might an 'ethics of alterity' alter our approach to human rights, discrimination, immigration? Do legal frameworks and processes – the common law, the courtroom, international bodies – have any place for Levinas' idealism, for his compassion, for the disturbing demands he makes of us?

Essays on Levinas and Law is applied ethics *and* applied law. If this accounts for its range and eclecticism, it accounts also for its passion and dynamism. The folly is to think there might be an audience for such an engagement. Are there students of philosophy and of ethics out there for whom legal institutions are not a dirty little secret but a crucial realm in which to put their ideas to the test? Are there students of law out there for whom ethics is not a dirty little secret but a vital realm against which to measure their structures and solutions? Kevin Costner in *Field of Dreams* famously says, of a ballpark being built in the desert (a folly in the strictly architectural sense), 'If you build it, they will come.' The current collection likewise aspires not only to respond to an interest in applying Levinas to law, but to constitute that interest. Ethics, in this way, is also a field of dreams, a folly.[5] As Levinas remarked, it 'is like goodness – the Desired does not fulfil it, but deepens it'.[6] This book is not intended to *satisfy* a need, but to awaken one.

* * *

This raises a question of tone or balance to which these chapters have responded diversely. To what extent should we assume a knowledge of law or a knowledge of Levinas amongst our readers? The present collection of chapters is not intended as an introduction to Levinas. It is instead intended bring together and sum up the state of the art. While many of these chapters begin from first principles, some of them assume a certain familiarity the better to engage with an ongoing debate.

Nevertheless, as much as possible references to both law and Levinas throughout this book have been articulated for a reader with only their curiosity to guide them. In addition, each of the four parts into which the rest of the book is divided starts with more generalized discussions and then moves to those which might require greater knowledge of the sources. In that way the chapters have been arranged not only to engage and converse with each other, but to help the reader become increasingly familiar with the nature and implications of Levinas' thought.

These *Essays on Levinas and Law* do not form a single coherent system but a gathering of forces, '*A Mosaic*' as its subtitle implies. The metaphor of a mosaic nicely describes the contributions to this volume, which build up a picture through chapters which each have their own colour, shape, and character. There has been no effort to impose a uniform writing style or perspective. The aim instead has been to give the reader a sense of possibilities in thinking about Levinas and the uniqueness of each of our responses to his work. A mosaic is fragmented but this fragmentation is the source of its strength. Indeed ethics for Levinas is similarly fragmentary in nature. Ethics does not attempt to reduce everything to a system, a structure or a set of rules in which uncertainty is rendered impossible and a single perspective is privileged at the expense of all others. This Levinas called 'totality': it renders impossible any engagement with another person which recognizes and affirms their strangeness rather than merely attempting to assimilate it or deny it. Ethics, then, is that which resists the urge to systematize, and allows the uniqueness and surprise of another person to show itself and in the process to call *us* into question. Ethics sees responsibility as an attentiveness to the unpredictable demands of each irregular and irreplaceable shard of us.

At the same time, the reference to mosaic in the title reminds us of the centrality of Judaism to all Levinas' thought, the philosophical as well as the rabbinical. 'We are faced with the great task of articulating in Greek those principles of which Greece had no knowledge', he wrote. 'The singularity of the Jews awaits its philosophy.'[7] But we are also reminded that the gulf between law and ethics has not always seemed as unbridgeable as it does now. What was Moses but the founder of a religion and a jurisprudence at once? The Moses of the Torah sees God in a burning bush, inexhaustible, ineffable, mystical; but also in stone tablets, finite, linguistic, practical. Yet even the Ten Commandments, written in God's own hand, are broken in anger when the Israelites turned to other gods while Moses was away. The second time, of course, the Ten Commandments are written in a human hand.[8] The imperfection of law or of humans in the face of law, which Moses found so infuriating, always requires the supplement of ethics. In that way, the legal code itself comes to resemble a mosaic, whose broken and irregular surface can only be properly seen by the continual exercise of imagination.

I want to tell you a story though I don't know what it means. When I was seven I was chosen to play the part of the narrator in the school nativity play. The words were painstakingly written out for me by my father in a beautiful Gothic hand, with the help of a dictionary we owned which had calligraphy in it, and placed in a folder of lapis blue to which he added lettering in gold paint. The night before the concert, I left the folder open and face down on top of the washing machine while I tried to memorize its contents – I could have just read the text but I was too clever for that. Around and around I span reciting my lines, while the ink ran and my father's beautiful work was ruined. He was livid or, thinking back to Moses, he went Baalistic. The text he wrote a second time, but in haste and in a much simplified script with only the occasional blackletter flourish. From the audience of course, the folder looked as marvellous as ever, but I knew that what I was reading was only a trace of its former glory. This instilled in me, then and now, a certain shame in my hubris and thoughtlessness. But I also know that the vague memory of that perfection is somehow more powerful an incitement for being lost. And I wonder if this was a moment when I first began to learn about ethics, which no words no matter how glorious or precise could teach me, and about which, no longer having access to the original, I am always learning, always failing, and always trying to express through some feeble second-hand reduction of my own, written in a much simplified script with only the occasional black letter flourish.

I don't know whether the folder still exists. The dictionary does. My father used it to press any four-leaf clovers he happened to find, and though he has been dead for almost 20 years, the clovers are still there. They will crumble if you so much as touch them now.

* * *

Essays on Levinas and Law is broken into five parts corresponding to the five Mosaic books. The next part, *Exodus*, speaks to the foundation of law. The four authors here debate what it means to try to apply Levinas' vision of fragmentary, singular, and infinitely demanding responsibility to law, which appears as the opposite of these things. Diane Perpich argues for a modest position, in which Levinas cannot provide us with any specific ethical content: Levinas does not stand 'for' or 'against' any particular norm. Levinas will not tell you what to do, whether the death penalty or bombing the Gaza Strip is justified, or whether you should visit your aunt in hospital Tuesday. But he does tell you why the question of our responsibility to others, no matter how it is answered in any specific context, is nonetheless of primary importance to our humanity and our legal system. For Perpich, Levinas does not tell us *what* norms we are obliged to hold or enforce; but he does tell us *why* we cannot ignore the normative question in thinking about our lives, our society, and our law. This point, it seems to me, is taken up in Jonathon Crowe's chapter. He too argues that Levinas' claim that ethics comes before philosophy, points to the necessity of some normative criteria in evaluating the legitimacy of law. Crowe has a familiar target in mind. H. L. A. Hart and the whole positivist tradition, in many law schools still the unchallengeable orthodoxy, attempts to defend exactly the opposite, insisting on an absolute separation of legal from moral questions.[9] Crowe, with Levinas, attempts to show us why it can't be done.

The two chapters that follow spread out in different directions from this beginning. Nick Smith, a pioneer in relating Levinas to law, prescribes us a salutary dose of scepticism. He does not merely doubt whether the ethereal Levinas can be pinned down to something as concrete as law. He further doubts whether 'infinite' and 'assymetric' responsibility, the extreme demands it makes on us, and its theological overtones would not in fact do more harm than good. The sacrificial nature of responsibility in Levinas' work seems to Smith alarming where it is not impractical, particularly in relation to areas such as discrimination law, where we are most in need of a legal system which effectively advances the interests of the disadvantaged. In cautioning us that Levinas might prove rather less 'progressive' than many writers assume, Smith presents a challenge to the merits of Levinasian ethics to which any defender will have to respond. It is a challenge which Jill Stauffer (amongst others in this book) takes up, going further than other writers in this part in claiming for Levinas important insights into justice and the rule of law. For Stauffer, the ambivalence which Levinas sets in motion between law's rules and an ethical responsibility which is unable to be pinned down in this way is 'productive'. The self-doubt and uncertainty thus generated is sometimes absolutely crucial to doing justice with, by, or in spite of the rules. In particular, using examples from international law, Stauffer demonstrates that the liberal framework of autonomy and freedom is in need of such ambivalence. In speaking instead of our indebtedness to others and our responsibility to them, Levinas offers to the legal norms of sovereignty and independence a supplement which demands more not only of governments but from every single one of us. She concludes,

> We all enter into the world late and helpless, only to find ourselves responsible for things we never did or intended, and affected by things that far exceed concern for our own safety. Levinas' revision of liberal subjectivity... is more likely to create the kind of person who will become the legal or political subject who would aspire to justice beyond socialized self-preservation.

The following two sections, *Leviticus* and *Numbers*, move from 'law' to 'laws', from form to content, and from the why to the how of applying Levinas. *Leviticus* is the Talmudic Gazette, as it were, the regulatory heart of the Torah which itemizes everything from the death penalty to procedures for the control of infectious diseases.[10] The three chapters in this part all attempt to convince us that Levinas can provide us with a distinct perspective on different areas of substantive law. In the process, all three deal with the question of judgment, that is with the day-to-day application of those rules.

Bob Gibbs, in thinking through the distinction we have already noted between rules which treat everybody the same, and an ethical *face à face* which pays full attention to the uniqueness of the person before us, draws our attention to a similar distinction which operates within the judicial system between the objectivity of the legal verdict and the subjectivity of sentencing. Drawing on Robert Cover, Gibbs helps us see the ethical significance of the singularity and discretion with which the common law has traditionally treated the moment of judgment. At the same time, Gibbs castigates both Cover and Levinas for paying insufficient attention to the details and nuances of the primary materials – case reports and Talmudic passages – and the divergences they reveal amongst the various interpreters – judges and rabbis – at the heart of both traditions. For Gibbs, the differences and doubt opened up by a careful and never tendentious reading of these enduring exegetical conversations are irreplaceable. His powerful and surprising conclusion is that the crossroads of Levinas and law, far from being a contradiction in terms, is in fact the very intersection where 'ethics at last finds its idiom'. My own chapter, which follows, likewise defends the common law against those of its critics who have noisily condemned its indeterminacy. Like Gibbs, I see ethical strength where others see only legal weakness. The legal area I focus on perhaps most immediately resonates with the language of Levinas: 'the duty of care'. On one level, here is where law attempts to explain why and how our responsibility to others arrives, not as a choice but a predicament; here is the legal discourse which dwells, with Levinas, on our infinite and unpredictable obligations to a 'neighbour'. On another level, the very way in which precedent works, inductively and discontentedly, from instance to instance, always reconfiguring its understanding, always circling back as it moves forward, brings us close to an ethical moment in law.

Yet Marinos Diamantides, in the final chapter in this part, warns against too optimistic a vision of law and too tame a vision of ethics. His study challenges our thinking about human beings who after catastrophic injuries, live on, on life support, in a 'persistent vegetative state'. They are the limit case for Levinas' fundamental insight: our responsibility to an other cannot be reduced to what we *know* about them but derives instead from their fundamental mystery and unknowability. But what does it mean to be responsible for a person who exists on the very border of all our knowledge about persons; whose very humanness is both undeniable yet impalpable? How can we act in the 'interests' of someone who has no interests that we can know? Diamantides argues that the affright that this challenge poses to judges, in particular, does not lead them towards an ethical and affective register, but instead to retreat to the safe vacuity of legal rules. While Gibbs and Manderson see the moment of judgment as allowing at least a partial embrace of ethics and human subjectivity, Diamantides suspects only a giddying vertigo as the ground opens up beneath them. For Diamantides, perhaps, the judge too is neither entirely dead like a machine, nor truly humanly alive – but inhabits the legal equivalent of a persistent vegetative state.

Numbers begins with a census[11] and asks, what does it mean to be a community, to 'count' to it, and therefore, to be excluded from it? So our attention shifts from the individual to the collective and in the process to the very heart of the political project that Levinas' attention to 'others' and 'otherness' might excite. In a way we are invited to think not just about our responsibility within a community but our responsibilities *as* a community. Sébastien Jodoin argues that the structure of international law itself is premised on exactly the assumptions of autonomy and choice that Levinas thinks cannot account for the emergence of human selfhood. At international law, States alone are accredited with this 'being'. Jodoin's chapter is at pains to show us the effects of this logic, the ways in which it avoids confronting global interdependence, and its profoundly limited capacity to address human oppression and suffering. An international law which takes the sovereign State as its threshold or horizon of visibility, so to speak, like the domestic law which takes the sovereign individual as its, will find itself equally unable to either see our interdependence or to accept the responsibility for others it entails.

The two chapters that follow take aim directly at the capacity of communities to treat with disinterest or disdain those who have been defined by law or society as outside their purview. Here too the legal system seems determined to shield its horizon of visibility against the other. Marie Failinger provides an intimate and poetic portrait of the legal stratagems through which the law of immigration justifies drawing a line between those that matter and those that don't. Through a careful meditation on the intimate demands of Levinasian ethics, she tries to get us to see the faces where law sees only numbers. This is not easy, 'but at least in acknowledging our *difficulties* as we behold the face of the other and the one more, we can refuse to allow ourselves to be comforted by the so-called justice of totalization... Equity takes risks on behalf of the face, the only risk worth taking in the law'. Dorota Glowacka tells an even more chilling story of what happens to those who are faceless and unbelonging. The massacre by the Polish townspeople of Kielce of 42 returning Holocaust survivors in 1946 shows a capacity to dehumanize those who are not 'us', which was the central problem and trauma with which Levinas struggled. The responsibility of the witness and the possibility of forgiveness lay at the heart of his efforts to expand our notion of community in order to welcome not those who are the same as us but those who are different. But the events at Kielce pose a painful challenge. After such an event, how is forgiveness possible, asks Glowacka, and what is the role of the 'negative' witness who actually participated in such deeds? It is a problem of memory; to murder and then to forget having murdered, and then to deny having forgotten. How deep we bury our conscience. Glowacka does not just offer a cautionary tale. Through Levinas, she suggests also a *relationship* between the transformation of the 'negative witness', forgiveness, and responsibility which, far from 'closing a chapter' or 'ending a conflict' should instead be understood as infinite, asymmetrical, and continuous. Memory, then, does not close the past but opens the future.

Deuteronomy, which was so named because it contains the second statement of the Ten Commandments,[12] might be said to inaugurate the iterative process of law. It marks the moment when the law-giver dies, when legal pronouncement becomes legal discourse and when instruction inevitably turns to debate. From the heights of Mt Nemo, each of the three very different chapters in this final part draw on Levinas to offer us perspectives on the beyond or destination, the Promised Land of law, which is to say, on justice. Simon Critchley, whose work on Derrida and Levinas has been of inestimable importance in the developing conversation between post-structural ethics and law,[13] argues that there is in Levinas an anarchic element which risks being domesticated at the hands of law. While not exactly a plea for ethical imperatives uncontaminated by legal systems, Critchley nevertheless concludes in a speculative mode with a series of questions which might well form a prospectus for future study:

> What if we thought of law in terms of this movement of ambivalence and oscillation between the Saying and Said, between the experience of proximity and the taking of legal decisions? What if the very movement of law were both informed and deformed by the experience of anarchic proximity, an experience that can only be conveyed at the price of its betrayal in the Said? ... Might this not be an anarchic law, a law that has no law at its base and as its basis, where anarchy is understood as the relation of proximity to the neighbour?

Concerning the promise of such an 'anarchic law', Jesse Sims is far from sanguine, echoing in a different register some of the reservations we have already seen expressed by Smith. Sims, in a complex argument, reminds us that Levinas is not the only controversial thinker to be undergoing a refurbishment in our changing world. Carl Schmitt (1888–1985), too, is a growing presence in contemporary debates on politics, authority, and power. Schmitt's close association with Nazism, and his views on sovereignty and war,[14] place him as an exponent of *Realpolitik* and as an anti-ethicist. One might even say that whereas for Levinas the social world begins with 'friendship and faces'[15] for Schmitt it begins with the need for an enemy. And while Levinas insists that our difference from others is both necessary and constitutive, for Schmitt the enemy is 'in a specially intense way, existentially something different and alien, so that in the extreme case conflicts with him are possible'.[16] Yet although their differences are undeniable, Sims boldly brings together the two, arguing that they each see the moment of decision or of action – whether we call it 'ethics' with Levinas or 'politics' with Schmitt – as something exceptional, transcendent, and entirely unbounded by established rules or conventions. For Sims, there is therefore a sub-stratum of *violence* in Levinas which he cannot eliminate and which has the potential to permit, without recourse, all manner of excesses. This violence is given a divine source and the name of ethics, and is instituted for the friend rather than against the enemy; but its unjustified and absolute character remains. 'If the ethical priority of singularity over universality translates into the grounding of law in the exception, we are left with the insoluble problem that the exception can, in practice, justify anything, and the characterization of the exception as divine adds to the justification without improving the practice.' We are left to reflect on how scholars who see ethics as a necessary supplement to law might respond to this criticism, either by seeking to distinguish the violence of ethics as 'this most passive passivity', a kind of non-violent resistance;[17] or again, by trying to articulate a *relationship* between ethics and justice such that their different modes of legitimation continue to inform each other – a movement of oscillation and modification rather than a mere over-riding of one by the other.

This it seems to me is Sarah Roberts' approach in the chapter which closes the volume. Clearly there is a difference between ethics, that personal, unique, and absolute responsibility from me to you, and the legal structure of justice, which concerns balancing 'universal and symmetrical' obligations within a social structure of equality. But the former is neither deracinated by the latter (as Critchley fears) nor supersedes it (as Sims warns). Can we really have justice and ethics at once? Roberts answers in the affirmative: ethics is both the moment in which we question our rules, and thus keep them alive, and at the same time the driving force behind justice. 'The face of the suffering other', she writes, 'does not reach me as an instance of a general or universal category . . . My relationship with the other in proximity gives *meaning* to my relationship to all others as citizens or abstract members of a moral community'. Without the intimacy of ethics, we can neither want nor have the sociality of justice. In the process, and significantly for the arguments throughout this book, Roberts insists that Levinas' failure to see ethics as implicated *within* justice led him to treat the latter, erroneously, as nothing but a rule-bound system. Roberts, then, must ultimately save Levinas from himself. 'Justice', he wrote, 'is written, becomes a book, law and science'.[18] In order to bring ethics and justice together, she begs to differ.

* * *

After reading these chapters we are left with a clearer sense of the issues which confront the application of Levinas to law. Those which comprise *Exodus* might be summed up as ontology, exploring the possibility and the desirability of inaugurating such a relationship. *Leviticus* is epistemology, searching for those fields or aspects of law in which Levinas might offer a promising path to understanding or reform. *Numbers* is topology; it looks to the relationship between the inside and the outside of our legal systems: these chapters critique how law thinks and how law might yet think about our responsibilities to the 'other' of our communities, and in these pages war, dependence, indifference, and genocide all emerge as frameworks for analysis. Lastly (and where else but last?) *Deuteronomy* is teleology, offering both highly sympathetic and sharply critical perspectives on what Levinas contributes to our understanding about the goals or the legacy of law. Anarchy, violence, and justice are each offered up in answer to that question. *Exodus, Leviticus, Numbers, Deuteronomy:* before the law – within the law – without the law – beyond the law. These are the four dimensions of the current book and the dimensions to which any project aimed at working through the implications of Levinas to law, or law to Levinas, must respond.

We are also left with a multitude of questions which should stimulate such projects. They haunt the book and I hope will provoke all who, having read it, wish to pursue its optics. Here, drawn eclectically from the words of all the authors to this collection, is a selection:

- *Can we do without moral dispositions and norms once we have Levinasian responsibility?*
- *Is the obligatory character of law separate from its ethical content?*
- *What is the significance of the rule of law within such an unruly conception of justice? If we should dissolve our reductive categories, for example, how can we advocate for those who suffer from the legacy of discrimination?*
- *Who is responsible for the refugee, the prisoner of war, the sufferer of poverty or famine, the one to whom I never consented to owe a thing? Might it be possible to retain what is important about the subject's autonomy while admitting that vulnerability is the real backdrop to most of our experiences of subjectivity, law, and politics?*
- *What is the meaning of asymmetric responsibility?*
- *What are the implications of the pervasiveness of the State as a category of thought in international law?*
- *Is it possible to take responsibility, even for our own violence and oppression of one more by the other, without conceding the necessity to objectify, reduce, enumerate?*
- *What is the significance of Levinas' emphasis on witnessing in the constitution of the subject with respect to bearing witness after the Shoah? What does it mean in the context of a lynching mob?*

- *What if the very movement of law were both informed and deformed by the experience of anarchic proximity, an experience that can only be conveyed at the price of its betrayal in the Said? Might this not be an anarchic law, a law that has no law at its base and as its basis, where anarchy is understood as the relation of proximity to the neighbour?*
- *Is the injustice of some of Levinas' own politics an aberration or a demonstration of that theory's own ethical grounding in divinely legitimated violence?*
- *Isn't this view of our ethical responsibilities excessive? How could I respond to the demands of so many others? If I can't respond to everyone, how do I choose between this other and that one? If ethics only concerns my responsibilities and I am responsible for the whole world, then am I not leaving myself open to exploitation and oppression? How does Levinas account for my right to protect myself and meet my own needs?*
- *Who am I? What is my responsibility to others? Am I my brother's keeper?*

Essays on Levinas and Law aspires to help constitute, to embolden but also to make more rigorous and more critical, the growing community of students and teachers, lawyers and ethicists, willing and ready for the task of responding to these questions and asking their own. That is what a community is: a group of people united by their disagreements. This *Mosaic* has not attempted to 'lay down the law', to devise a list of Levinasian commandments that all must follow or burn in hell. In resisting such a temptation, the chapters in this collection instead seek to embody an ethics in which both scholarship and law are understood in terms of an open-ended dialogue. This jurisprudence is a difficult freedom,[19] to be sure, but it offers the only chance in which responsibility, learning, and innovation remain possible.

For the authors assembled here, the dangers of an ethical openness across disciplinary boundaries are real: one might not be understood or, worse (like the Emperor's new clothes in the old fable), one might be understood all too well. But these are risks worth running[20] because of the commitment we all share. Levinas is not just musing or amusing or bemusing. The ethics he offers us *matters*, matters to the life we live and the institutions that constitute it. Perhaps now more than ever, when the actions of terrorists against citizens and States against citizens alike contemplate neither ethics nor law as imposing any limits on acceptable conduct; when the crises of global warming and global transformation promise to create unprecedented levels of global dislocation, driving us both towards an acute awareness of our responsibility with others and yet also inciting heightened feelings of fear and selfishness; when the model of justice as an agreement of enlightened self-interest seems to bring us no closer to peace in the Middle East, or Chechnya, or the Sudan, or anywhere else for that matter. Although the authors in this collection do not always agree as to the meaning or value of Levinas' contribution, they do believe that the discussion about ethics and law is one which we urgently need to have.

For my own part, I don't think it is either melodramatic or clichéd to say that we live in worrying times. I think that Levinas, for all his difficulties, offers us new ways of thinking about who we are and how we are connected to others, and new ways therefore of understanding the role of law and the nature of justice. Whether that will be enough to help us through the next little while, I really don't know. What we need, I suppose, is a bit of luck where we least expect it. In honour of which, if you stumble upon a four-leaf clover you might press it between these leaves. In another 20 years perhaps a trace of the foolish hope and the fond memory symbolized here – first verbally then herbally – will remain.

March 2008
Australian National University, Canberra

Notes

1. *Genesis 1:1; John 1:1.*
2. E. Levinas, *Totalité et infini: essai sur l'extériorité* (Paris: Kluwer, 1961); *Autrement qu'être ou au-delà de l'essence* (Paris: Kluwer, 1974); *Totality and Infinity*, trans. A. Lingis (Pittsburgh: Duquesne University Press, 1968) [hereinafter TI]; E. Levinas, *Otherwise Than Being, or Beyond Essence*, trans. A. Lingis (Pittsburgh, Duquesne University Press, 1981) [hereinafter OBBE].
3. See S. Critchley, *The Ethics of Deconstruction: Derrida and Levinas* (Oxford: Blackwell, 1992); D. Cornell, *The Philosophy of the Limit* (London; Routledge, 1992); J. Derrida, *Adieu to Emmanuel Levinas* (Stanford: Stanford University Press, 1999).
4. Levinas, OBBE, pp. 157–159.
5. 'To be good is a deficit, waste and foolishness in a being; to be good is excellence and elevation beyond being': Levinas, 'God and Philosophy' (1975) in E. Levinas, *Collected Philosophical Papers*, trans. A. Lingis (Dordrecht/Boston: Martinus Nijhoff, 1987) 153, p. 165.
6. Levinas, TI, p. 34.
7. S. Hand (ed.), *The Levinas Reader* (London: Basil Blackwell, 1989), p. 87.
8. *Exodus 32:19; 34:27–28.*
9. H. L. A. Hart, 'Positivism and the Separation of Law and Morals,' *Harvard Law Review* 71(1957–1958) 593–629.
10. For example *Leviticus 20; Leviticus 13 & 14.*
11. *Numbers 1–4.*
12. *Deuteronomy 5:6–21*; the first statement is to be found in *Exodus 20:2–17.*

13. See Critchley, *The Ethics of Deconstruction: Derrida and Levinas*.
14. C. Schmitt, *Political Theology: Four Chapters on the Concept of Sovereignty*, trans. G. Schwab (Cambridge: MIT Press, [1922] 1985).
15. Levinas, OBBE, pp. 159–160.
16. C. Schmitt, *The Concept of the Political*, trans. G. Schwab (Chicago: University of Chicago Press, [1927] 1996), p. 26.
17. Levinas, OBBE, p. 115.
18. Ibid., pp. 158–159.
19. E. Levinas, *Difficult Freedom*, trans. S. Hand (London: Athlone Press, 1990).
20. Levinas, OBBE, p. 120.

Part II

Exodus

1
Getting Down to Cases: Can a Levinasian Ethics Generate Norms?

Diane Perpich

Normativity without norms

There is a widespread view according to which Levinas is not engaged in 'ethics' in any of the usual senses in which philosophers, legal scholars, political theorists, or others generally employ the term. As one scholar puts the point, 'Levinas does not treat "ethics" as one branch of philosophy amongst others. And neither does he attempt to construct a normative moral philosophy. Rather his work is a search for the significance of ethics and the ethical.'[1] The parallel with Heidegger's fundamental ontology is clear: just as *Being and Time* is not an ontology in the usual sense but a fundamental ontological inquiry into the question of the meaning of being, so too Levinas's thought is not an ethics per se, but a radical rethinking of the question of the meaning of the ethical. In *Ethics and Infinity*, Levinas himself seemingly endorses this view. Asked about the practical moral implications of his thought, he famously says, 'My task does not consist in constructing an ethics; only try to find its meaning.'[2]

Though one can hardly disagree with this estimation of the aims of Levinas's thought, difficulties arise when his inquiry into the meaning of ethics is held to be entirely separate from normative forms of ethical reflection. In the first place, almost no one – Levinas included – actually adheres to the idea that his thought is completely outside the scope of normative ethics traditionally conceived. When his work is invoked in the name of a respect for alterity, difference, or those construed as 'other' by the dominant culture, when his thought is employed to analyze social, political, and economic injustices, when it is cited as a way to rethink the ethical dimension of relationships between teachers and students, caregivers and patients, judges and defendants, or when it is appealed to by a host of disciplines from psychology and sociology to literary theory and communication studies as they make the 'turn to ethics,' it is well-nigh impossible to see these appropriations as having nothing to do with normative ethical concerns. Indeed, to the extent that Levinas's thought has had an impact outside of narrowly phenomenological and theological discourses, it is his *ethical stance* that has captured readers' attention. Robert Bernasconi makes it plain that this is as it should be: 'the reorientation of thinking that is Levinas's goal... matters *not at all* unless it impacts on our approach to concrete situations so that we come to see them as ethical.'[3] If Levinas's notion of responsibility as a manner of being for the other has no practical impact, if it does not change the way we see ourselves or the situations we confront, then there is little point to invoking his work as a fundamental investigation into the meaning of something all too vaguely called 'the ethical.' But what sort of impact is Levinas's thought supposed to have? What sort *can* it have if it foregoes all connection to normativity and norms? Is it enough merely to be inspired by Levinas's writings to see ourselves as in an ethical relation to the other? Surely this concedes too much to those who are already tempted to view Levinas as no more than a pious moralizer whose poetic or religious writings are accepted by 'disciples' without the benefit of justification.

In order to employ Levinas's thought in all the ways we currently employ it – that is, in a host of practical ethical and political contexts – the relation of Levinas's thought to normativity and, by extension, particular norms needs to be rethought. Levinas's notion of responsibility has a distinctly normative dimension: it is an elucidation of the sense in which we are *bound* by an ethical relation. Moreover, being bound to the other in an ethical relation means, for Levinas, being bound to give an account of oneself – one's actions, judgments, and broader form of life – to the other. But this normative relation does not entail and cannot be used to construct a set of rules or principles that would specify universally and abstractly what it is right or good to do or how we ought to live. In other words, being bound to give an account of oneself is not the same as construing ethics as a matter of moral accounting – of toting up balance sheets or producing algorithms that distinguish right from wrong actions. If Levinas offers us an original and compelling account of normativity, it is nonetheless a normativity without norms.

In what follows, I begin with two fundamental features of Levinas's account of responsibility – its ambiguity with respect to grounds and its simultaneous status as constitutive of subjectivity. I then construct an argument to show how responsibility in this sense responds to the moral skeptic who professes indifference to the other's moral demands. In effect, seeing how Levinas responds to the skeptic allows us to see how normativity is at work in his thought. Finally, I address the question of why normativity in Levinas's sense nonetheless does not produce or underwrite specific norms or moral principles.

Two features of responsibility

As Levinas's notion of responsibility is no doubt well known to readers of this volume, let me recall just two features of his account. In the opening sections of *Otherwise Than Being*, responsibility is described as 'a response answering to a non-thematizable provocation.'[4] The provocation or call cannot be thematized because that which provokes it is not an object for consciousness or something that appears:

> This response answers, before any understanding, for a debt contracted before any freedom and before any consciousness and any present, but it does answer, as though the invisible that bypasses the present left a trace by the very fact of bypassing the present. That trace lights up as the face of a neighbor....[5]

The *trace*, in the Levinasian sense, is not a mark within the world; it is not like the tracks of an animal or the prints left by a thief, both of which represent absence through the presence of a sign. A sign 'is a mark *in* the world, the *effect* of a cause *in* the same world... [and] accessible to an interpreter who would decode them.'[6] The trace, in Levinas's sense, is like the mark that occurs when a thief wipes away his prints. It is an 'overprinting' that is not perceptible as such.[7]

Since responsibility for Levinas has the structure of a trace, that is since it is a response to a face that never appears as such, the face may be said to be something like the site of normativity but not its origin or source. Indeed, there will be nothing that functions so foundationally in the Levinasian account. With respect to the face, Levinas emphasizes that it 'does not function... as a sign of a hidden God who would impose the neighbor on me. It is a trace of itself, a trace in the trace of an abandonment, where the equivocation is never dissipated.'[8] The face is misunderstood if it is thought to operate like a cause or origin of our responsibility and Levinas is clear that it cannot serve as the point of departure for a demonstration of the truth or reality of responsibility. One can neither deduce ethical obligation from the trace, nor find unambiguous evidence of the passing of a face in ethical responsibility. The infinite that calls for or commands my response is thoroughly 'ambiguous,' 'enigmatic,' and 'equivocal.'[9] In an evocative description, Levinas compares the trace to diplomatic language and sexual innuendo in which 'if one likes, nothing has been said.'[10] Thus the face that 'commands' or 'ordains' one to an infinite responsibility is nothing certain or unambiguous. If one likes, one has never been called! This intractable ambiguity is the first point to be noted for the reading developed here.

Levinas further describes responsibility as a matter of 'doing before hearing' or as a situation in which I respond before having been called.[11] To be obliged by a face that passes only in a trace means that 'I am obliged without this obligation having begun in me, as though an order slipped into my consciousness like a thief.'[12] Levinas notes that this will appear paradoxical to views, like those he credits to phenomenology, according to which nothing can be totally alien to the consciousness that thinks it. It is 'as though' responsibility consisted in a movement of obeying before an order had been formulated or as though the order was 'formulated in the very obedience of the one who obeys.'[13] The response to the other is thus paradoxically the very site in which the order to respond is given. In later sections of *Otherwise Than Being*, Levinas speaks of a command that commands me 'by my own mouth'[14] and of an order that is heard only in the response that obeys: 'The order has not been the cause of my response, nor even a question that would have preceded it in a dialogue. I find the order in my response itself.'[15] I am subjected to this order 'before hearing it' or 'I hear [it] in my own saying.'[16] This strange structure of an order that forms in the syllables and on the lips of the one who responds corresponds 'concretely,' Levinas says, to the ordinary event of responsibility for the neighbor.[17] This proximity to the neighbor 'is already an assignation, an extremely urgent assignation – an obligation.'[18] Prior to any commitment on my part, before I can invest this assignation with meaning or make of it a theme for consciousness, I am affected by the other. Indeed, Levinas goes so far as to say that before being for myself, I am for another. It is as if the other were the condition of my own subjectivity. And this is the second feature of the account to be particularly noticed.

The skeptic's question and exposure to the other

Asked 'what would you respond to someone who said that he did not... feel this call of the other, or more simply that the other left him indifferent,' Levinas replied, 'I do not believe that is truly possible. It is a matter here of our first experience, *the very one that constitutes us*, and which is as if the ground of our existence.'[19] Suppose that Levinas's account of responsibility were meant to respond to the moral skeptic who claims indifference to the face of the other and who expresses doubt that there is any such ethical relation to the other or any such moral demand being made. The skeptic asks, 'what is the other to me?' or 'why ought I value the other's demands?' Such questions imply that only a fool is duped into thinking that the other's claims to moral consideration have any kind of binding force apart from that already provided by utility or other prudential considerations.[20] In effect, the skeptic doubts that there are uniquely moral reasons and doubts that such reasons have a normative force that cannot be reduced to self-interest. The skeptic thus asks what reasons there are to value something or someone she has been told she has an obligation to value. She asks why she should think that the other has *moral* value or deserves moral consideration.[21]

Faced with this ordinary sort of moral skepticism, a Levinasian response might[22] begin like this: the idea of valuing something presupposes a world in which this something is meaningful or intelligible. If I value something – regardless of the value I assign to it – this implies I have taken its measure, weighed it against other objects or possibilities, and in some manner understood its connection to my own life or that of others. To be sure, I can be wrong in any of these estimations. I can underestimate the value of what I have and realize my error only too late. Equally, I can overestimate something's value and later come to see that, after all, it was something I was able to live without. Further, my valuing something need not mean that I have gone through an explicit or conscious process of evaluation or reflection. Much of our valuing, in fact, comes about without direct reflection, but a relationship is not one of valuing unless it is possible for it to have been accompanied by some such reflective process. On this account, valuing requires and expresses the fact that I am already reflectively in a world.

To be 'in the world' can be understood here with the full richness Heidegger gives to the term: to be in a world is to be immersed in an open-ended system of relationships, many of which I understand and control, some of which I do not, all of which refer to possibilities of the kind of being that I am myself. What are we to say about how I came to be in a world? While Heidegger takes the question of the worldhood of the world to be one of the fundamental questions of ontology, he would no doubt read the question of *how* we come to find ourselves in a world as an ontic question of little direct interest. On the Levinasian account, however, how we answer the question is crucial. Being in the world, for Levinas, is neither the achievement of a self-supporting subject nor the ontological birthright of *Dasein*. Being in a world presupposes an other who has *opened that world to me and with me*. I do not meet the other *in* the world, rather to have a world (which means being capable of reflection) is already to be in a relationship to the other. Without the other, there is no world; without the world, there is no ego, no 'I' who could be the subject or bearer of experiences within the world.[23] The relation to the other is thus constitutive of my having a world at all.

Though Levinas shies away from developmental models almost as much as Heidegger, we might consider the case of a newborn to illustrate this point: even when only a few months old, a child will use another's hand to grasp what he wants. He holds his father's hand, for example, as that hand grasps a toy or a spoonful of fruit. The other's limbs become an extension of the infant's body as he reaches for something out of his grasp or beyond his ability to manage. Likewise, the toddler's early words, her first demands and observations, are intelligible only to those who have been keenly watching for them and who can interpret the rough syllables as meaningful words and phrases. Context in such cases is everything. Knowing which objects are the child's favorites, and which things she is likely to be 'talking' about, a parent mediates the child's early attempts at conversation to others, helping her be a part of the world long before she can hold her own there. Such observations are as much in an Irigarayan vein as in a Levinasian one, perhaps, but then Irigaray's notion of the touch and the caress is deeply indebted to Levinas's own elaboration of these themes in *Totality and Infinity* and later texts. What is clear in any case for Levinas and Irigaray is that others are not just 'there' *with* me in a world; they are the condition for my having a world *at all*. Others are not co-originary with the world, for Levinas, they are the pre-original condition for any subjectivity and any relation to the world whatsoever.

In *Otherwise Than Being*, Levinas writes somewhat enigmatically that responsibility arises in an 'overemphasis of openness.'[24] The suggestion developed here is that we can read this openness as the opening of and to a world. If subjectivity signifies for Levinas as 'being affected by the other whom I do not know,'[25] this need not mean that the other is literally a stranger or a remote and absent Other. She may well be unknown because there is as yet no 'I' to do the knowing. By the time I become *me* – by the time, in other words, I achieve subjectivity – I am not just susceptible to a single other but deeply vulnerable to a host of others because my subjectivity has been constituted within a series of intimate and dependent relationships that make my meaningful relations to the world possible. Responsibility – exposure and non-indifference to the Other – is thus the condition of subjectivity and mediates its formation. The relation to the other mediates the subject's entrance into the world, though, strictly speaking, the subject does not pre-exist the relation itself.

Levinas's thought, both early and late, insists that the ethical relation precedes the possibility of reason in us and by reason he means the possibility of critical rational activity or thinking. He rarely concerns himself with the question of what sort of thing reason is, except to insist that it is not an abstract, universal Reason with a capital 'R,' but something embodied and creaturely.[26] Rationality, like subjectivity itself for Levinas, is a distinctly social product. To be in a world, to be reflective, to be rational, all have the same condition: the relation to an other who even as he or she is constituted by my reflective, conscious activity, is equally the condition of its possibility.

This realization prepares the final step in the argument which now reads in full as follows: (1) the idea of holding anything as a value presupposes a world in which the thing valued is already meaningful or intelligible. To value thus means that I am already reflectively situated in a world. (2) Being reflectively in the world is the product of a social relationship, which is to say that the relation to the other is constitutive of my being able to value anything whatsoever. (3) Thus, the other person is not merely something or someone that I can value or fail to value. Without an other, there is no world and no meaningful valuing. Hence, the skeptic's question of whether one is obliged to value the other and on what grounds always comes *too late*. It mistakes the other for an object within the world rather than seeing the relationship to the other as the condition of my having a world at all and being able to find value in it. If I value *anything* at all, then, I am already in a relationship to the other. He or she *already* concerns me. What could my continuing to ask for proof of this mean except that I have failed to understand what sort of relationship we have? The other can never be only an object of value within the world concerning which I might rightfully ask why she or her needs should matter to me. By the time I ask these questions, I have already shown myself to be immersed in a complex evaluative practice. In effect, to ask for reasons, to ask why I should concern myself with the other, is itself already indicative of such concern. The skeptic's question thus indicates that the other has already passed that way, already introduced her into a world in which critical reflection is possible.

The reading advanced here, though it often departs from Levinas's own idiom, nonetheless conforms closely to the structure of his thought. If Cain (and sometimes Hamlet) is Levinas's exemplar of the moral skeptic, the skeptical question is this: 'Why does the other concern me? What is Hecuba to me? Am I my brother's keeper?'[27] Levinas maintains that such questions are meaningful only for a subject who pre-exists its encounter with an other: 'These questions have meaning only if one has already supposed that the ego is concerned only with itself, is only a concern for itself. In this hypothesis it indeed remains incomprehensible that the absolute outside-of-me, the other, would concern me.'[28] By contrast, for a subject whose very subjectivity is formed as a response to the other such questions always come on the scene *too late* and it is always too late to be concerned *only* with oneself. Responsibility is not the concern of the subject who already has a history, who already exists; rather, Levinas says, responsibility 'speaks' in the 'pre-history' of the ego.[29] To capture this idea Levinas employs the figure of the *hostage*. I am already bound to the other, already his or her hostage, when 'I' take up my position in being: 'The self is through and through a hostage, older than the ego, prior to principles.'[30] For this reason Levinas is doing more than playing on words when he says that to posit oneself in being, to be posited there or to pose oneself there (*se poser*), is to be exposed *(s'exposer)* to the other, to be already outside oneself, not oneself, or unable to close oneself up in oneself. From the very first moment that one takes up a position as a subject, one is already exposed to and in relation to an other.[31]

Election and reflective endorsement

Totality and Infinity repeatedly tells the reader that the face of the other calls the egoism of the ego into question and subsequently commits that ego to a path of infinite responsibility for the other. The reading proposed here has interpreted that moment not as an empirical, psychological event in the life of an adult ego but as the moment in which the subject or ego is first constituted. This is consistent with Levinas's insistence that being called into question by the other is not equivalent to being conscious of having been called into question. By the time such consciousness has occurred, that is by the time I am explicitly or consciously aware of being challenged by another, I have already become a subject with the ears to hear the other's demands. (Of course, as will be emphasized momentarily, by then I am also someone who can try and even succeed somewhat in turning a deaf ear to the other.) In either case, for the other's demand or question to be intelligible to me *as a demand or question*, for me to receive it as such, I already have to have been constituted – in a past I cannot assume or recuperate within memory – as a subject vulnerable to an other who makes demands and poses questions. The relations by virtue of which I have come to be constituted as a subject able to be addressed and capable of responding are not the product of my own will even if I can make them 'mine' in a subsequent intentional act. Subjectivity thus arises in the accusative before it achieves nominative status.[32]

If this argument is right, then reflection for Levinas does not indicate a consciousness that turns its 'ray' back upon itself, grasping its own thoughts or actions as a new object for thought. Rather, to be capable of reflection means being susceptible to the other, which in turn means being susceptible to the other's demands. In 'Humanism and Anarchy,' we read, 'The subject is a responsibility before being an intentionality.'[33] Formed or brought into being as a subject through its exposure to an other, responsibility – a fundamental social relation – both precedes subjectivity and is a condition for 'concrete' or everyday moral responsibility. Levinas argues that 'Subjection [*asservissement*]' to the Good happens effectively 'before' the subject is a subject, that is before reflection has arrived or is possible. The Good 'is not the object of a choice for it has taken possession of the subject before the subject had the time – that is, the distance – necessary for choice.'[34] To be able to take a distance from one's object means being able to represent it and hence to have presented it in consciousness as an object of reflection. But the Good 'seizes' the subject prior to the possibility of reflection. This does not mean that the Good sneaks up on an ego unaware; it means that the relation to the Good is prior to and facilitates the emergence of a subject. Since a relation to the Good – here synonymous with being for the other, with responsibility, with exposure to the other, and so on – precedes the very being of the subject, it is inescapable: 'There is indeed no subjection more complete than this possession by the Good, this election.'[35]

Is this a kind of servitude or enslavement to the good? Levinas denies the violence this suggests and maintains that 'the subjecting character of responsibility... is nullified by the goodness of the Good that commands. The obeying one recovers his integrity on the hither side of subjection.'[36] I am 'formed' by social relations before I have the capacity to represent them to myself and thus to choose or reject them. Were it not for the other who opens the world to me, I would not become an 'I' capable of reflection and judgment. But once I *am* an 'I' and *am* capable of reflection, I can reflect critically on my being so and think it better to have been subjected to the other in this relation and to be capable of reflection than not. I reflect that it is better to be subject to the Good than not. Thus, according to Levinas, the ego recovers its 'integrity' in the midst of its subjection.

The argumentative strategy Levinas employs here is not unlike the reflective endorsement found in Hume and other moral sense theorists. In brief, reflective endorsement acknowledges a basis for morality over which the subject has no control – in the Humean case because it is a matter of our human nature and our developed dispositions. But this basis nonetheless survives the scrutiny and meets the approval of the moral faculty (which it also forms). Reflective endorsement asks, 'all things considered, do we have reason to accept the claims of our moral nature'?[37] Calling the mental operations that give rise to normative judgments in whatever field a 'faculty' and the normative judgments themselves are 'verdicts,' Christine Korsgaard explains that 'a faculty's verdicts are normative if the faculty meets the following test: when the faculty takes itself and its operations for its objects, it gives a positive verdict.'[38] As she points out, for Hume the faculty of understanding fails the test: 'the harder we press the question whether we ought to believe our beliefs... the more the degree of our conviction – that is, the liveliness and vivacity of the ideas – will tend to diminish.'[39] The faculty of the moral sense, by contrast, passes the reflexivity test. 'Reflection on the origin of our moral sentiments only serves to strengthen those sentiments. The moral sense approves of its own origins and workings and so approves itself.'[40] While it is unclear how to distinguish this approval from the biased approval of a prejudice, this is not necessarily a problem since it only suggests that indeed 'there is no place outside of our normative points of view from which normative questions can be asked.'[41]

Let me be perfectly clear: Levinas is not here being classed with moral sense theorists. To the extent that he rejects unequivocally the view that ethics is a matter of naturally arising moral feelings, he is far from the views of Shaftesbury, Hume, or others in this tradition. The similarity is limited to the *form* of the argument he employs to offset the heteronomous beginnings of ethical life. For Levinas, the relation to the other is the condition for reflection. Reflection, to say it again, is not a naturally occurring capacity but the evidence and product of a prior social relationship; though it is a relationship which *brought forth* or which constitutes the subject who is then said to have been one of the terms of the relationship. It is by grace of the other, then, that rational critique or critical reflection – evaluation and the acceptance of responsibility – is possible for me. Once the other introduces me into critically reflective practices, I can reflect on reflection itself and endorse both its origin and its operation. To express this in Levinas's terms, sometimes people have been thankful for finding themselves able to thank.

From this vantage point, moral skepticism is put in a new light. The would-be amoralist asks for proof or evidence that the other is his concern: 'What is my brother to me or I to him that I should concern myself with his welfare?' The skeptic effectively demands a *reason* that would justify the other's demand for care or concern. In so doing, the skeptic implicates herself in the very practices of reflection that indicate just the sort of relation she would like to deny. That is, the skeptic uses a practice granted to her by the social or ethical relationship in order to question whether such a relation could really be attributed to her. Her question thus involves her in a performative contradiction and is in this sense self-defeating or refuting.

Two further points can be made in this connection. First, responsibility as it functions in Levinas's thought is never naturalized: 'nothing in this passivity of possession by the Good... becomes a natural tendency. The relation to the other is not convertible into a nature.'[42] Specifically, Levinas seems to have in mind erotic relationships as the exemplar of a naturally occurring concern for the other, but his point can be generalized. Possession by the Good is not evidenced in nor does it result in natural sentiments of care, affection, love, or compassion. Levinas's is *not* an ethics of care and he does not see a naturalized concern for the other as either the locus or the expression of pre-original responsibility. The 'anarchical bond between the subject and the Good... is made without the subject having been a will. It is not the constitution of a "divine instinct" of responsibility, an "altruistic or generous nature," or a "natural goodness."'[43] Responsibility is a matter of a pre-subjective subjection to the Good and a posterior approval of it that does not and cannot amount to an experience of this Good or an assuming of it as my choice. It is only my election that I approve.

Second, reflection does not guarantee morality in the conventional sense; that is, subjection to the Good is not a guarantee of what we ordinarily call ethical goodness, moral character, or right action. The birth of an ego with a will and judgment – that is to say, the coming into being of a subject through its election by the Good – is certainly, in Levinas's view, the condition for moral responsibility in the ordinary sense. But it is *equally* the condition for the 'seductions of irresponsibility.'[44]

'This temptation to separate oneself from the Good is the very incarnation of the subject or his presence in being.'[45] Levinas is careful to point out that incarnation is not the cause or source of such a temptation – his is not the tale of a fall from grace, nor does he view the body as that which impugns or corrupts an otherwise perfect or holy will. To be faced with 'axiological bipolarity' or the choice between good and bad one has to already have been constituted as a subject which means being constituted through an exposure to the other.

Sounding similar themes in *Otherwise Than Being*, Levinas denies that subjection to the Good is the 'naïve unconditioned "Yes" of submission.'[46] It is submission both before and after the fact, both in the original election and in the later endorsement, but it is not the unconditioned *yes* of 'infantile spontaneity.'[47] It is, Levinas says, 'the exposure to critique, the exposure prior to consent.'[48] The subject is constituted in a manner that makes it unable to be totally deaf to the other's demands, whether those be a demand for reasons, a cry for compassion, an expression of pain, or the pangs of hunger. To be in a world as an ego means being exposed to the other in a manner that makes perfect indifference to her expressions impossible. I can harden my heart against the other, but I cannot claim literally that she is meaningless to me. Subjectivity is ever too late to say that the other in no way concerns it. This lateness signifies, as Levinas says, 'the necessity that the Good choose me first before I can be in a position to choose.'[49]

We can return to the skeptic's question to see this. In demanding a justification, the moral skeptic is trapped in a performative contradiction between the content of her question and its practical conditions. The skeptic's question presumes a neutral, pre-social subject who has no constitutive relation to the other and thus must be provided with a reason to take the other into account. But the practices of reason-giving in which the skeptic's own question participates already belie her introduction into a socially or intersubjectively constituted world. When the skeptic asks 'Why be moral?' or 'What is the other to me?,' she demands a reason for acting in one way rather than another. Far from casting doubt on the possibility of ethical life through such questions, skepticism is in fact its prolongation. It is the *enactment* of ethical life. If it were not for the other who opens the world to me, I would not be able meaningfully to ask the skeptic's question. Thus, being chosen before I can choose is the condition for all of my later choosing, for all my affirming or denying. I cannot without contradiction deny my ability to engage in the process of critical reflection and, by extension, I cannot without contradiction deny my exposure to the other. This inability to turn a deaf ear, this non-indifference to the other, *is* the moment of normativity in Levinas's thought. What now remains to be examined is the relation of normativity in this sense to norms.

Concrete norms and ethical life

Writing of a responsibility that 'commits me . . . before any truth and any certainty,' Levinas says it makes 'the question of trust and norm an *idle* question.'[50] The formulation is provocative. Can we do without moral dispositions and norms once we have Levinasian responsibility? Are we to assume that Levinasian responsibility makes us morally good or virtuous, to the point where discussion of these is now unnecessary? If nothing else, Levinas's comment reinforces a supposed gap between his reflections on 'responsibility' and our usual understanding of the term. A few lines later he notes further that the 'ethical language we have resorted to does not arise out of a special moral experience' and insists that 'responsibility is not comprehensible on the basis of ethics [i.e., moral rules or norms].'[51] None of this comes as a surprise, but what of the reverse? Can one derive moral norms from the condition of being bound to the other in an original responsibility? Here we arrive back at a consideration of the practical import of Levinas's thought – and back at the role of the skeptic.

Levinas treats skepticism as the legitimate child of philosophy; the moment of the ethical saying *within* philosophy.[52] The full-grown, self-positing subject – the ego of Western philosophizing – thinks itself within its rights in demanding an account that shows that others must matter to it. But even as it thus attempts to chase off or dismiss the other's demands, the fact of its recognizing them *as demands* (that it may want to cast as illegitimate but that it nonetheless cannot claim are meaningless) means that it remains dogged by an ethical recognition enacted in its own discourse. Skepticism is both a figure for and an enactment of the fate of ethics: 'It is as though skepticism were sensitive to the difference between my exposure without reserve to the other, which is saying, and the exposition or statement of the said in its equilibrium and justice.'[53] If the truth of ethical saying (exposure to the other that opens a world that can become intelligible and in which critical reflection is possible) is put on the same level as the truths made possible by it (the *logos* or meanings of that opened up world), it no longer registers. The statement 'you are infinitely responsible to the other' is always open to contestation. Why am I responsible? How so and to what extent? The skeptic is right to pose such questions, but in doing so she enacts the responsibility – the original election by the good – that her words would like to consign to the ash heap. The skeptic can challenge individual moral statements, but she cannot, without contradiction, challenge her engagement (in the very act of posing her question) in an ethical relationship and by extension a form of ethical life. Or, as Levinas puts it, she cannot evade her election by the Good without denying herself and her own uniqueness.[54]

Norms belong to the class of particular moral statements and share their fate. Generated contingently (though not arbitrarily) by the history, culture, and material practices of a given society, norms belong to what Levinas calls 'the said.' They are a kind of thematization and sedimentation of the life of a people at a particular time in its history. As such, existing norms may always be contested in the name of new self-understandings, emerging or changing social and cultural practices, and ever varied forms of life. Each norm registers a demand, and each norm may be contested in the name of making another or a different demand heard. Whether I assent to this demand or another is a historical question and the question of justice in such cases cannot be decided in abstraction from the given conditions and practices of a society. Indeed, particular conceptions of justice themselves have a history that intersects with the cases and norms that are the objects of their judgment. But whatever my position with respect to a given norm, what cannot be claimed without contradiction, from the Levinasian perspective, is that there is no normativity, or that I am not bound to see or hear these demands *as* moral demands necessitating a response. In effect, I cannot claim to be deaf to the fact that a demand has been registered. I can try to dismiss it as wrongheaded or pernicious, but I cannot claim that such demands are literally meaningless nonsense or none of my affair. And if I cannot do that, then I am already enmeshed in ethics. In short, for a Levinasian, every particular norm is contestable but the *moment* of normativity – that the other makes a claim on me to which I cannot be entirely indifferent – is incontestable. To say 'there is no normativity' or 'there is no responsibility' is to make a claim that enacts the ethical relation even as it attempts to deny its existence.

Does this mean that Levinas's thought cannot be called on to help us adjudicate the moral and ethical controversies of our own time? Not exactly, but this much is clear, Levinas's thought will not function in relation to ethical controversies as might Kantian or utilitarian ethics. It does not provide a principle or algorithm that could be used to determine the rightness or wrongness of some given action. Someone might object that by Levinas's own account the face provides at least one principle: thou shalt not kill. After all, Levinas attributes these words to the other on more than one occasion. To read this as a king of categorical imperative prohibiting killing is, however, a misunderstanding the sort of thing Levinasian responsibility is. Levinas's account of responsibility, on the view of it developed here, can no more be used to argue against just war theory than it can be used to intervene *directly* in debates on euthanasia, abortion, animal rights, ethical vegetarianism, capital punishment, or a right to self-defense. All of these cases involve the possibility of killing another – and they are only the tip of the iceberg – and in them we reflect on questions of the justice of taking another's life. To claim that killing is prohibited in any or all of these spheres is to propose a moral principle or norm. It is to make a demand. Levinas's thought does not give us a direct or indirect way to decide these cases. But it does tell us why we cannot walk away from them in utter indifference. Non-indifference to the other, as has been argued here, is not a matter of valuing the other or, by extension, of valuing what she values. It is rather a matter of a certain kind of vulnerability to the other being constitutive for my own possibility of being a subject. One is not an ego without being in relation to an other in such a way that one is already vulnerable to the other's demands at the very same moment in which one is first capable of making demands of one's own. My own demands, my 'self-interest,' have no priority, logically, chronologically, morally, or ethically, in the Levinasian view. To be exposed to the other is constitutive for being myself. When it comes then to the other's demands – for rights, freedoms, benefits, opportunities, or whatever – Levinas's view explains why the infinite task of responding to those rights is incumbent on us and why, though we can in fact act irresponsibly,[55] we can never argue that this is none of our own affair. Levinas would agree with Lyotard when he writes, 'And so, when the question of what justice consists in is raised, the answer is: "It remains to be seen in each case."' But while justice must be taken case by case, our obligation to seek justice, to hear and weigh the other's demands, and to weigh them against the demands of *all* the others (including also ourselves) is not just categorical but constitutive of who we are.

Notes

1. F. Ciaramelli, 'Levinas's Ethical Discourse between Individuation and Universality' in R. Bernasconi and S. Critchley (eds), *Re-reading Levinas* (Bloomington: Indiana University Press, 1991), p. 85.

2. E. Levinas, *Ethics and Infinity: Conversations with Philippe Nemo*, trans. R. Cohen (Pittsburgh: Duquesne University Press, 1985), p. 90.
3. R. Bernasconi, 'What is the Question to Which "Substitution" is the Answer?' in S. Critchley and R. Bernasconi (eds), *The Cambridge Companion to Levinas* (Cambridge: Cambridge University Press, 2002), p. 250, emphasis added.
4. E. Levinas, *Otherwise Than Being or Beyond Essence*, trans. A. Lingis (Pittsburgh: Duquesne University Press, 1998) [hereinafter OBBE], p. 12.
5. Ibid.
6. J. Robbins 'Tracing Responsibility in Levinas' Ethical Thought' in A. Perpezak (ed.), *Ethics as First Philosophy* (New York: Routledge, 1995), p. 177.
7. E. Levinas, *Collected Philosophical Papers*, trans. Alphonso Lingis (Dordrecht: Martinus Nijhoff, 1987) [hereinafter CPP], p. 104.
8. Levinas, OBBE, p. 94.
9. Ibid., p. 12.
10. Levinas, CPP, p. 66.
11. On this phrase in Levinas's thought, see E. Wyschogrod, 'Doing Before Hearing: On the Primacy of Touch' in F. Laruelle (ed.), *Textes pour Emmanuel Levinas* (Paris: Editions Jean-Michel Place, 1980), pp. 179–203.
12. Levinas, OBBE, p. 13. When he uses this phrase again on page 150 a footnote gives the reference as *Job 4:12*. See Levinas, OBBE, p. 199, note 19.
13. Ibid.
14. Ibid., p. 147.
15. Ibid., p. 150.
16. Ibid.
17. Ibid., p. 100.
18. Ibid.
19. J. Robbins (ed.), *Is it Righteous to Be? Interviews with Emmanuel Levinas* (Palo Alto: Stanford University Press, 2001), p. 184, emphasis added.
20. That Levinas imagines the skeptic in this way is evident in the opening lines of *Totality and Infinity* where he writes, 'Everyone will readily agree that it is of the highest importance to know whether we are not duped by morality' (E. Levinas, *Totality and Infinity*, trans. A. Lingis, Pittsburgh: Duquesne University Press, 1969) [hereinafter TI], p. 21.
21. To avoid misunderstanding, it needs to be emphasized that 'valuing' in the ordinary sense in which it is used here is not in any way a synonym for 'responsibility' in the Levinasian sense. The skeptic's question is 'why need I value the other's demands' and the account of responsibility is, in a certain sense, the answer to this sort of question. However, as will be shown, to be responsible to and for the other person is not a matter of *valuing* the other; it is a matter of owing him or her an accounting of oneself.
22. That this is not Levinas's own way of going about the question of responsibility will be clear to even the most casual reader of his texts. Nonetheless the proposal here follows the structure of his thought even if it illuminates his position from a different perspective and in a different idiom.
23. It is worth noting that Heidegger, too, recognizes something like this structure when he makes the self a secondary formation not identical to the mode of being of *Dasein*. However, to the extent that *Dasein* is either an individuated being or the abstract mode of being of all beings such as we are, the role of others is left ambiguous at best. Heidegger says of *Mitsein* that it is

co-originary with being-in-the-world. For Levinas, it is primary. There is no being in the world that could pre-exist or exist independently of others.

24. Levinas, OBBE, p. 119.
25. Ibid.
26. The human being, he notes in an early text, is not a rational animal in the sense of being an animal who *in addition* to sensing and other instinctual behaviors is also capable of reason. If we use the term 'rational animal' it must indicate 'an original structure' (Levinas, CPP, p. 27).
27. Levinas, OBBE, p. 117.
28. Ibid.
29. Ibid.
30. Ibid.
31. Levinas, *Of God Who Comes to Mind*, trans. B. Bergo (Stanford: Stanford University Press, 1998) p. 89.
32. The case being attributed to Levinas in this respect is structurally similar to Jane Gallop's reading of Lacan's mirror stage (though the similarity will be limited to a single feature). Before the child sees itself in the mirror, it is a fragmented body or body in bits and pieces [*corps morcele*]. The reflected image that the infant assumes and identifies as his own – the *imago* – is not preceded by a subjectivity which recognizes itself (as if it had already grasped itself or known itself). Rather, the recognition *is* the birth of subjectivity and not the act of a pre-existing subject. But, as Gallop emphasizes, we can have little confidence in this story which purports to say how each of us goes from the condition of a *corps morcele* to that of a fully imaged ego. After all, the fragmented and unorganized body cannot be the object of an experience since experience is possible only for one who has achieved subjectivity. Following Laplanche and Pontalis, Gallop writes, 'The mirror stage would *seem to come after* "the body in bits and pieces" and organize them into a unified image. But actually, *that* violently unorganized *image only comes after* the mirror stage so as to *represent what came before*' (J. Gallop, *Reading Lacan* (Ithaca: Cornell University Press, 1985) p. 80). What came before cannot be represented except retroactively. Levinas might speak here of a dis-integrated body that belongs to an immemorial or an-archic past, one that cannot be made present except in a trace structure. So, too, with the pre-history of subjectivity itself in the Levinasian account. To have undergone without there being a subject who undergoes is possible because the locus of subjectivity is in sensibility and corporeality.
33. Levinas, CPP, p. 134.
34. Ibid., p. 134.
35. Ibid., pp. 134–135.
36. Ibid., p. 135.
37. C. Korsgaard, *The Sources of Normativity* (Cambridge: Cambridge University Press, 1996), p. 19.
38. Ibid., p. 62.
39. Ibid.
40. Ibid., p. 63.
41. Ibid., p. 65.
42. Levinas, CPP, p. 137.
43. Ibid.

44. Ibid.
45. Ibid.
46. Levinas, OBBE, p. 122.
47. Ibid.
48. Ibid.
49. Ibid.
50. Ibid., p. 120.
51. Ibid.
52. Ibid., p. 168.
53. Ibid.
54. Ibid., p. 122.
55. For a discussion of irresponsibility in Levinas, see R. Visker, 'Is Ethics Fundamental? Questioning Levinas on Irresponsibility,' *Continental Philosophy Review* 36 (2003), pp. 263–302.

2

Levinasian Ethics and the Concept of Law

Jonathan Crowe

Most people think they have an obligation to obey the law. They think the mere fact that a particular action is required by law gives them a reason to behave in that way. This popular view of law has provoked considerable academic discussion. The influential legal theorist, H. L. A. Hart, responds to the popular view by positing a systematic distinction between legal and moral obligation.[1] He suggests that we have a distinctive obligation to obey the law, regardless of its moral character. This line of argument has not been without its critics. Perhaps the most prominent dissenter from Hart's view on this point has been Joseph Raz, one of Hart's distinguished former students. Raz denies that we have any generic obligation to obey the law; whatever obligations we have to obey specific legal rules depends upon their moral content.[2]

Emmanuel Levinas does not engage directly with this debate. However, his theory of ethics holds fundamental implications for our understanding of legal obligation. That, at any rate, is my argument in this chapter. I begin by briefly examining one of the key tenets of Hart's conception of law: namely, that law is a distinctive species of social rule. This view forms the basis for Hart's distinction between legal and moral obligation.

I then ask whether Hart's approach is tenable in the light of Levinas's ethical theory. I begin by emphasising two aspects of Levinas's views that have influenced my approach to this question. First, I examine Levinas's emphasis on the face-to-face encounter as the fundamental unit of ethical experience. I then go on to consider the social dimension of Levinas's theory. I suggest that social judgements about the ethical significance of particular forms of action may be understood as arising from the passive synthesis over time of repeated encounters between ethical beings.

These social judgements then form the basis for the reflective process of moral reasoning, made necessary by the role of the 'third party' [*le tiers*] in disrupting the primary ethical structure of the face-to-face.

In the final part of the chapter, I explore the implications of Levinas's view of ethics for theories, such as Hart's, that distinguish systematically between legal and moral forms of obligation. I suggest that such views are incompatible with Levinas's depiction of ethical experience as a primordial element of social discourse. If law presents a generic obligation, it must be ethical in nature. This point has important consequences for how we understand the concept of law.

Hart on legal obligation

Hart views law as a distinctive species of social rule. It is therefore necessary to ask both what he means by a social rule and what makes law a distinctive instance of this type. Hart's account of social rules has come to be known as the 'practice theory'.[3] According to this theory, a rule has two components: first, the existence of a pattern of conduct generally followed by members of the social group; and, second, a distinctive normative attitude towards the relevant practice, according to which members of the group both use the practice to guide their own conduct and criticise others who do not conform to it. It is this reflective normative attitude that, for Hart, distinguishes social rules from mere habits; he famously calls it the 'internal aspect of rules'.[4]

Hart identifies many different types of social rules, including rules of etiquette, language, morality and law. The question therefore arises: what makes legal rules special? Hart's answer has two parts. First, legal and moral rules are distinguished from other types of social standards by the seriousness of the normative pressure that lies behind them.[5] Second, legal rules are distinguished from moral rules because their authority derives from their sources and not their content. It is because legal rules stem from an authoritative source – such as a legislature, court or legal official – that members of the community recognise them as binding.

Hart describes the social rule that gives legislators, judges and other officials the authority to enact legal norms as the 'rule of recognition'.[6] This rule gives us a master test for legal validity. The rule is likely to be both vague and complex; as such, it may be difficult to apply in some cases.[7] In principle, however, it enables us to distinguish consistently between legal rules and other social standards. In this way, Hart seeks to separate law from morality.

It is important to be clear about the extent of this separation. Hart does not commit some of the more obvious fallacies that are sometimes attributed to legal positivists. He does not deny that judges and legislators often consider moral values in formulating new legal rules; indeed, he openly recognises and endorses this practice.[8] Nor does he deny that law must have a minimum level of moral pull in order to be considered authoritative.[9] He even argues – contrary to some other legal positivists[10] – that open-ended moral standards may be incorporated into law if recognised by legal officials.[11] Where Hart *does* separate law and morality is in his account of the normativity of legal rules.[12] He not only thinks, like other positivists, that there may be valid laws that are not morally binding; he also regards such laws as giving rise to a special type of social duty. In this way, Hart draws a clear distinction between moral and legal forms of obligation.

Hart argues in *Essays on Bentham* that the key to understanding legal institutions lies in the concept of an 'authoritative legal reason', which he describes as a 'content independent and peremptory' reason for action of a special kind.[13] Since authoritative legal reasons provide judges and other legal actors with peremptory reasons for action, we can meaningfully regard them as expressing duties. However, Hart denies that the terms 'duty' and 'obligation', when used in the purely legal sense just outlined, express any necessary *moral* meaning. He further denies that judges who view themselves as holding legal obligations necessarily see those obligations as morally binding.[14] For Hart, then, law presents a generic form of social obligation that is non-moral in character. I wish to ask whether such a view of legal obligation is sustainable in the light of Levinas's ethical theory.

Levinas on ethical experience

Levinas suggests that ethical experience has its foundations in the irreducible relation between oneself and other people, whom he describes collectively as 'the Other' [*l'autrui*]. He argues that the irreducible strangeness of the Other presents an unavoidable ethical demand, which radically resists definition. Levinas famously holds that ethics is first philosophy. He sees the relation between Self and Other as the primary question presented in concrete human existence. The centrality of the ethical encounter to human experience makes ethics unavoidable.

Levinas's first enquiry in exploring ethical experience is into the nature of subjectivity. In order to recognise ourselves as individuals, it is necessary to achieve solitude, in the sense of separating ourselves from that which we are not.[15] According to Levinas, the isolation of the subject is found initially in enjoyment. In enjoyment, 'I am absolutely for myself' (*TI*, 134); I adopt an attitude that is entirely self-regarding. In pure enjoyment, the subject appears self-sufficient, familiar, cocooned from the world. Enjoyment is interiority (*TI*, 118).

The isolation associated with pure enjoyment, however, is not sustainable. Our concern for ourselves inevitably 'becomes a consciousness of objects' (*TI*, 139). We appropriate and represent objects as aids to our enjoyment. Our awareness of objects leads to language, as objects are communicated and thematised. It also leads to an awareness of the Other.

The subject initially attempts to thematise other people in the same way. Her attitude towards the Other is thereby 'cast in the relation of language' (*TI*, 69). However, our attempts to appropriate and represent the Other as an aspect of interiority prove fundamentally at odds with the phenomenological character of interpersonal exchanges. As soon as I purport to encapsulate the Other, it becomes clear that 'the invoked is not what I comprehend'; the Other 'is not under a category' (*TI*, 69). My attempts to thematise the Other conflict with her 'strangeness', her 'very freedom' (*TI*, 73).

Simon Critchley usefully links Levinas's observations about the alterity of the Other to the epistemological problem of other minds.[16] Suppose I hear someone crying out in pain and rush to her aid. When I get there, the person denies that she was in pain at all. How can I know whether the remark is sincere? Ultimately, I cannot; the other person's state of mind radically resists my knowledge.[17] For Levinas, this inevitable resistance to knowledge defines my encounter with the Other.

Levinas contends that the radical alterity of the Other demands recognition. In the first place, objects no longer exist simply for my enjoyment. They also exist for the Other. I am obliged to negotiate with the Other by approaching her through the medium of language. In speaking to the Other, I surrender my pure interiority. I invite the Other into my conceptual universe, creating 'the world in discourse'. I offer the Other 'things that are mine' (*TI*, 76). In this respect, conversation with the Other is a 'gift', albeit a necessary one. In admitting the Other to my world, I make possible a new type of commerce. For Levinas, commerce with the Other is *ethical* (*TI*, 73). In recognising the Other as exteriority, I acknowledge her 'rights as a stranger' (*TI*, 77).

Levinas's discussion of the encounter with the Other is a claim about everyday experiences. It can be illustrated using commonplace examples. Recall, for example, encountering another person while walking along a corridor. Our first instinct is to negotiate the person as we would an object, but we are simultaneously aware that such a straightforward response is not possible. In regarding the other person, we immediately apprehend her ability also to change course in response to our appearance. We are obliged to move from simply regarding the person like an object to anticipating her intentions and accommodating them by our own movements. The other person demands acknowledgement. When, as sometimes happens, both parties alter course only to find themselves once again facing one another, we are immediately aware of the other person as an unpredictable, irreducible entity.

Our initial mode of encountering the Other is to negotiate her presence in pursuing our own desires. We are not immediately inclined to acquiesce to her perspective, especially where it conflicts with our own. However, we are unavoidably aware of the need to alter our plans to at least traverse her intentions. We cannot simply ignore or dismiss the Other in pursuing our own enjoyment. The significance of her presence is ambiguous and undefined. We must reach out to the Other, addressing her through language. The needs of the Other come face to face with our own. Our world becomes a world of values, an ethical world.

Levinas locates the revelation of the Other in what he terms the *face-to-face* encounter (*TI*, 202). The face of the Other represents a kind of 'epiphany', in which 'the sensible, still graspable, turns into total resistance to the grasp' (*TI*, 194, 197). In facing the Other, I am hostage to her expressions. It is not the juxtaposition of her desires to my own that strikes me, so much as the unpredictability and irreducibility of her responses. In the 'total nudity of [the Other's] defenceless eyes', I encounter a 'primordial' demand for recognition; the infinity of the face 'paralyses power' (*TI*, 199). Confronted with the gaze of the Other, my freedom becomes 'inhibited', 'guilty' and 'timid' (*TI*, 203). In the ethical moment, I am compelled to acknowledge that affirming my own subjectivity necessarily involves assuming responsibilities 'for which no one can replace me and from which no one can release me' (*TI*, 245).

The demand encountered in the face of the Other is primordial (*TI*, 199). It is prior to subjectivity, prior to choice. I cannot posit myself as a subject without distinguishing myself from that which I am not. I must thematise the world around me. However, it is not possible to conceptualise the world without reaching out to the Other and addressing her radical resistance to thematisation. I have no choice but to respond to the ethical challenge that the Other represents.

In affirming myself as subjectivity in the face of the Other, I posit myself as responsible (*TI*, 215). Subjectivity and morality 'constitute one sole and same process in being' (*TI*, 245). It follows that it is impossible to avoid assuming ethical obligations, while maintaining my self-image as an autonomous subject. The assumption of ethical responsibility is 'passive' and 'non-voluntary'.[18] As Levinas says, 'to be unable to shirk: this is the I' (*TI*, 245).

Ethics and social discourse

There is a problem in Levinas about the relationship of ethical experience to social discourse. The problem arises in two ways. In the first place, the particularity of the ethical encounter, as described by Levinas, seems to cast doubt upon the possibility of shared judgements about ethical significance. There is also a problem about the nature of moral reasoning. Moral deliberation requires a framework of general normative concepts; in short, it requires rules. However, if ethics has its basis in the immediacy of the face-to-face encounter, according to Levinas, it is far from clear how reflective moral engagement is either necessary or possible.

The face-to-face encounter may be described as *particular* in two distinct but intertwined senses. First, the experience of the encounter is primordial and therefore resists expression through general terms and concepts; and, second, the encounter generates a unique and inescapable responsibility that rests on the subject alone. Given these features of the ethical encounter, it is hard to see how the experience could be either genuinely shared by multiple subjects or accurately communicated between them. Indeed, Levinas is saying ethics is about what is *not* shared, that which is prior to any communication. At this level, the very idea of ethical *discourse* appears to conflict with the particularity of the face-to-face.

Levinas hints at a partial response to this problem when he speaks about time as the deepening of ethics. Through repeated interactions with the Other, 'the alterity of each face increases and deepens ever more profoundly' (*TI*, 283). Here, Levinas adapts Henri Bergson's conception of time as a continuous duration or movement. Levinas's remarks on duration can be developed to yield a picture of ethical significance that transcends the immediate case.

We might usefully draw here on an illustration employed by Bergson.[19] Suppose that I wave my hand across my body. My hand passes through an infinite series of points on the way to its destination. However, the watcher perceives the action, not as a punctuated series of locations, but as a continuous movement between two positions.

We might regard repeated ethical encounters in the same light. Each encounter with the Other involves an epiphany. Over time, however, our repeated ethical experiences show themselves in a general attitude towards social life. In Bergson's terms, this attitude is not 'a series of distinct psychological states', but rather 'the continuous melody of our inner life – a melody which is going on and will go on, indivisible, from the beginning to the end of our conscious existence'.[20] We come to regard ourselves as oriented towards the social environment, assuming responsibility for the Other wherever we find her.

We might summarise this analysis by saying that *social judgements about ethical significance* arise from the coincidence of multiple ethical experiences synthesised by individual actors.[21] They are social habits that carry with them the weight of repeated ethical encounters. The synthesis in question is passive; it involves the pre-reflective accretion of a sequence of experiences, as when we form unconscious habits and acquire intuitive skills, such as learning to ride a bicycle.[22] It follows that our basic understanding of ethical significance is already in place before we engage in any conscious moral reflection.

At this point, Levinas's account of ethics raises a further issue. What is the relationship between our primordial social judgements of ethical significance and the rational process of moral engagement? In order to engage in moral reasoning, we must translate the passive synthesis of ethical experience to a reflective framework of principles and rules. However, the temporal character of social judgement militates against such a reductive enterprise. Ethics is constantly requiring something new of us, changing direction and altering its shape as we are thrown into new forms of proximity with the Other. It therefore resists expression as a set of formal rules.

Levinas acknowledges this tension by distinguishing the saying [*le dire*] from the said [*le dit*]. The saying is revealed through my interaction with the Other. It resists phrasing and therefore comes to my awareness only through the way it speaks to me in the ethical moment. The said, by contrast, comprises statements or propositions to which truth values may be assigned. As Critchley puts it, the said is 'the content of my words', whereas the saying 'consists in the fact that these words are being addressed to an interlocutor'.[23]

The said thematises and conceptualises, while the saying displays an inherent resistance to categorisation. It is tempting to conclude that the saying and the said are entirely alien to one another. However, Levinas resists such an outcome. Although my responsibility for the Other is 'prior to anything said', it is both necessary and possible that the saying be 'thematised, that is, manifest itself, that it enter into a proposition and a book'; it must 'spread out', 'posit itself', 'let itself be seen' (*OB*, 43–44). The saying must find expression in propositional form in order to support the possibility of justice (*OB*, 46) – as well as, one might add, the concept of law.

Why are justice and law necessary? For Levinas, the answer lies in the phenomenon of 'the third party' [*le tiers*]. The third party is the neighbour of my neighbour; she is all those, other than the Other, who may be affected in some way by my response to the face-to-face. The appearance of the third party adds an extra level of complexity to the ethical environment. The Other demands my full and undivided attention; I am compelled to acknowledge her needs and desires. The presence of the third party, on the other hand, prevents me from simply embracing the Other's entreaties. The third party necessitates 'assembling, order, thematisation... the intelligibility of a system' (*OB*, 157) – in a word, justice. If the subject and the Other were alone in the world, the problem of justice would not arise. The third party, however, 'interrupts' the cosiness of the face-to-face (*OB*, 150).

It is tempting to view the third party as an intruder who appears on the scene only after the relationship between the subject and the Other has already been formed. In some passages, Levinas seems to endorse such an interpretation. 'The responsibility for the other is an immediacy antecedent to questions, it is proximity. It is troubled and becomes a problem when a third party enters' (*OB*, 157). Elsewhere, however, Levinas warns against such a rigid chronological view of the appearance of the third party. 'It is not that there first would be the face, and then... justice; the epiphany of the face qua face opens humanity' (*TI*, 213). In other words, the third party makes her presence known contemporaneously with the face-to-face encounter. 'The others [in the plural] concern me from the first' (*OB*, 159).

Robert Bernasconi depicts these two alternative accounts of the third party as partly symptomatic of Levinas's own 'uncertainty' regarding the issue.[24] He views Levinas as making a deliberate choice to privilege the latter interpretation. For Levinas, then, my awareness of the third party is not a mere supplement to the face-to-face; it is already present in the ethical encounter. 'The third party looks at me in the eyes of the Other' (*TI*, 213); 'in the proximity of the other, all the others than the other obsess me, and already this obsession cries out for justice' (*OB*, 158). The point is far from insignificant; as Bernasconi notes, it bears directly on the relationship between ethics and political justice.[25] If the appearance of the third party is subsequent to the ethical encounter, ethics and justice appear as two separate realms, with the latter a simple modification of the former. If, however, the ethical and the political are contemporaneous in the face-to-face, the relationship between them becomes potentially much more fluid. They would seem to sit side by side, each potentially shaping the other.

Levinas cautions us not to over-simplify the necessarily ambiguous relationship between pre-reflective ethical experience and the conceptual framework imposed in moral deliberation. It is not that moral concepts are somehow embedded, *in nuce*, in the phenomenology of ethical life. Rather, they are layered onto the ethical context in reflective engagement, mediated by the requirement of good conscience. The saying does not *become* the said; moral language arises as a necessarily imperfect attempt to represent the saying and thereafter sits alongside it. There is a continuing, unresolvable interplay between the saying and the said – mediated by the hermeneutic context of social judgements.

On this view, then, moral deliberation consists in reflective, good faith engagement with primordial social judgements of ethical significance. This view of moral reflection is social in two distinct ways. First, our experiences of discrete ethical encounters are passively synthesised into social judgements of ethical significance. This continuous melody of social life takes shape at a pre-reflective level. Second, the appearance of the third party in the face-to-face reveals the necessity of reflective engagement with the primordial ethical context. This social dimension of the ethical encounter creates a need for overarching rules and principles. However, these reflective concepts must always be viewed as subsidiary to the demands of the pre-reflective ethical environment.

In the said, the saying begins to be understood (*OB*, 38); at the same time, however, the conceptual framework of moral reasoning is constantly unsettled, called to account, by the ineluctable demand for recognition presented in the saying. In this way, 'the saying is both an affirmation and a retraction of the said' (*OB*, 44). Philosophy must be alert to the betrayal that takes place when ethical experience is reduced to language (*OB*, 6–7, 44). Yet this does not necessitate silence on ethical questions – indeed, the presence of the third party makes silence impossible – but rather sensitivity to the areas where moral concepts fail to capture the full significance of the ethical environment.

The concept of law

I wish to conclude this chapter by exploring the implications of a Levinasian approach to ethics for views, such as that of Hart, that propose a systematic distinction between legal and moral species of obligation. We have seen that, for Levinas, ethical value is primordial; it permeates social discourse at a pre-reflective level. This suggests that the basic commitments that feature in moral reasoning are in place before any *positive* legal obligation enters the picture. It follows that legal reasons can prompt action independently of moral motivations only where the relevant ethical judgements are systematically set aside.

Now, it is quite plausible, in specific cases, for an individual to set aside ethical motivations in favour of legal reasons. Consider the legal official who applies the letter of the positive law, while realising that it yields an oppressive outcome. Such an attitude may be unethical, but it is far from impossible. The prevailing legal and social culture may even entail that such attitudes are not uncommon among legal actors. However, I would argue it is impossible to found a systematic picture of legal obligation on such an account; it therefore does not support a *generic* conception of legal authority.

It is useful, in this context, to examine the following question. How are we to grasp the meaning of normative language, as used in relation to legal standards? Let us begin by considering a game of chess. Suppose I move my rook diagonally across the board and you say to me, 'you ought not to move your piece in that way'. How am I to grasp the meaning of your statement? Presuming that I am intending to play chess and not merely moving the pieces without any sense of their significance, it is straightforward for me to conclude that you are talking about what, in the context of the game of chess, I ought to do. In other words, you are referring me to a specific rule of the game.

However, suppose that you have just heard someone threaten me that, unless I stop moving my rook diagonally, an innocent person will be killed. The situation now bears unmistakable moral significance. Might you nevertheless reiterate, with the same meaning as before, 'you ought not to move your piece in that way'? Given the context, your statement inevitably takes on an ethical meaning. You can no longer restrict your frame of reference to the rules of the game; the underlying ethical context dominates the hermeneutic field.

Legal theorists have often compared law to a game. Hart, in particular, compares law to games such as cricket and baseball.[26] It is easy to see why: for Hart, law is a set of rules, similar (in many ways) to the rules of a game. Even in a game like chess, however, it is impossible to make normative statements without preserving a trace of ethical meaning. And, in this context, it is relevant to note a sense in which law is decidedly *not* a game. Law, unlike chess or baseball, is specifically concerned with matters of ethical significance. Law claims authority over all aspects of social life;[27] it inevitably has ethical consequences. It follows that legal discourse is *particularly* vulnerable to infiltration by ethical meaning.

We have seen that, in the context of a game of chess, where a normative statement holds possible significance both within the rules of chess and within the broader framework of ethical life, it is impossible to drain the utterance of ethical significance. Is the situation any different when we are playing the game of law? The question is not whether one could occasionally state a legal norm without also conveying ethical meaning; no doubt this is possible in some situations. (In the highly striated environment of the courtroom, normative statements might perhaps be understood in a purely legal light.) The question is whether one could do this systematically, preserving a morally neutral sense of obligation across the whole range of contexts where legal rules apply.

Hart notes in *The Concept of Law* that 'those who accept the authority of a legal system ... express their sense of its requirements in internal statements couched in the normative language which is common to both law and morals', which commonly includes reference to obligations.[28] He nonetheless claims that legal obligation can be distinguished systematically from its ethical counterpart. On Levinas's theory, however, the context for all normative language is primordially ethical. It follows that ethical meaning permeates the legal context from the outset.

Law, if conceived as a self-contained normative order, faces the permanent task of pushing aside competing layers of ethical meaning in order to motivate action. Such a view of law is permanently constituted as open; it is always probable that ethical judgements will come to dominate the process of normative reasoning. It is, at best, a partial system; it appears far too weak to support Hart's conception of law as a generic network of peremptory rules. On the one hand, law's attempts to maintain itself as an autonomous normative discourse are prone to be infiltrated and undermined by the insistent weight of ethical context. On the other hand, any systematic attempt to accommodate ethical significance within legal discourse makes it unfeasible to maintain the separate nature of the discipline. It seems impossible either to permanently set aside ethical demands or to consistently admit them into legal judgements while retaining the institutional closure of law.

It is useful to consider the above point in the light of Hans Kelsen's concept of the basic norm [*Grundnorm*]. Kelsen views law as a self-contained order of norms; the basic norm is the ultimate source of intra-systemic validity within a particular order, to which all the other norms in that order can trace their authority. Kelsen explains the basic norm of the legal order by reference to the 'constitution that is the first historically';[29] it is from this historically first constitution that the binding force of all subsequent constitutions is ultimately derived. He goes on to note that 'the first constitution is a real constitution, a binding norm, only on the condition that the basic norm is presupposed to be valid'. The basic norm is 'the validity of [the] first constitution'; 'it is postulated that one ought to behave as [the individuals] who laid down the first constitution have ordained'.[30]

Kelsen treats the basic norm as rendering the other norms in the order conclusive. The fundamental assumption that the historically first constitution is valid gives other norms within the legal order decisive force; it therefore constitutes the legal order as a self-contained system. We might say that the basic norm is both binding and blinding; it obviates the need to refer outside the legal order to decide whether to recognise a legal rule. As Kelsen puts it, the basic norm 'represents the empowering of an ultimate moral or legal authority'.[31] The blindingness of the basic norm of the legal order leads Kelsen to hold that it is not possible to assert at the same time a legal norm and an inconsistent moral norm.[32] This aspect of Kelsen's view has been strongly criticised by Hart.[33]

From a Levinasian perspective, however, Kelsen is right and Hart is wrong. Kelsen bases his argument on the logical structure of law as a normative order; he argues it is logically incoherent for two contradictory norms to co-exist from the point of view of the same system. However, a similar result follows from Levinas's views on the primordial place of ethics in social discourse. If social experience is viewed as primordially ethical, it is impossible to have an assumption of blindingness that does not claim moral force. A normative order is bound to find the meaning of its terms permeated with the weight of ethical experience whenever it purports to govern a morally significant field of action. As such, any order that purports systematically to exclude moral considerations will be only a partial order; it will lack a genuine basic norm.

Law as ethical non-closure

It is impossible to have a stable, self-contained normative system of general application that does not claim moral significance. If we accept this premise, our account of legal obligation must proceed in one of two ways. One option would be to deny, as Raz does, that law presents any *generic* obligation.[34] On this view, legal standards possess no general authority; only those particular legal rules that hold moral force present us with obligations.[35] In other words, the legal order lacks a genuine basic norm, in the blinding sense intended by Kelsen.

The problem with this approach is that it strays a long way from our ordinary understanding of the concept of law. As we saw at the beginning of this chapter, most people think they have an obligation to obey the law, just because it is the law. Raz's response to this popular view is to distinguish between the claims and the force of law. According to Raz, law claims generic authority; this is why people commonly view law as presenting them with obligations.[36] However, Raz continues, this popular view is mistaken; in fact, law possesses no generic normative force. Effectively, Raz presents an error theory of legal obligation.[37] On this view, the concept of law that figures in everyday social discourse has no firm basis in reality; law, as we commonly understand it, simply does not exist.

Raz seems restricted in his analysis by the legal positivist framework bequeathed to him by Hart. In particular, he is at pains to avoid imbuing the concept of law with any necessary moral content; since he does not accept Hart's distinction between legal and moral forms of obligation, this leads him to conclude that law, qua law, presents no generic obligation at all. The result is an understanding of the concept of law that appears strained, at best.

Fortunately, this is not the only possible analysis consistent with the primordial character of ethical experience. The other option, for those who wish to retain the view that law does indeed present a generic obligation, is to hold that legal obligation is a species of moral obligation. This approach would entail that the term 'law', in the focal sense,[38] extends only to those positive standards that are morally binding. On this account, the basic norm of the legal order is perhaps best understood as a stipulation of *non-closure*, according to which ethical experience permeates and shapes the legal framework – not just once, not just at a particular moment in the past, but continually.

This view of law casts legal reasoning as a communal enterprise of reflective engagement with the primordial social context of ethical meaning. Legal materials come to light against a backdrop of pre-reflective judgements of ethical significance; legal deliberation involves a hermeneutic engagement with these social understandings.[39] The meaning of legal texts is always and already prefigured by the surrounding context – including the shared ethical judgements of members of the legal community. In this sense, law and ethics are inevitably intertwined and never entirely settled. Talking about ethics and justice is a central part of what it means to engage in the process of legal argument.[40]

Levinas shows us that law, conceived in a purely positive sense, does not possess any generic authority. The obligatory character of law depends upon its ethical content. We should not conclude, however, that the popular understanding of legal obligation is in error. Rather, it is the positivist insistence on a morally neutral test for legal validity that misrepresents the concept of law.

Acknowledgements

I would like to thank James Allan, Nicholas Aroney, Julian Lamont, Desmond Manderson and Suri Ratnapala for their helpful comments. Earlier versions of this chapter were delivered at the Australian Society of Legal Philosophy Conference in May 2005 and the Centennial Conference on Levinas and Law in September 2006. I am grateful to all who participated in the discussions.

Notes

1. H. L. A. Hart, *Essays on Bentham: Studies in Jurisprudence and Political Theory* (Oxford: Clarendon Press, 1982) pp. 147–161, 262–268.
2. J. Raz, *The Authority of Law* (Oxford: Clarendon Press, 1979) chapter 12.
3. See H. L. A. Hart, *The Concept of Law*, 2nd ed. (Oxford: Oxford University Press, 1994) pp. 254–255; Raz, *The Authority of Law*, pp. 50–58.
4. Hart, *The Concept of Law*, p. 56.
5. Ibid., p. 87.
6. Ibid., p. 100.
7. Ibid., pp. 147–154.
8. Ibid., pp. 203–205.
9. Ibid., pp. 193–200.
10. See, e.g., Raz, *The Authority of Law*, pp. 45–52; J. Raz, 'Incorporation by Law', *Legal Theory* 10 (2004) 1–17.
11. Hart, *The Concept of Law*, pp. 250–254.
12. See, in particular, Hart, *Essays on Bentham: Studies in Jurisprudence and Political Theory*, chapters 6, 10; Hart, *The Concept of Law*, chapter 5. For further discussion, see A. Oladosu, 'H. L. A. Hart on Legal Obligation', *Ratio Juris* 4 (1991) 152–176; J. Raz, 'Hart on Moral Rights and Legal Duties', *Oxford Journal of Legal Studies* 4 (1984) 123–131.
13. Hart, *Essays on Bentham: Studies in Jurisprudence and Political Theory*, p. 243.
14. Ibid., pp. 147–161, 262–268; Raz, 'Hart on Moral Rights and Legal Duties', p. 129.
15. E. Levinas, *Totality and Infinity: An Essay on Exteriority*, trans. A. Lingis (Pittsburgh: Duquesne University Press, 1969) p. 117 [hereinafter TI].
16. S. Critchley, 'Introduction' in S. Critchley and R. Bernasconi (eds), *The Cambridge Companion to Levinas* (Cambridge: Cambridge University Press, 2002) pp. 1–32 at 25–26.

17. It may well be possible to observe scientifically the other person's brain and map her neural activity during the experience in question. However, knowing about a person's physiological state is quite different to knowing about the phenomenal quality of her mental experiences. For a classic exposition of this point, see F. Jackson, 'Epiphenomenal Qualia', *American Philosophical Quarterly* 32 (1982) 127–136.
18. E. Levinas, *Otherwise Than Being or Beyond Essence*, trans. A. Lingis (Pittsburgh: Duquesne University Press, 1998) p. 15 [hereinafter OBBE].
19. H. Bergson, *The Creative Mind*, trans. M. L. Andison (New York: Philosophical Library, 1946) pp. 167–186.
20. Ibid., p. 176.
21. For further discussion, see J. Crowe, 'Dworkin on the Value of Integrity', *Deakin Law Review* 12 (2007) 167–180, 172–178; J. Crowe, 'Existentialism and Natural Law', *Adelaide Law Review* 26 (2005) 55–72, 71–72.
22. The concept of 'passive synthesis' is drawn from the work of Edmund Husserl. See E. Husserl, *Cartesian Meditations*, trans. D. Cairns (The Hague: Martinus Nijhoff, 1960) pp. 77–81; E. Husserl, *Analyses Concerning Passive and Active Synthesis*, trans. A. J. Steinbock (Dordrecht: Kluwer, 2001). More recently, it has been adopted by Gilles Deleuze in his engagement with Bergson's philosophy of duration. See particularly G. Deleuze, *Difference and Repetition*, trans. P. Patton (New York: Columbia University Press, 1994) chapter 2.
23. Critchley, 'Introduction', p. 18.
24. R. Bernasconi, 'The Third Party: Levinas on the Intersection of the Ethical and the Political', *Journal of the British Society for Phenomenology* 30 (1999) 76–87, 76–77.
25. Ibid., p. 77.
26. See, for example, Hart, *The Concept of Law*, pp. 141–147.
27. Compare J. Raz, *Practical Reason and Norms* (Oxford: Oxford University Press, 1999) p. 154.
28. Hart, *The Concept of Law*, p. 203.
29. H. Kelsen, *General Theory of Law and State*, trans. A. Wedberg (New York: Russell and Russell, 1961) p. 115.
30. Ibid. (emphasis added).
31. H. Kelsen, *General Theory of Norms*, trans. M. Hartney (Oxford: Clarendon Press, 1991) p. 256.
32. Kelsen, *General Theory of Law and State*, pp. 373–376, 407–410.
33. H. L. A. Hart, 'Kelsen Visited', *UCLA Law Review* 10 (1963) 709–728, 722–728.
34. Raz, *The Authority of Law* chapter 12.
35. Ibid., pp. 233–234.
36. Ibid., pp. 30, 33; Raz, *Practical Reason and Norms*, pp. 149–154. For further discussion, see J. Crowe, 'Natural Law in Jurisprudence and Politics', *Oxford Journal of Legal Studies* 27 (2007) 775–794.
37. The term 'error theory' is commonly used to describe J. L. Mackie's view of moral discourse. See J. L. Mackie, *Ethics: Inventing Right and Wrong* (Middlesex: Penguin, 1977).
38. For a discussion of the idea of 'focal meaning' and its role in legal theory, see J. Finnis, *Natural Law and Natural Rights* (Oxford: Clarendon Press, 1980) pp. 9–18.

39. Compare L. L. Fuller, 'Positivism and Fidelity to Law: A Reply to Professor Hart', *Harvard Law Review* 71 (1958) 630–672.
40. The importance of ethical context in constructing legal discourse finds some expression in the work of Ronald Dworkin. See particularly R. Dworkin, *Taking Rights Seriously* (London: Duckworth, 1978); *Law's Empire* (London: Fontana, 1986). For Dworkin, however, the ethical context of law derives substantially from the contingent social and legal structures of the community, rather than from the basic character of ethical interaction. For further discussion, see Crowe, 'Dworkin on the Value of Integrity'.

3
Questions for a Reluctant Jurisprudence of Alterity

Nick Smith

Introduction

Much has changed in the ten years since I argued for Levinasian alternatives to the law and economics movement in one of the first articles on Levinas to appear in a US law review.[1] Levinas scholarship has expanded considerably, especially with respect to the practical applications of his purposefully impractical philosophy. Despite his well-known aversion to the subject, Levinas' political philosophy now receives considerable attention.[2] This seems inevitable given his status as one of the great thinkers of Judaism in an age in which Zionism plays such an enigmatic role in global affairs. Our desperation for a light to pierce the ethical fog of modernity and its imperialist wars also makes Levinas' unyielding challenge to violence a welcome beacon. And as this volume, the spirited conference that gave rise to it, and Desmond Manderson's *Proximity, Levinas, and the Soul of Law* demonstrate, Levinas now also provides inspiration for many legal theorists.[3]

I should warn readers that my previous enthusiasm for Levinas' importance for law has waned somewhat. I recently discussed my general concerns about Levinas and Levinasianism at some length, evaluating the disagreements between his writings and those of T. W. Adorno.[4] The kinship between Adorno and Levinas is incontrovertible and has received some attention in recent years.[5] At root, they share: (1) a personal confrontation with National Socialism, the horrors of which motivated both to define their theoretical positions negatively against authoritarianism; (2) a critique of (a) the ubiquity, (b) the inadequacy, and (c) the violence of instrumental reason; (3) a similar understanding of that which is occluded by abstract thinking as auratic concrete particulars, what Adorno names the 'non-identical' and Levinas marks as the 'other'; (4) a claim that the conceptual subsumption of the particular to the universal amounts to an ethical failure; (5) an engagement with the possibility of rerouting philosophy toward a highly self-reflective mode of thinking as an attempt to relate to what is exterior to thought non-violently; (6) an ultimate appreciation of the impossibility of sustaining a non-instrumental relationship with the particular; (7) a demand that this difficulty regarding a non-violent relationship to the other remain at the fore of thinking, making philosophy an inherently ethical undertaking; (8) a belief that this ethical task of philosophy is interminable and that all acts of philosophizing become complicit with the violence they seek to eradicate; and (9) an elevation of actual concrete things into a dialogical relationship with philosophy despite our damaged relationship with the world, making the face for Levinas and the modernist work of art for Adorno bearers of exclusive truths.

I argued in that paper that we should understand Levinas' assertion of the transcendence of the face as the most telling point of departure between his and Adorno's critiques of instrumental reason. I attempted to explain why Adorno might understand Levinas' notion of illeity – the property of the other that endows her with an infinite positive ethical charge and thus elevates her from the normative cipher of the absolutely unknown – as a potentially dogmatic by-product of a culture desperate for non-instrumental meaning. Adorno's historical and sociological account of the disenchantment of the world and the destruction of aura within a culture fully administered by scientific rationality and economic reductionism sharply contrasts to Levinas' transcendental phenomenology, and I explained why I find Adorno's dialectical methodology and his close attention to the cultural forces driving instrumental rationality ultimately more compelling.

I also share many of the concerns enumerated by Simon Critchley in his 2004 essay on the difficulties facing a Levinasian political theory.[6] In addition to the occasional sexism, racism, monotheism, extolling of the 'marvel of the family,' and the uncomfortable relationship with Zionism that Critchley flags in Levinas' work, I explained why I find Levinas' speciesism both telling and disturbing.[7] Many contributors and readers of this volume will disagree with my arguments in that paper, and I admit that I offered those rather uncharitable interpretations in response to the dangers that I see in over-sympathetic readings of Levinas. Although we might occasionally need to be more Levinasian than Levinas himself, I wonder which aspects of his work we can alter without undermining the spirit of his critique. That paper questioned whether we can easily amend his views on art and non-human animals, for instance, and therefore I want to be forthcoming about my uneasy relationship with Levinas and my preference for Adorno's materialist critiques.

Having said that, for the purposes of this volume – which considers Levinas' contribution to debates regarding law and justice – I think Levinas and Adorno share the same problem. Levinas and Adorno both refuse to translate their stringent ethical convictions into a programmatic social theory because translating their theories of non-identity into models of governance would necessarily perpetrate, en masse, the very subsumptive violence they denounce.[8] Although Levinas and Adorno have come to provide ethical guidance to Continental philosophers, their outright refusal to be drawn into applied theory has caused innumerable difficulties for progressive theorists compelled by their critiques of instrumental reason but handcuffed by their skepticism toward practical reform. I do not mean to suggest that Adorno and Levinas were not personally engaged with political causes or that numerous interpreters have not extrapolated political content from their work, but rather that Levinas and Adorno expressly blocked the conversion of ethics into political and legal programs on ethical grounds. This chapter outlines the procedural and substantive questions that I find most worrisome for a 'Jurisprudence of Alterity' motivated by Levinas or Adorno.

Levinas, Adorno, and the depracticalization of philosophy

Attempts to glean applied ethics, political philosophy, or legal theory from Levinas or Adorno face a serious problem. At root, what I find most distinctive and important about their thought is its challenge to philosophy *as instrumental rationality*. Levinas and Adorno keep alive the idea of meaning beyond the purview of the modes of thinking that lead us to evaluate and understand everything from the egocentric perspective. Because they question the limitations and transgressions of cognitive habits that relate to the world exclusively in terms of its worth within our instrumental totalities, Levinas and Adorno present a difficulty if we hope to *use* them as a means to achieve some social, political, or legal end. As soon as we speak of the instrumental value of their critiques of instrumentality, we seem to offend the basic spirit of their contribution. We can look to many philosophers for theories of justice, but both Levinas and Adorno thought that their contributions lay elsewhere. Problems of justice, for both of them, were more fundamental than legal and political systems. Violence begins in the subsumption of the particular to the universal, and pretensions otherwise only allow the roots of injustice to grow deeper.

I imagine readers of this volume are familiar with Levinas' critique of the sorts of practical philosophy common to legal and political theory. Other commentators have made these difficulties clear, and I will not rehearse those arguments here other than to remind us of the nature of the dilemma. For Levinas, I lose the experience of the radical particularity of the other as I shift my attention away from my immediate responsibilities to her and toward abstract considerations regarding the well-being of the community. As soon as I think of my responsibilities to the many before those to the singular second person, I cannot sustain my level of attentiveness to the other.[9] Law deals in rules and legal principles that apply across time, places, and populations and requires us to evaluate the demands of the many, but Levinas insisted that ethical responsibility originates in the confrontation with the singularity and incommensurability of the other. Law, in other words, operates at the level of abstract universals but ethics can only be found in the singular relationship with concrete particulars. Regardless of their content, theories of justice appear inextricable from totalizing viewpoints that categorize, organize, and codify alterity. The other becomes one generic citizen among many, and we revert to a unified ontology: 'Political totalitarianism rests on an ontological totalitarianism.'[10] Hence Levinas' most often-repeated missive against politics: 'The art of foreseeing war and winning it by every means, politics... is opposed to morality, as philosophy to naiveté.'[11] We can therefore distinguish several interrelated sorts of problems for a Levinasian theory of justice. Law, by its customary definition: (1) reduces the other according to a given onto-political totality; (2) diminishes attention to the singular other; (3) denies the radical particularity of ethical responsibility by relying on the practical maxims provided by laws and legal principles; (4) introduces a new authoritarianism with such laws, regardless of their self-reflexivity and revisability; and (5) enables the most brutal forms of instrumental rationality.

Similar challenges face those hoping to practicalize negative dialectics, which levels its critique of instrumental rationality with a materialist and sociological methodology rather than from Levinas' phenomenological approach. Adorno's abstinence from politics extends Lukács' diagnosis of the reification of proletariat consciousness. To summarize, Marx's expectation that the contradictions of capitalism would generate class resistance became suspect as the objective conditions for revolution divorced from the subjective conditions. Adorno attributed this to the decerebrating tendencies of the culture industry: as inequalities grow and technoscience extirpates traditional sources of value, commodity fetishism numbs the mind. Exchange value supplants the values that should drive revolutionary action. Desperately in need of a transfusion of new lifeblood, humans 'must act in order to change the present petrified conditions of existence, but the latter have left their mark so deeply on people, they have deprived them of so much of their life and individuation, that they scarcely seem capable of the spontaneity necessary to do so.'[12]

For Adorno, true reform would require a transformation of the modes of cognition that dominate modernity. Until we can interrelate beyond the pure instrumentalities of identity thinking, all social, political, and legal reform will sacrifice the concrete particular to the abstract universal. For Adorno, 'even the best intentioned reformer who uses an impoverished and debased language to recommend renewal, by his adoption of the insidious mode of categorization and the bad philosophy it conceals, strengthens the very power of the order he is trying to break.'[13] Until the enlightenment becomes enlightened about *how* it thinks, *what* it thinks about justice will necessarily lead to the violence of totalizing thought. We cannot speak of justice, in other words, within a conceptual framework that views the world in strictly instrumental terms.

Under these conditions, the public can only muster 'the feeble resistance which that very industry has inculcated in it.'[14] The crippled protest itself becomes integrated into the system, as the culture industry 'embraces those at war with it by coordinating their consciousness with its own ... [because] what subjectively they fancy as radical, belongs objectively to the compartments reserved for their like.'[15] What appears critical, today exemplified by all of the forms of 'alternative' life, merely diversifies the products bought and sold. Identity thinking and its practical apotheosis in global commodification go effectively unchallenged. The illusion of resistance gives culture a placebo that leads its members to believe they are treating their condition when in fact the dose of consumerism coated with false negativity further degenerates them.

As an heir to the Marxist emancipatory project, Adorno's skepticism for practical reform created predictable animosity amongst his revolutionary-minded colleagues. Lukács famously castigated Adorno for taking up residence at '"The Grand Hotel Abyss" ... equipped with every comfort.'[16] Hans-Jürgen Krahl, an activist in the German student movements denounced by Adorno, found Adorno incapable 'of translat[ing] his private compassion for the wretched of this earth into a . . . theory for the liberation of the oppressed.'[17] This notion that Adorno's negative dialectics cannot constructively engage theories of justice has become the standard reading over past 40 years, as Drucilla Cornell summarizes:

> For Adorno, the 'end of philosophy,' which must come with the full acknowledgment of the horror of the holocaust, left him only with 'negative dialectics' . . . . To try to abstractly portray the conditions of redemption, to give form to the hope of reconciliation as if it existed now, only promotes accommodation of a fallen world. As a result, Adorno does not reflect on the conditions of justice and the relation of these conditions to positive law, either through quasi-transcendental inquiry or through empirical analysis . . . . [E]ven if his negative dialectics carries with it an ethical message that can be decoded, this message cannot be translated into an account of justice and its relation to law.[18]

The pretensions of theories of justice 'accommodate' the status quo by treating the symptoms of identity thinking rather than addressing the underlying cognitive disease. In addition, political movements depend upon the abstract classification of peoples, and these classifications indubitably result in categorization, repression, and domination.[19] Whatever advance is won in substantive reform comes with a regression in the struggle against identity thinking.[20]

For both Levinas and Adorno, we cannot salvage theories of justice from their practices of reducing the other by classifying concrete particulars into abstract, generic, and lifeless institutional beings. The transition from the ethical to the legal and political codifies collective violence, and therefore both raise the bar of political justification beyond the range of any legislation by enforcing the uncrossable divide between law and justice. Thus while non-identity theory problematizes the vanity of all theories of justice, it abstains from determining substantive policies. This refusal to collude with the violence of law relegates non-identity theory into a position of *permanent* dissent regarding theories of justice.

The costs of Levinas and Adorno's sacrifice of immediate practical concerns to more fundamental critique are high considering their popularity amongst post-Marxists. Leftist critics of economic injustice, commodification, essentialism, and other issues inclined to look to Levinas and Adorno are mired in what has been called the 'post-socialist condition,' a period Habermas describes as devitalized by 'the exhaustion of [leftist] utopian energies' since 1989.[21] While neo-liberalism encircles and digests the globe, the left struggles to identify principles around which to mount a unified opposition. All of this helps to explain both the awkwardness and the importance of the contributions in this volume. It also discloses my own reservations about the questions I am about to ask.

Procedural and substantive questions

Procedures of alterity

Although it often proves difficult to sustain such distinctions, theories of alterity have tended to speak to procedural rather than substantive issues of justice. Since the influential volume *Deconstruction and the Possibility of Justice*, the bulk of Levinasian and deconstructive critiques of law has emphasized the tenuous relationship between law and justice.[22] Although this may seem like a rather banal contribution to legal theory, I find this shift in cognitive and emotional disposition quite profound because Levinas and Adorno remind us of the fragility of all decisions. Incommensurable loss accompanies all choice, regardless of our purported justifications. We minimize these losses in order to fortify our resolve, and Levinas and Adorno incessantly press us to confront our lack of justification.

In this respect, theories of alterity provide a counterbalance to binary determinations that dominate law by imparting much needed humility to considerations of justice. Adversarial legal systems reframe the competitive tendencies of capitalism into contests for justice where we are guilty or innocent, winners or losers. Unlike normative theories that vie to out-fundamentalize others and pronounce determinations of justice with absolute certainty, ethical phenomenology and negative dialectics bring about the anxiety of radical open-mindedness. Certainty becomes the enemy of justice, and both recent and ancient examples corroborate the belief that a lack of humility, facile moralism, inattention to nuance and context, and unwillingness to revise one's beliefs leads to authoritarianism. This is especially poignant when we contrast the interruptive capacities of theories of alterity with the methodological commitments of the Law and Economics movement, which unflinchingly reduces all human value to an economic metric and provides a powerful example of the totalizing ideology of capitalism digesting the entirety of existence.

We can also notice how Levinas and Adorno might shift the source of authority in law from abstract moral principles and legislation to concrete particulars, which might prove pioneering in several respects. First, reorienting the normative source of law in this way would address the deficiency in the motivational structures of Kantian theories of morality. Enlightenment rationalism vacates our motivations for obeying moral laws because it becomes unclear why we should care about justice once we adopt the disinterested perspective to realize its nature. When we empty ourselves of all of our self-interest in order to become unbiased rational agents, what remains to motivate us to honor principles of justice?[23] Instead of being compelled by the immediate suffering of a being, the Kantian's duty is to the moral law rather than to the person in need. If this seems backwards, Levinas and Adorno reorient the foundations of justice toward the actual suffering of a particular other. According to J. M. Bernstein, only 'the normative authority of the factual' can fill the motivational deficit resulting from our reliance on moral argumentation rather than the force of unique suffering things.[24] Hence the experience of the other triggers a kind of moral insight in the sense that a painting provides a moving experience of beauty. Just as we cannot experience the full beauty of a painting through a verbal description of it, we cannot experience the force of justice without confronting the intricacies of individual injuries. Given this, legal disputes generally seem better suited to reflection on concrete particulars than political theory. Whereas political thought tends to consider populations from a macrological distance, legal thinking must tarry with the micrological details of individual cases. Judges must develop the *phronesis* to mind the infinite particularities of justice because every case invokes the intuitions of reflective judgment rather than the rote application of law to fact, and this seems amenable to a jurisprudence of alterity.

Continental philosophers of law often sound as if they prefer the untamed version of law to the more predictable varieties, but I worry about the dialectic swinging too far in either direction. What, for example, is the significance of the rule of law within such an un-ruly conception of justice? Do we trust judges to exercise their reflective judgment on the merits of radically particular cases, as if methodologically oriented by Kant's *Third Critique* rather than their nation's constitutional code? Likewise, should *stare decisis* remain a guiding principle or should we abandon the practice of 'treating like cases alike' for one that emphasizes their absolute difference? Although allowing incommensurability and non-identity to guide legal judgment may sound like a cornerstone of progressive jurisprudence, we would doubt the prudence of affording such latitude to a court if it drifted from the favored ideology. An emphasis on concrete particularity, in other words, can serve all points on the political spectrum.

The belief that re-orienting law to incommensurable particulars will result in a less violent justice system rests on the notion that the other holds a positive ethical charge and its influence will pull law toward responsibility. If law genuflects before the other, we might think, it will show us the way toward justice. But how can we know that the other exerts such normative gravity? Can we be certain that the other – that which is beyond all categorization – belongs to the category of things of ultimate meaning and authority? If that which is beyond our concepts is *unknowable*, how can we *know* that it triggers infinite ethical responsibility?[25]

As I have written elsewhere and Critchley and Caygill have discussed in some detail, Levinas' conception of responsibility seems inextricable from his notion of illeity.[26] Illeity refers to the 'He-ness' of the other, interesting not only because of its gender but because it describes something like the presence of god. I do not wish to overstate this point, but Levinas' use of illeity causes me to worry about the role of god in any Levinasian jurisprudence. Illeity endows the other with its 'absolute' force, and he often derives the authority of the other from its relationship with god despite his attempts to think beyond onto-theology. Does the force that shines from the other and pulls us toward responsibility ultimately emanate from god? Does god give the other its normative authority? Consider the following passage from 'Meaning and Sense':

> To be in the image of God does not mean to be an icon of God but to find oneself in his trace. The revealed God of our Judeo-Christian spirituality maintains all the infinity of his absence, which is in the personal 'order' itself. He shows himself only by his trace, as is said in Exodus 33. To go toward him is not to follow his trace, which is not a sign; it is to go toward the Others who stand in the trace of illeity. It is through this illeity, situated beyond the calculations and reciprocities of economy and of the world, that being has a sense. A sense which is not a finality.[27]

It becomes evident that the Other's ultimate significance does not arise from the enigmatic nature of its concrete particularity, as it does for Adorno, but instead results from a supplement added to its trace from on high.[28] Although Levinas did not strictly identify the Other with god, he does not deny that the normative power of the Other is generated by god. The emphatic redundancy from *Entre Nous* leaves little room for doubt in this regard:

> When I speak to a Christian, I always quote Matthew 25; the relation to God is presented there as a relation to another person. It is not a metaphor: in the other, there is a real presence of God. In my relation to the other, I hear the Word of God. It is not a metaphor; it is not only extremely important, it is literally true. I'm not saying that the other is God, but that in his or her Face I hear the Word of God.[29]

'God is personal,' Levinas continues, 'insofar as He brings about interpersonal relations between myself and my neighbors.'[30] Adriaan Peperzak summarizes how there can be no path to transcendence for Levinas without God leading the way: 'The only chance of contacting God, the only possibility for "transcendence," is walking in the trace he or it left, a trace that always leads to a human face.'[31]

As an agnostic philosopher, this makes me uneasy. I appreciate Levinas' challenge to prevailing models of normativity, and I am genuinely moved by his challenge to rethink the relationship of ethics and theory to the infinite. Levinas wrests questions of ultimate meaning away from the debate between the dueling dogmas of reductive scientism and religious fundamentalism, and his alternative can transform our basic understanding of the relationship between thought and value. Indeed, I often wonder about the presence of a god in the quiet moments when I look into the faces of loved ones and I find devout atheists as dogmatic as those who unquestioningly affirm monotheism. For me, the relationship between god and the infinite remains an open question.

It seems more troublesome, however, to shift from private considerations of the role of god in a phenomenology of the other to a public 'Jurisprudence of Illeity.' How, for instance, would a jurisprudence of illeity respond to those unmoved by the face? How would it arbitrate between those who invest the Other with infinite authority and those who do not? Does an assertion of ethics as first philosophy, even prior to the dialectics between cognition and violence that Adorno prefers, risk preaching to the converted? Might a 'Law of Levinas' lend authority to the most unsavory aspects of his philosophy or to those who adopt his views unreflectively? Perhaps my concerns are unwarranted, but I find these to be important questions to ask.

Even if we could imagine a justice system controlled by Levinasians, could there be a prevailing jurisprudence of alterity? Or is it better suited to occupy a minority position, offering a kind of regulative ideal against which we measure all other legal theories and actions? If Levinas provides a kind a regulative ideal for law, what can we say about the substantive commitments that such a view would entail?

Substance of alterity

With these procedural concerns in view, we can wonder if a jurisprudence of alterity would advocate particular substantive doctrines. Here we first run up against Levinas and Adorno's shared inability to compare the relative merits of laws and legal systems. Notice, for example, how little practical guidance Levinas offers given his prioritization of the saying over the said. According to Levinas, 'the saying is the fact that before the face I do not simply remain there contemplating it, I respond to it.'[32] We can understand the saying as the ethical *event* of speaking to another, and the said as the content of any saying. For Levinas, the 'said does not count as much as the saying itself,' because '[t]he latter is important to me less through its informational contents than by the fact that it is addressed to an interlocutor.'[33] 'It is as though,' Levinas writes, 'saying had a meaning prior to the truth it discloses, prior to the advent of knowledge and information it communicates, free of everything said, a saying that does not tell anything, that infinitely, prevoluntarily, consents.'[34] The 'unsaying of the said' testifies to my ethical imperative to alterity by speaking and relentlessly examining the inability of that very speech to relate non-violently to the other. Thus the saying, or the very gesture of response to the other, takes priority over the said, or the content of any cognitive insight.

Because the said always reduces the other regardless of its content, Levinas offers no means to determine which saids fail less. All substantive claims totalize, so we are left to wonder how to differentiate between the content of any assertions. In a rather alarming passage, Levinas writes:

> The other is maintained and confirmed in his heterogeneity as soon as one calls upon him, be it only to say to him that one cannot speak to him, to classify him as sick, to announce to him his death sentence; at the same time as grasped, wounded, outraged, he is 'respected.'[35]

If calling the other to the gallows can offer a saying that 'respects' her, I wonder if Levinas can make any substantive distinctions relevant for law. Does he allow us any means of evaluating which substantives are less ethically impoverished? Remaining with the example of punishment, can Levinasians distinguish between executing, incarcerating, or rehabilitating? Although Levinas claims that the other commands us not to kill, can he advise us regarding whether imprisonment or torture is necessarily better than death? Adorno's infamous declarations that everything is equally bad present the same difficulty. Any legal systems and judicial decisions, from the most barbaric to the most progressive, appear to arrive at the same ethical dead end by their standards. How, then, can we evaluate the comparative merits of competing forms of governance or principles of law? How might legal actors – whether legislators, judges, attorneys, probation officers, litigants, or others – apply theories that go to such extremes to resist application? Their disengagement from the concrete world of pain and suffering seems inapposite to the very ethos of non-identity thinking. Both Levinas and Adorno attempt to reorient thought toward the normative force of particulars, yet they cannot speak to the concrete suffering of individuals within our legal institutions. Thus they advocate for concrete particulars *in the abstract* but say little regarding *actual* concrete and particular ethical situations.

Here we can wonder if the aversion to rule-making, abstraction, classification, and commensuration disables attempts to dissolve repressive identifications within law? Surely even if all legal institutions are woefully totalitarian and we cannot draw a bright line between democratic and fascistic practices on this ground, we should not consider them ethically equivalent. Two orders of reduction appear to be at issue. First, we can call the initial reduction of objects to concepts 'formal reduction.' Levinas and Adorno meditate on the ethical and cognitive difficulties that arise in this first order. The second order of reduction concerns the undesirable social, political, and legal consequences of the use of reductive categories. Second order reduction necessarily requires first order reduction. The question receiving far too little attention is whether the first order necessarily, and to what extent, entails the second order. A jurisprudence of alterity should be sensitive to the interplay between first and second order reductions, considering how reductive concepts result it domination and suffering.

Neither Levinas nor Adorno, however, can reform the reductive tendencies of law without differentiating between grievous and hateful reductions and their comparatively benign counterparts. Although all legal concepts perpetrate a reductive violence, they are not all equally repressive. As Nancy Fraser understands this dilemma, undiscriminating forms of deconstruction or negative dialectics that denounce all identity concepts, like undiscriminating forms of multiculturalism that celebrate all identities, fail to connect critique with social justice.[36] If all identity concepts are equally insidious, we lose the ability to differentiate between the concepts and their social-political consequences. We must differentiate, for example, between concepts utilized to promote economic equality and those that are openly exploitative and degrading. Without this ability, theories of alterity become, in Fraser's terms, a night in which all cows are gray: 'all identities threaten to become equally fictional, equally repressive, and equally exclusionary.'[37]

Critchley attempts to avoid this danger by arguing that Levinas' slogan that 'politics begins as Ethics' means that 'political space is based on the irreducibility of ethical transcendence, where community takes on meaning in difference without reducing difference.'[38] Such a claim, however, seems rather unhelpful unless it can distinguish between policies that respect difference and those that exterminate it. Legal and political concepts are indeed reductive, and perhaps such violence is never justified in any simple sense. Yet are not some concepts, such as those identifying classes of people in need of special protections from the law, appropriate considering the dangers of not using such concepts? Guyora Binder and Robert Weisberg have stated this need frankly: 'How human beings should be represented in social thought is a pressing moral question, but whether they should be represented is not.'[39] *How* to represent can be addressed with sensitivity to the shortcomings of representation as such, and this would be a welcome alternative to writing off all theories of justice as hopelessly reductive. Yet the problem remains: how can we distinguish between justifiable and unjustifiable violence in law without reverting to the traditional moral theories that Levinas and Adorno find so problematic?

Consider, for instance, the difficulties of weighing the dangers and benefits of a notion like 'equality' in law. Given the centrality of this abstract generalization to so many progressive programs, how can we determine whether social justice warrants the continued use of a commensurating by-product of Enlightenment rationalism? If notions of equality reduce others to the same, should we continue to honor them? Recent history tells the story of the parallel ascendance of democratic forms of governance and free markets wherein formal equality – as in the equality to compete in the global marketplace – becomes a justification not only for treating humans as interchangeable commodities but also for the material inequality between them. The notion of equality can thus be a means of repression as well as liberation, and it seems unclear whether a jurisprudence of alterity can distinguish between these uses.

Critchley claims that although 'my ethical relation to the Other is an unequal, asymmetrical relation to a height that cannot be comprehended,' it also 'opens unto a relation to the third and to humanity as a whole – that is, to a symmetrical community of equals.'[40] Because of this ultimate equality, Critchley writes, 'I can feel myself to be an other like the others – that is, one of a community that can demand its rights regardless of its duties.'[41] Critchley further claims that '[d]emocracy is the form of society committed to the political equality of all its citizens and the ethical inequality of myself faced with the Other,' but what does he mean by this rhetorically powerful but often ambiguous term?[42] *Who* deserves equality and of *what* do they deserve equal proportions? Can Levinas or Adorno help us to determine whether notions of equality hinder or advance our 'openness to the other' or to distinguish between repressive and responsible conceptions and uses of the term?

Notice the extent of these difficulties for matters of legal identity and distributive justice.[43] Rather than adopting the multicultural position that celebrates group identity, for instance by recognizing and ennobling diverse racial classifications, a jurisprudence of alterity would presumably favor antiessentialist conceptions of personal identity that understand individuals as radically particular. If we deny the particularity of the other by categorizing her according to racial indicia, this would appear to violate the particularism advanced by Levinas and Adorno. Instead of reinforcing totalizing identity concepts, antiessentialists attempt to overcome such identifications by deconstructing their meanings and exposing them as fallout from totalizing narratives. Radical otherness exists beyond the binary classifications of personal identity, and philosophers of alterity therefore appear to support a kind of 'politics of non-identity.'

Where does this leave the antiessentialist committed to social and economic justice? If we should dissolve our reductive racial categories, for example, how can we advocate for those who suffer from the legacy of such discrimination? How do we improve the economic status of racial minorities if race requires an illusory metaphysics? Should we instead respond to the individual demands of each radically distinct other and thereby look past racial concepts? It seems that we cannot think in terms of structural violence and structural reform without adopting a totalizing view, but should we not nevertheless consider the potential benefits? A jurisprudence of alterity would surely resist the sorts of reductive identifications used in racial profiling, but what about those necessary for affirmative action programs? How can we maintain antiessentialism without abandoning the ability to redress the harms visited upon those subordinated because of their historical classification within disfavored groups? When advocating for equal pay for women, for example, how can we provide special protections and remedies for women without reifying essentialist gender categories? Neither Levinas nor Adorno provide guidance regarding how an antiessentialist legal orientation can sustain its recognitive position while working toward redistributive and other remedial ends. From their perspective, the current methods of achieving social justice in law are always Pyrrhic victories.

I imagine that Levinas would be much more helpful for the analysis of contemporary social and legal issues if we could supplement his insights with something like Adorno's materialist sensitivities. Although other commentators may disagree and cite Levinas' occasional references to economic injustice, I find his transcendental phenomenology unsatisfying when compared to Adorno's refusal to consider the non-identical outside of its sociological environment.[44] For Adorno, identity thinking is an anthropological practice that originates in the drive for survival and develops into universal commodification. While Levinas offers a largely ahistorical and transcendental critique, Adorno engages the gritty details of the central features of life in a post-Holocaust culture increasingly ordered by capitalism: meaning is lost as cosmological narratives deflate, scientific rationality piles on reasons why our lives and suffering are irrelevant, and the money economy makes the most insidious forms of abstract classification global and compulsory. This account of the relationships between identity thinking, instrumental rationality, and domination contextualizes alterity in a manner largely unavailable to Levinasian ethical phenomenology despite his appreciation of the specific difficulties presented by the 'famished stomach that has no ears, capable of killing for a crust of bread.'[45] In my view, a jurisprudence of alterity would be compromised without an acute sensitivity to the contours of legal culture within modern economic structures. Perhaps we should supplement Levinas with Marx, and Adorno with even more Marx.

Levinas and Adorno create obstacles on certain paths toward economic reform, yet economic justice seems like an essential means to the ends they envision because their ethical demands are far more practicable when supported by favorable social and political conditions. Hunger, repression, and war are considerably less likely to foster the type of non-instrumental relations they advocate because of the instrumental demands individuals under such circumstances face. Although both Adorno and Levinas argue that we should not subordinate ethical responsibility to survival itself, the motivations underlying repressive identification are strongest in times of fear and competition. It will be most difficult, but perhaps most critical, to genuflect before and bracket instrumentalizations of another when her boot is on my throat. Economic and political circumstances condition cognitive habits, and, as current events have made clear, a perceived threat from members of a class will reinforce rather than dissolve repressive identifications. Constitutive feedback reverberates amongst economic conditions, legal frameworks, and the cognitive behavior of citizens, and any hope to reform ethical habits should be mindful of this dialectic.

Most generally, I fear that the problems for law created by the indiscriminate critique of traditional normative theories risk stalling all progressive legal reform. Of all the problems that face contemporary legal reformers, I wonder whether we can consider Levinas and Adorno allies with respect to any particular issues. In addition to the concerns related to redistributive justice, for instance, what might a jurisprudence of alterity contribute to theories of punishment as mentioned earlier? Although they undermine the confidence of all justifications for punishment, does this entail that Levinas and Adorno would support a complete abolition of all punitive activity? Should we adopt a radical passivity toward all offenders, from corporate tax evaders to war criminals? Would this prohibit even rehabilitative punishment? And although we might extrapolate a Levinasian position on any number of debates, this may lead toward potentially unwelcome conclusions. Given his clear advocacy for non-violent relations with the other and his disdain for liberal conceptions of freedom, for example, I suspect that extending Levinas' views to abortion or assisted suicide would require us to denounce both. Or how would Levinas address French immigration policy, especially considering his surprising claim that that the war with Germany was justified 'in order to defend the French language'?[46] Moreover, Levinas was quite clear that non-human animals did not deserve the sort of ethical considerations afforded to humans.[47] Should we look to his philosophy when regulating industrial slaughterhouses? Perhaps these questions are generally outside the scope of theories of alterity, but they seem difficult to avoid if we are serious about applying philosophers like Levinas and Adorno to law. Of course, Levinas' own statements and misstatements need not be the last word on Levinasianism. Just as we can bracket Kant's sexist and racist remarks as we take Kantianism forward, we can correct Levinas on his own terms. But as many now argue that Kant's unsavory remarks point to deeper flaws in his system – for instance that his racism and speciesism reflect a bias for the white European male as the prototype of the rational agent – we should be open to engaging in a similarly critical relationship with Levinas.

Conclusion

These are sobering questions for me. I find the challenges that Levinas and Adorno pose to modernity and the history of philosophy quite powerful, yet their resistance to practical philosophy is deeply frustrating. Surely not all philosophers must satisfy our desire to put philosophy to use, but Levinas and Adorno seem to have relinquished their ability to judge legal and political activity. This seems far from an apolitical, pre-political, or meta-political position. I cannot help but think that no politics is bad politics – politics stripped of evaluative thought. This worries Fraser as well because such a position

> is tantamount to surrendering any possibility of distinguishing emancipatory and oppressive identity claims, benign and pernicious differences. Thus, deconstructive antiessentialists evade political questions of the day: Which identity claims are rooted in the defense of social relations of inequality and domination? And which are rooted in a challenge to such relations? Which identity claims carry the potential to expand actually existing democracy? And which, in contrast, work against democratization? Which differences, finally, should a democratic society seek to foster, and which, on the contrary, should it aim to abolish?[48]

Although 'we are not now in a position to envision a full-scale successor to socialism,' Fraser encourages us to 'try nevertheless to conceive provisional alternatives to the present order that could supply a basis for a progressive politics.'[49] There may be no leftist utopia, and all campaigns claiming otherwise should be treated with deep suspicion. We will not overcome identity thinking in grand political reformations, but we can fight it in the minutiae of each conflict, policy, and practice. Laws do identify and categorize, but they do not all do so with equal violence and disregard for particularity. Levinas and Adorno, however, deny us any means of drawing comfortable distinctions between the justifiable and unjustifiable.

Given the current state of law and politics, the prospects of achieving reform through non-identity thinking seem quite grim. Even if we could – against Levinas and Adorno's spirit – activate a coherent program of reform around theories of alterity, I doubt they could match the powers promoting their antithesis. Prevailing instrumental institutions gain momentum and crush or integrate theories of alterity, and the strategy of abstaining from political life in order to preserve the protest against instrumentality seems more desperate than ever. Our objective should not merely be to use thought to remember the non-identical, but rather to safeguard the thought of the non-identical while acting to release it from blind domination. Without both a practical orientation toward transforming material conditions and a tolerance for the organizational categories necessary to implement such reform, deconstruction and critical theory seem severed from their radical traditions. Pretending that these critiques provide a form of resistance when they live harmlessly in their academic niche only reinforces the status quo.

As Adorno and Marx recognized, reason struggles to navigate a course that gives it effect in the concrete world without sacrificing it to the instrumentalities of that world. I like to think that law is an ally in this project, but I now wonder if there is any practical upshot for a jurisprudence of alterity. Any attempt to discover legal praxis in Levinas and Adorno will traverse such heights that the reformer, if not forced to turn back, will ultimately find herself in air so theoretically rarified that one might doubt if any community could survive at its altitude. From this perspective, a jurisprudence of alterity seems most relevant as a regulative ideal for all legal activity. Yet for those of us inclined to seek guidance for law in Levinas or Adorno because we are moved by the threats of authoritarianism and consumerism, we find ourselves on strangely familiar ground as we stand on this summit. Though separated by miles of conceptual elevation, we arrive at the familiar practical values recognized by the traditions we seek to overcome: dignity, respect, difference, non-violence, dialogue, participation, and so on. Did we find these practical principles at the height of Levinas and Adorno's works, or did we bring our interpretive biases with us? It seems odd, for instance, to rely on a radical critique of Western metaphysics to support rather pedestrian arguments against racial profiling, capital punishment, violations of human rights, or the recent wars in Iraq. We can make such arguments with much less controversial premises, and hence I am suspicious of myself. Am I, as Adorno accused Lukács, 'guilty of smuggl[ing] back the most pitiful clichés of the conformism to which the critique had once been directed?'[50] Can law ever be more than such a cliché?

Notes

1. N. Smith, 'Incommensurability and Alterity in Contemporary Jurisprudence,' *Buffalo Law Review* 45 (1997) 503–553.
2. For recent discussions of Levinas' relevance to political theory, see B. Bergo, *Levinas between Ethics and Politics: For the Beauty that Adorns the Earth* (Pittsburgh: Duquesne University Press, 2003); H. Caygill, *Levinas and the Political* (New York: Routledge, 2002); and S. Critchley, 'Five Problems in Levinas' View of Politics and a Sketch of a Solution to Them,' *Political Theory* 32 (2004) 172–185.
3. D. Manderson, *Proximity, Levinas, and the Soul of Law* (Montreal: McGill University Press, 2007).
4. N. Smith, 'Adorno vs. Levinas: Evaluating Points of Contention,' *Continental Philosophy Review* 40 (2007) 275–306.
5. See, for example, H. de Vries, *Minimal Theologies: Critiques of Secular Reason in Adorno and Levinas*, trans. G. Hale (Baltimore: Johns Hopkins University Press, 2005); C. F. Alford, *Levinas, The Frankfurt School, and Psychoanalysis* (Middletown: Wesleyan University Press, 2003); J. Cohen, *Interrupting Auschwitz: Art, Religion, Philosophy* (New York: Continuum Press, 2003); A. Horowitz, "'By a Hair's Breadth": Critique, Transcendence, and the Ethical in Adorno and Levinas,' *Philosophy and Social Criticism* 28/2 (2002) 213–248, 221.
6. Critchley, 'Five Problems in Levinas' View of Politics.'
7. Ibid.
8. For recent discussions of Adorno's relevance to political theory, see E. Hammer, *Adorno and the Political* (New York: Routledge, 2005); L. Jager, *Adorno: A Political Biography*, trans. S. Spencer (New Haven: Yale University Press, 2004); L. Zuidervaart, *Social Philosophy after Adorno* (New York: Cambridge University Press, 2007); and R. Berman, 'Adorno's Politics' in N. Gibson and A. Rubin (eds), *Adorno: A Critical Reader* (New York: Blackwell, 2003).
9. See S. Critchley, *The Ethics of Deconstruction: Derrida and Levinas* (New York: Blackwell, 1992) p. 222: 'politics is the primacy of the synoptic, panoramic vision of society, wherein a disinterested political agent views society as a whole. For Levinas, such panoramic vision, not only that of the philosopher but also that of the political theorist, is the greatest danger, because it loses sight of ethical difference – that is, of my particular relation to obligations toward the Other.'
10. E. Levinas, *Difficult Freedom: Essays on Judaism*, trans. S. Hand (Baltimore: Johns Hopkins University Press, 1997) pp. 206–207.
11. E. Levinas, *Totality and Infinity: An Essay on Exteriority*, trans. A. Lingis (Pittsburgh: Duquesne University Press, 1969) p. 21 [hereinafter TI].
12. M. Horkheimer and T. W. Adorno, *Dialectic of Enlightenment*, trans. J. Cumming (New York: Continuum, 1972) p. 275.
13. Ibid., p. xiv.
14. Ibid., p. 145.
15. T. W. Adorno, *Minima Moralia*, trans. E. F. N. Jephcott (New York: Verso, 1974) p. 46.

16. G. Lukács, *The Theory of the Novel*, trans. A. Bostock (Cambridge, MA: MIT Press, 1974) p. 22.
17. H. Krahl, 'The Political Contradictions in Adorno's Critical Theory' in J. Bernstein (ed.), *The Frankfurt School: Critical Assessments, Vol. 4* (New York: Routledge, 1994) p. 117.
18. See D. Cornell, *The Philosophy of the Limit* (New York: Routledge, 1992) p. 181.
19. Ibid., p. 39. Cornell states: 'twentieth century experience has presumably taught us that the appeal to community ineluctably slides into an appeal to totality, closure, and exclusion.'
20. Iris Marion Young has followed Adorno's critique of the inadequacy and violence of political concepts. See I. M. Young, 'The Ideal of Community and the Politics of Difference,' *Social Theory and Practice* 12 (1986) 1–26, 1–2: 'I criticize the notion of community on both philosophical and practical grounds. I argue that the ideal of community participates in what . . . Adorno calls the logic of identity, a metaphysics that denies difference. The ideal of community presumes subjects who are present to themselves and can understand another as they understand themselves. It thus denies the difference between subjects. The desire for community relies on the same desire for social wholeness [and] identification that underlies racism and ethnic chauvinism, on the one hand, and political sectarianism, on the other.'
21. J. Habermas, 'The New Obscurities: The Crisis of the Welfare State and the Exhaustion of Utopian Energies,' *Philosophy and Social Criticism* 11 (2) (1986), 1–18.
22. D. Cornell, M. Rosenfeld, and D. Gray Carlson, (eds), *Deconstruction and the Possibility of Justice* (New York: Routledge, 1992).
23. See N. Smith, 'Adorno vs. Levinas' and Smith, 'Making Adorno's Ethics and Politics Explicit,' *Social Theory and Practice* 29 (3) (2003) 487–498 (reviewing J. M. Bernstein, *Adorno: Disenchantment and Ethics* (New York: Cambridge University Press, 2001).
24. See Bernstein, *Adorno: Disenchantment and Ethics*.
25. For similar concerns, see E. Hammer, 'God Squaddy,' *Radical Philosophy* 134 (2005); and R. Visker, 'Is Ethics Fundamental?' *Continental Philosophy Review* 36–3 (2003) 263–302.
26. See Caygill, *Levinas and the Political*, p. 31 and Critchley, 'Five Problems in Levinas' View of Politics,' p. 174.
27. E. Levinas, 'Meaning and Sense,' in A. Peperzak, S. Critchley, and R. Bernasconi (eds), *Emmanuel Levinas: Basic Philosophical Writings* (Bloomington: Indiana University Press, 1996) p. 64.
28. Levinas' assertion that 'the enigma comes to us from Illeity' contributes to this sense of the force of the Other being channeled from above. See Levinas, 'Enigma and Phenomenon' in *Basic Philosophical Writings* 75.
29. E. Levinas, *Entre Nous: Thinking-of-the-Other*, trans. M. B. Smith and B. Harshav (New York: Columbia University Press, 1998) p. 110.
30. Ibid.
31. A. Peperzak, '*Illeity* According to Levinas,' *Philosophy Today* 42 (Suppl) (1998) 41–46, 45.
32. E. Levinas, *Ethics and Infinity*, trans. R. E. Cohen (Pittsburgh: Duquesne University Press, 1985) p. 88.

33. Ibid., p. 42.
34. E. Levinas, 'No Identity,' in *The Levinas Reader*, trans. S. Hand (Oxford: Blackwell: 1989) p. 146.
35. Levinas, TI, p. 69.
36. N. Fraser, *Justice Interruptus: Critical Reflections on the Post-Socialist Condition* (New York: Routledge, 1996) p. 175.
37. Critchley, *The Ethics of Deconstruction*, p. 253.
38. Ibid.
39. G. Binder and R. Weisberg, *Literary Criticisms of Law* (Princeton: Princeton University Press, 2000) p. 462.
40. Critchley, *The Ethics of Deconstruction*, p. 226.
41. Ibid., p. 231.
42. Ibid., p. 239.
43. I consider these issues at length in 'Social Justice and Anti-essentialist Legal Identity,' *Continental Philosophy Review* (forthcoming).
44. Levinas once claimed that 'justice can have no other object than economic equality.' See E. Levinas, 'The Ego and the Totality,' in A. Lingis (ed.), *Collected Philosophical Papers* (Pittsburgh: Duquesne University Press, 1987) p. 44. On page 39 of this essay he also claims that ' "earthly morality" is rightly suspicious of every relation between beings which has not first been an economic relation.'
45. Levinas, TI, p. 118.
46. F. Poirié, *Emmanuel Levinas: Qui êtes-vous?* (Lyon, France: La Manufacture, 1987) p. 74, cited in Critchley, 'Five Problems in Levinas' View of Politics,' p. 177.
47. See Smith, 'Adorno vs. Levinas.' For discussions of Levinas' position on animals, see P. Atterton, 'Face to Face with the Other Animal?' in P. Atterton, M. Calarco, and M. Friedman (eds), *Levinas and Buber: Dialogue and Difference* (Pittsburgh: Duquesne University Press, 2004) pp. 262–281; M. Calarco, 'Deconstruction Is Not Vegetarianism: Humanism, Subjectivity, and Animal Ethics,' *Continental Philosophy Review* 36 (2004) 175–201; D. Clark, 'On Being "The Last Kantian in Nazi Germany": Dealing with Animals after Levinas' in J. Ham and M. Senior (eds), *Animal Acts: Configuring the Human in Western History* (New York: Routledge, 1997) pp. 165–198; J. Llewelyn, 'Am I Obsessed by Bobby? (Humanism of the Other Animal)' in R. Bernasconi and S. Critchley (eds), *Re-Reading Levinas* (Bloomington: Indiana University Press, 1989) pp. 234–245.
48. Fraser, *Justice Interruptus: Critical Reflections on the Post-Socialist Condition*, p. 182.
49. Ibid., p. 4.
50. T. W. Adorno, 'Extorted Reconciliation: On Georg Lukacs' Realism in Our Time' in trans. S. W. Nicholsen, *Notes to Literature I* (New York: Columbia University Press, 1991) p. 217.

4
Productive Ambivalence: Levinasian Subjectivity, Justice, and the Rule of Law[1]

Jill Stauffer

Introduction

The weight of justice hangs on the distinction between consent to obligation and responsibility for what no one would choose. What could this mean? It is often thought that the philosophy of Emmanuel Levinas gives us valuable insight into the field of ethics, but has little to offer when it comes time to make the difficult decisions imposed on us by politics and institutional legality. However, if the weight of justice does hang on the distinction between consent to obligation and responsibility for what no one would choose, then what Levinas offers us with his philosophical description of human subjectivity sets in motion a much needed correction to a tradition we might wish to preserve in some of its aspects. That tradition – of liberal rule of law legality and equal rights – assumes that the subject of law and of rights is autonomous and self-sufficient, capable of consenting to take on any duty he or she would bear. That narrative respects individuals and supports liberal ideas about justice but cannot explain to us why we might bear duties beyond our legitimate legal duties. And yet such duties are indelible in our current political landscape: Who is responsible for the refugee, the prisoner of war, the sufferer of poverty or famine, the one to whom I never consented to owe a thing? If we want to answer those questions with any lasting success, we need to amend the theoretical pre-history of liberal individualism, starting with the narrative of subjectivity we inherit from that tradition. This chapter will set forth Levinas' revision of subjectivity, show its affinity with the tension between formalism and responsiveness we find in rule of law theory and practice, and gesture toward a new way to conceive of a liberatory form of individualism, all for the sake of justice.

It's not that theorists of liberal individualism deny or fail to appreciate that individuals need the protections granted by rights only in the context of a prior plurality – a plurality on which the individual is, in some measure, dependant. That dependency is, after all, the reason why individualist theories create a self-sufficient subject: calling the individual autonomous accords with liberal ideas about how the subject ought to be treated – by law and by other human beings. But how do we harmonize that fiction with the fact that protections put forth by philosophies of liberal individualism are efficacious only when made formal by means of their promulgation as legally binding standards recognized and enforced by institutionalized legality? What becomes, then, of the subject's primordial self-sufficiency and innate rights? Might it be possible to retain what is important about the subject's autonomy while admitting that vulnerability is the real backdrop to most of our experiences of subjectivity, law, and politics?

Such an approach would also help to explain why ideas about autonomy do more than support existing law; they also strengthen aspirations to a broader form of justice not yet attained by institutional legality. Rights often function simultaneously as legal standards and as objections to existing legal forms that do not award rights equally. The two functions – of legality and aspiration – can be at odds with each other while cohabiting in space and time. It is not controversial to claim, however, that only *legal* rights protect individuals in any reliable way – hence the aspiration always to expand the sphere of rights to accommodate more claims of justice within legal institutions. While the expansion of rights may be a just project, it may also neglect to observe something about what justice is beyond rights and legality. Part of my argument will be that revising the pre-history of liberal subjectivity brings us back to something that rights-based theories sometimes miss.

It is not that formal institutional legality is *bad*. It is simply that justice requires more than formal legality. Levinas' philosophy helps us understand this by asking us to balance formality with more chaotic demands of ethics that nonetheless also stand for justice. Levinas' use of the terms 'ethics,' 'politics,' and 'justice' is idiosyncratic, and must always be defined against other usages, whether in daily speech or political philosophy. 'Ethics,' for Levinas, is not order or a set of rules, but disorder, chaos, the challenge to all systematic instantiations of justice. In turn 'justice' and 'politics,' for Levinas, both stand for institutional legality – for its better and its worse – more than they do for aspirations beyond institutions.

Some accounts of Levinasian justice assume that what Levinas calls ethics (something beyond or outside of institutions) saves us from the excesses of what Levinas calls politics or justice (institutionalized forms of governance).[2] Those accounts are mistaken not only because they do not describe adequately what Levinas writes, but because choosing ethics over justice simply subjects existing structures to a reversal. Reversals, like some revolutions, can occur even while leaving underlying structures undisturbed, to be taken up by new powers who will preside over regimes organized much like what was overthrown.

In short, reversal is not radical enough to do justice to Levinas' philosophy, and Levinas is careful to demonstrate to us that reversal on its own will not do. His aim is to draw us into disorder, to upset our presuppositions about how ethical responsibilities work and are incurred. Then, once we are disoriented, ejected from our legal and ethical formalisms, Levinas reminds us that the point was not to destroy formalism but to balance it with important responsibilities that cannot be formalized but which do matter to any true account of justice. Calling for an unending weighing of competing demands ends up being more radical than the project of total reversal.

The self

First we need to amend the theoretical pre-history of liberal individualism. And so we begin with the Levinasian subject: a hostage, persecuted by a responsibility it never chose. Instead of an original freedom, Levinas posits an absolute subjection to a responsibility it is not possible to choose or refuse. He writes:

> responsibility for another is not an accident that happens to a subject, but precedes essence in it, has not awaited freedom in which a commitment to another would have been made. I have not done anything and I have always been under accusation – persecuted.... Responsibility... is the impossibility to come back from all things and concern oneself only with oneself. It is to hold onto oneself while gnawing away at oneself.[3]

Levinas' narrative of subjectivity describes a subject always already split because of the demands of others, and lacking the freedom to choose different circumstances. This is not the primordially self-sufficient liberal individual. Nevertheless, despite the unchosenness of the self's response to others, the self is not a saint. As Levinas conceives it, the self does try to escape from the unchosen sense of responsibility that occurs because of the other's demand. The self (*soi*) is affected by an ego (*le Moi*) and also by 'me' (*moi*), the part of the self we might call pre-political. *moi* senses the demand of an other and thus is pressed by a responsibility it never chose. Fleeing into itself in an attempt to evade the demands of responsibility, *moi* finds *le Moi*, the ego, and disturbs the ego's tranquility. This movement of 'me' (*moi*) into the self, where it encounters the ego (*le Moi*), fractures or interrupts the sovereignty that the ego formerly thought it possessed. One might say that *le Moi* thought it was all of *soi* until *moi* came along to trouble the seamlessness of that narrative.

The subject's identity, in this moment, is revealed as something other than A=A. I am 'ego' *and* 'me.' Or, better, given that this whole self-revelation is put in motion by what is not-me – 'the other' – I am 'ego' and 'me' and 'other,' all at once, deep within myself. That is what it means to be a human being and be affected by others regardless of anything we might have wished. The self just is an ambivalence, a double movement, between self and other.

For Levinas, to become a self is to accept enchainment to one's body. In his 1934 essay 'Reflections on the Philosophy of Hitlerism,' Levinas contends that Hitlerism gains currency in part because, despite its manifest racism, it contains a truth of the body: its rootedness in material conditions. A problem with liberalism, according to Levinas, is the abstraction of its freedom: thought's freedom from rootedness in the body harbors the danger that thought can become a game. The power to doubt becomes a lack of conviction wherein there is no need to commit to any truth.[4] Paradoxically, this lack of commitment means that the ideals of freedom and equality can be embraced and made the objects of fervent belief without ever being actualized. Levinas writes in 'Humanism and Anarchy' that 'the postponement ad infinitum of the *Sollen* [the "ought"], which devolves from the subject posited as ego...announces the failure involved in human action.'[5] When freedom and equality are abstractions without issue, human beings become alienated from them precisely because they fail to materialize in real human living conditions.

The self and justice

Perhaps the experience we have of being 'embodied' gives us a better basis for pursuing a persuasive account of humanity than does the abstract autonomous individual always-already endowed with an intellectual freedom regardless of the various forms of physical, psychical, or other oppression that the concrete person might undergo. Perhaps an 'embodied' philosophy will also give us a rule of law legality capable of seeing beyond rule of law formalism. I have written elsewhere about how theories of the rule of law are conspicuous in their inability to agree about what the rule of law is and what it requires of us, even as they lay out rules or offer descriptions.[6] If we read Hart, Fuller, Raz, Dworkin et al. on the rule of law, we can't help but emerge with more questions than answers. That is as it should be, I contend, because it points us to the limits of formalism, or of theory, in describing for us what law is and ought to be. However, one thing remains clear amongst all the divergent views. As Annabel Herzog puts it, 'hunger in the face of the Other is not an anonymous and formal expression; it indicates the collapse of all formalism: *This* Other's hunger opens *this* humanity's hunger.'[7] It is the same with justice, we might say. The call for justice issued by the other is not anonymous and formal, even if it issues from halfway around the world in a person or persons whom I will never meet. When I read testimony of victims of rape as a crime against humanity, or hear a report about a woman who bribes her jailer to kill her quickly instead of slowly, I undergo a passion for justice that is not a product of reason and has nothing to do with deducing what I owe. Gross injustice indicates the collapse of all formalism.

The problem is that I don't know with certainty, when formalism collapses, what to do with my ethical response. How does my response become a form that will do justice? I know, from reading Levinas, and from observing how legal institutions work and malfunction, that turning my response into a form, or submitting it to institutional procedures, may be fair, but it will not always be fair. And, even when procedures are fair, they are not always just. There are, as Levinas points out in the discussion following his essay 'Transcendence and Height,' the tears the civil servant can't see.[8] In addition, formal equality may help us guide our interactions with other people in stable and orderly ways, but the differences and distinctions institutions awarding formal equality must ignore in order to make subjects formally equal may at times need to be asserted and maintained *rather* than ignored if we are to do justice. To put it in Levinasian language, institutions can only assimilate the Other into the Same. That is not always an injustice, formally speaking. But justice requires more. And that is why the question that must be answered, really, by anyone who wants to speak of a Levinasian politics or justice, is: What is the relation of ethics to justice, or ethics to politics?

Levinas calls the relation a necessary one. But he does so in a way that won't answer, to our satisfaction, the question we have about what we ought to *do* about our response to others. To answer that question with any finality would be to commit Levinasian ethics to a system and thereby betray the infinite responsibility for which ethics stands. The relation between ethics and politics is not unidirectional, nor causal or temporal. It is an oscillation, an indecision, a constant balancing, an endless vigilance. That is what justice requires. Institutions of law call what is needed in instances such as these, *judgment*. Part of my point is that the uncertainty of Levinas' ethics is already contained in any system of law, and in most accounts of what the rule of law is or ought to be. Rigorous attention to one idea of what the rule of law requires might tempt us to overlook the ways in which every system of law is involved in an unending process of balancing competing demands. But consideration of theories and practices of the rule of law reveal to us an endless oscillation that never rests finally on one idea.

Productive ambivalence

And so we turn to ambivalence. We've seen that there is an ambivalence in subjectivity, between self and other, or between security and responsibility. When I am called by the other, it is despite myself. In turn there is a tension within liberal thought between belief in rule of law standards (security, the part of the law that tends toward stability) and impatience with regard to rule of law safeguards (responsibility, the part of the law that tends toward responsiveness).

The rule of law, then, is wrought of the tension between stability and responsiveness. For instance, in the international arena, many thinkers and observers were impatient following World War II when it came time to set up the Nuremberg Tribunal. Lawyers worried about the legality of the tribunal because of the retroactive status of its powers – retroactivity undermines what is stable in law by holding people to standards by which they could not have been guided, since those standards were not yet in effect at the time of commission of the actions being judged. Others couldn't understand why anyone would worry about the retroactivity of law for something that was so manifestly a grave crime. They were impatient with the idea that we might not be able to rule on something we had not had the foresight to call unlawful in advance. That tension stands for an ambivalence – a *productive* ambivalence – that reflects competing demands of justice faced by law. One demand is that the law be knowable, obeyable, non-retroactive, stable. That is what is often called 'the rule of law.' But another, equally important demand is that law be responsive to claims of justice it may not yet have had time or opportunity to accommodate. Thus the paradox of the rule of law is that sometimes we have to ignore what it demands in order to adhere to what it stands for.

We must be careful with how we make the foregoing claim, however, because concern for rule of law formality is neither rule fetishism nor the product of an analytic mind gone wildly strict – though that could be the impression given by the idealist claim made by some readers of Levinas that ethics ought to guide politics. Such a claim seems to assume that usually, in the contemporary world, politics guides ethics, and politics is necessarily corrupt; hence, the claim might continue, politics would be better if it were guided by an ethic of saints. One can't say of Levinas that he means for ethics to guide politics unless one also notes that he expects politics to guide ethics, as I will demonstrate. So, it's not that those who would cling to the rule of law are stubborn and can't see the larger picture formed by a better view of what it means to be just.[9] Institutional legality is, whatever else it is, monopolized power backed by violence. And so it matters – not only to lawyers – when we decide that an institution may judge things it hasn't judged before.

To illustrate this, I'll offer another example from international law. In a 1999 report, UN Secretary-General Kofi Annan posed a set of questions in the aftermath of the Rwandan genocide.[10] The questions address the tension inherent in the rule of law as it emerges in conflicts over what international humanitarian law forbids and requires. In them we witness again the simultaneity of concern for strict adherence to rule of law standards and impatience with regard to the injustice such strictness can sometimes create. Thomas Franck summarizes Annan's questions:

> Suppose there had been a coalition of the willing able to act preemptively, but consent for such rescue had been blocked by the opposition of a permanent member of the Security Council. Had there been a choice, would it have been better to sacrifice the Charter rules if it were possible thereby to save a multitude? Or, would it have been better, at least in the long run, to sacrifice those lives in order more firmly to uphold the letter of the law? What would be the costs to the system of allowing the rules to be bent or... of 'setting dangerous precedents for future interventions without clear criteria to decide who might invoke those precedents and in what circumstances?' What, on the other hand, would have been the cost to the credibility of the normative system were strict adherence to the laws to have been the proximate cause of mass slaughter of innocents?[11]

Annan's set of questions reminds us that the rule of law will not guide people if it demonstrates itself to be *capable* of ignoring or facilitating gross injustice, and *incapable* of saving 800,000 lives. But it also reminds us that any exceptions we make to it for the sake of justice may well be claimed in the future by those whose aims are not just.

Consider the NATO intervention in Kosovo, which was undertaken without UN Security Council approval. Those who call that event lawful in retrospect ignore traditional methods of interpretation of international law, citing instead a 'jury of nations' or a consensus on what the best course of action was, given the political and temporal constraints. Such thinkers and practitioners do this because they recognize a need for intervention that cannot be met by existing UN practices and rules. However, if there is a 'jury of nations' coming to a consensus, it is a jury that does not include Russia, China, India, Namibia, Belarus, Ukraine, Iran, Thailand, Indonesia, and South Africa, nor any of the 133 developing states of the G77 that adopted two different declarations affirming that unilateral humanitarian intervention is illegal under international law.[12] The dissent is considerable, and worth considering. Sometimes a rigid adherence to the letter of the law reveals the limits of procedural forms or the nihilistic indecision of powerful nations, as when Article 4.2 of the UN Charter (the article on state sovereignty) is used as justification for not intervening in the Rwandan genocide. But at other times such legalism stands for the 'rule of law' that protects all subjects of law equally, defending them from frequent changes in law that would render law difficult to follow and that would also leave law prey to majority interests or the interests of those with greater political power. I have claimed that just law transpires as a balance of stability and responsiveness. We see now that too much stability is inhuman, whereas too much responsiveness can undermine the formal equality for which the rule of law ought to stand. What Levinas gives us with his revision of human subjectivity in *Otherwise Than Being* is reflected in the contemporary 'ethical history' of the international order: we cannot choose ethics *or* politics to lead us, placing one as permanent sovereign over the other, because either choice leads to insupportable conclusions.

Indeed, the principle of the equality of sovereign states is respected in international law to such an extent (despite current glaring exceptions) by so many UN member-states large and small, that even when interventions are conducted for humanitarian reasons – as they were in Bangladesh, Cambodia, and Uganda – they are often justified on other terms, such as national security. Alternate terms are chosen in order to avoid setting a dangerous precedent for intervention that other states might take up for reasons that do not tend toward justice. In short, there is reason to be cautious about changes in international law – despite its manifest defects – if only because there is no guarantee that changes forced by exceptional practice would tend toward justice.[13] It is very possible that such changes would end up undermining whatever exists of equality among states, installing hegemonic powers in exceptional positions that would be not only privileged but also newly *justified* by international legal standards.

So, while it is surely important to question both legal formalism and any unquestioning adherence to existing rules (as does most any use of Levinas' work for political or legal theory), it is unrealistic to suggest that something uncodifiable like Levinasian ethics can do much more than interrupt the seamlessness of law's formalism. The Levinasian arguments I've called linear or causal tend to propose a logic of reversal, whereby instead of judging ethics by politics or placing politics over ethics, we judge politics by ethics or place ethics over politics. That claim is not supported by Levinas' philosophy, nor does it give us a hope of greater justice; it may even be dangerous. Levinas' point is more subtle and more challenging, and requires of us a great and endless effort on behalf of justice – what I've given the odd name of 'productive ambivalence,' and about which I will soon say more. My point for now is that this does not make Levinasian ethics weaker or hopelessly abstract, but rather endows such ethics with their radical potential.

Concrete demands and a problem

In *Otherwise Than Being*, Levinas writes that his ethics of the other is not 'a deforming abstraction.'[14] He continues: 'In [ethics] justice is shown from the first.... This means concretely or empirically that justice is not a legality regulating human masses, from which a technique of social equilibrium is drawn, harmonizing antagonistic forces. That would be a justification of the State delivered over to its own necessities.' In other words, justice, which for Levinas means institutional legality (with some characteristic slippage of definition in the above quotation), is shown in ethics, the irreducible relationship to the other that summons forth in me a responsibility I had neither time nor opportunity to choose. I bear this response to others *and* the responsibility it bespeaks much as I bear the pains and pleasures that come along with being inescapably situated in a body – it is *that* concrete. Levinas adds that 'justice, society, the State and its institutions' come to be known only on the basis of this prior ethics. As such, he reminds us that 'it is important to recover all these forms beginning with [ethics], in which being, totality, the State, politics, techniques, work, are at every moment on the point of having their center of gravitation in themselves, and weighing on their own account.'[15] These forms, sometimes even these formalisms, are knowable to us – they form and are formed by the structure of our knowledge. We use them to order our lives and to govern our interactions with others. As such they are always on the very edge of being declared the totality of how we must and do govern our relations with others. But Levinas demonstrates that these forms are comprehensible only because of a prior ethics, something utterly concrete – our unchosen response to others. Ethics animates justice, and then also balances the tendency of justice to forget that its procedural form loses something of what inspired it in the first place: the human relationship.

But it is equally true that ethics on its own is inhuman in some way. As much as law and politics are always trying to be their own center of gravity, ethics, with its infinite demand, threatens to engulf the self, who is incapable of infinity. This installs deep within Levinas' philosophic oeuvre a difficulty from which it may seem impossible to escape: how can the finite self carry an infinite demand? (And, important for any theory of human happiness: why *would* the self do so?)

The problem and two solutions

The impossibility of the finite self fulfilling the demand of infinite responsibility is met by Levinas in two ways: the first is that we simply answer the demand by taking it up, and thereby undo the impossibility: 'it is experienced precisely by constantly running up against it, and crossing over its own contestation.'[16] That is the enigma of the Infinite in Levinas' thinking, and also one argument for why his ethics are resolutely secular despite the theological language in which they sometimes appear. Levinas writes: 'The enigma of the Infinite, whose saying in me, a responsibility where no one assists me, becomes a contestation of the Infinite. By this contestation everything is incumbent on me.'[17] An infinite responsibility hangs on me, and yet I am mortal, therefore incapable of Infinity. As such we might think that an infinite responsibility expressed through a mortal body becomes a contestation of infinity. One might then conclude that this responsibility is impossible and thus cannot be owned. We throw in the towel and return to the liberal theory of socialized self-interest, glad for its rational justifications. But Levinas reasons differently. This responsibility *is* mine despite its infinity; there can be no disputing it just as there can be no disputing the body's physiological pains (in both cases 'disputation' is beside the point and almost farcical). What do I take, then, from the impossible weight of this responsibility on me? 'Everything is incumbent on me.' I do not wait for something infinite like a god to take on this weight. It is mine – like my own arm, or my shoulder – and so I shoulder it. Levinas calls this 'the enigma of a God speaking in man and of man not counting on any god.'[18] Nothing less is required of a post-Holocaust world wherein the certainty that no God will intervene even in the greatest human evil has been secured without ambiguity. It is not a theology.

Everything is incumbent on me. That is his first solution. The second helps to humanize it. In diachrony, the situation outside of linear temporality where the self is responsible for the other and owed nothing in return, the self shoulders an infinite weight. But the self also co-exists with multiple others in time, and that necessitates building and adhering to just institutions and stable rules that will treat all subjects equally. In synchronous time even the infinitely responsible self is protected, and rules are offered whereby responsibilities can be shared. These institutions are 'an incessant correction of the asymmetry' of ethics.[19] Justice can be established only if I, despite my being divested of being and in a non-reciprocal relationship with the other, can become an other like the others.[20] The subject given to us by Levinas is not a saint or a masochist, and hasn't lost what liberalism names its human status, wherein it is owed rights much as it grants them. The Levinasian view of justice I have developed here, of balancing infinite weight with formal equality, may even get us closer to human equality than the rights-based formal equality awarded by institutions, as institutional rights so often become privileges when they are attached to institutions that cannot or will not protect all human beings even as they protect some. Levinas writes:

> My lot is important. But it is still out of my responsibility that my salvation has meaning, despite the danger in which it puts this responsibility, which it may encompass and swallow up, just as the State issued from the proximity of the neighbor is always on the verge of integrating him into a 'we,' which congeals both me and the neighbor.[21]

Infinite weight is too heavy, yes, but the State's legal equality forgets that its formality was meant to protect human individuals in their uniqueness – legality is too light. And so we engage in the work of weighing.

Ethics is too heavy for the individual – burdensome to the point of injustice – if it is not tempered by institutions, while institutional legalism becomes a tyranny of procedure unless it is balanced by a weight no one had time to choose or refuse. We cannot rely on an ordered collection of set rules to administer justice for all time; nor can we do without the stability of set rules. The problem: an infinite weight hangs on a finite self. Solution one: I shoulder it anyway – no one can replace me; I am unique. Solution two: Human-made institutions help us share burdens precisely by recognizing each of us as unique and also equal. These 'solutions' don't transpire in the linear ordering of synchronous time, but rather oscillate, require balance, leaving us with nothing more solid than an endless vigilance.

Freedom and subjection

The rule of law is wrought of ambivalence – but ambivalence is multidirectional, and thus doesn't lead only to nihilistic resignation to the world's inevitable injustices. Ambivalence might also lead us to ask anew after justice and its demands; it can be productive – it stands as a reminder of all that is importantly human that cannot be held in one timeframe or caught in the permanent daylight of even the most lucid text. There are always shadows. We see this, and undergo the truth of it, whenever we view or experience the rule of law in theory and in practice – what we 'know' is never so certain when we face the hard cases. You might say that we undergo the truth of this also in the very way we become subjects, always already haunted by responsibilities we never had time to consent to bear.

The rule of law might begin as a set of procedures or guidelines aimed at ensuring fairness and equal treatment, and at protecting individuals from law's potentially arbitrary power – so the story goes. But then Levinas reminds us that its aspiration to equality comes from a prior subjection. It does not arise solely as a product of self-sufficiency. Self-sufficiency is a useful fiction aimed at protecting vulnerability, and it arises out of that vulnerability – but loses sight of this. Then, often, somewhere on the way to a procedural utopia, the rule of law finds itself allied with a form of justice that knows all too well the limits to its jurisdiction, and which thus leaves whole categories of persons unprotected, on principle. It can become the kind of equality that relies on the inequality of others, where things that get called rights are really more like privileges.

At the same time, however, the power of the idea of the rule of law is largely responsible for developments in international justice that award legal rights to more and more people, and give us international criminal tribunals instead of summary executions of those who are both war criminals and war losers. The rule of law, though it is often thought to be a formal limitation on what law can do, on occasion equips law to do more than anyone would have thought it could do. How could it do all this? Levinas writes, in another context:

> It is through its ambivalence which always remains an enigma that infinity or the transcendent does not let itself be assembled. It leaves a trace of its...inordinateness in my proximity with the neighbor, where I state, in the autonomy of the voice of consciousness, a responsibility, which could not have begun in me, for freedom, which is not my freedom.[22]

The autonomous subject can take on responsibilities that could never have devolved from her autonomy. The rule of law can open up new avenues of justice that never could have proceeded out of a bare concern for procedure. Of course, the autonomous subject can also refuse any responsibility that she did not create, and the rule of law can limit itself to being a set of procedures. That's the thing about ambivalence. Sites of ambivalence point to phenomena not readily captured in the form of reason, but which continue to have their sway nonetheless. Our responsibility for others, sensed in the materiality of our bodies long before it could have been reached by reason, is one such phenomenon – though a better word for it would be 'enigma.'

It's not that I am ever *really* solely the responsibility-hostage persecuted by an asymmetrical responsibility, but nor, really, am I ever absolutely free, limited only by duties I would consent to bear. Both descriptions of subjectivity are too extreme; both radically misrepresent what it means to be a human being living in society with others. The truth is somewhere between these oppositional forms, and each human subjectivity is a balancing act managing the conflicting demands of freedom and subjection. In turn, law will never be captured entirely by statute and procedure, but nor could institutional legality *be* lawful without those forms.

We all enter into the world late and helpless, only to find ourselves responsible for things we never did or intended, and affected by things that far exceed concern for our own safety. Levinas' revision of liberal subjectivity – if it joins with autonomy in the background of our thinking about justice and about what it means to be a self – is more likely to create the kind of person who will become the legal or political subject who would aspire to justice beyond socialized self-preservation. The autonomous self-sufficient individual may also undergo the demands of responsibility but, because of her narrative of what a subject is, would then have at her disposal any number of reasonable terms for rationalizing a lack of debt to others – a refusal of responsibility justified by ethical principles. Levinas' account allows us no such escape. It demands more of us, but it won't tell us what, specifically, we should do, and it even undermines the basis on which most of us have conceived our responsibilities throughout our lives. It asks not only for our altruism, but for our recognition that we might bear responsibility – in a way finally separable from legal guilt – for things we never did or intended.

Conclusion

Could it be that revising subjectivity, endowing individualism with a radically different origin and goal, undermining an overconfident faith in human autonomy and self-sufficiency, and replacing all this with disorder, vulnerability, and even a persecutory narrative of responsibility that does not begin with 'me,' would give to us a truly liberatory philosophy? I suggest that it is a start, for anyone interested in justice – and I take justice to be the aim of anyone interested in liberation that isn't just concern for the self's own freedom.

That is why we might, even against the background of our subjection to what we could not have chosen, *choose* to rewrite the free and autonomous liberal political subject's prehistory to emphasize the frailty of our entrance into this world rather than the robust character of our primordial freedom. The material vulnerabilities that in no small way define us cast a shadow over our attempts to reason our way out of responsibility for things we did not directly do, harms we never intended, and violence beyond our jurisdiction. That shadow is responsible for every accomplishment of justice that exceeds self-interested measures. One might say that it even makes the rule of law possible, despite the fact that the rule of law sometimes makes the shadow more difficult to see. That is what Levinas means when he suggests that our thoughts about justice are not games we play without committing to their truths, but rather are risks we take, and dangers we undergo, because they are inscribed in the formation of our selves. It is a strange kind of law. The responsibility for others that affects us in our materiality is a necessity, but it does not assert itself as force. What we do is up to us.

Notes

1. Some sections of this chapter have appeared in publication elsewhere, though in much earlier versions, and animated by a different constellation of thinkers. See J. Stauffer, 'The Rule of Law and its Shadow: Ambivalence, Procedure, and the Justice Beyond Legality,' in *Journal of Law, Culture and the Humanities* 3 (2007) 225–243, and 'Can a Theory of Justice Be Freed of its Weight?: Levinas and Rawls,' forthcoming in R. Cohen (ed.), *Levinas and Liberal Democracy.*
2. For instance, Sara Roberts reads Levinas to say that institutions of justice make formal the ethical responsibilities that call on us prior to their instantiation in legality. This leads her to conclude that Levinas 'seems to think that the only way to achieve justice for the singular other before me is through traditional avenues' (S. Roberts, 'Rethinking Justice: Levinas and Assymetrical Responsibility,' *Philosophy & the Contemporary World* 7 (2000) 5–12, 11). Roberts misses what is radical in Levinas' revision of subjectivity – he redesigns what it means to be a self from the ground up such that questions other than those posed by Roberts, about rights and symmetry, become the questions asked about law and politics – Roberts reads Levinas as conservative because she assumes Levinas is arguing for liberalism as it is rather than a radical revision of liberalism. William Paul Simmons, though he does recognize that the relationship between ethics and politics is mutually interdependent rather than unidirectionally causal, follows some of Levinas' late writing about rights and the liberal state to argue that Levinas gives us a justification of the liberal state because 'the Levinasian liberal state is always trying to improve itself': W. P. Simmons, 'The Third: Levinas' Theoretical Move from An-archical Ethics to the Realm of Justice and Politics,' *Philosophy and Social Criticism* 25 (1999) 83–104. That is less conservative than Roberts, but not as radical as I think Levinas' work can be. Despite the fact that Levinas did write such things about the liberal state (as it aspires to be rather than as it is, as Simmons properly notes), I think his philosophy in *Otherwise Than Being* lends itself to a revision of liberalism more radical, more interesting, and more *just*, than that suggested by Levinas in some of his later work. On that point it seems apt to point out that when Levinas agreed to republish his 1934 essay 'Reflections on the Philosophy of Hitlerism' in 1990, his new preface contained the question: 'We must ask ourselves if liberalism is all we need to achieve an authentic dignity for the human subject. Does the subject arrive at the human condition prior to assuming responsibility for the other man in the act of election that raises him up to this height?': E. Levinas, 'Reflections on the Philosophy of Hitlerism,' *Critical Inquiry* 17 (Autumn 1990) 62–71. What Levinas gives us is not a proposal for a form of law or politics but a revision of the subject who makes law and politics what they are. In my view, any reading of Levinas that locates a program for law or politics in his work has fallen into error.

3. E. Levinas, *Otherwise Than Being or Beyond Essence*, trans. A. Lingis (Pittsburgh: Duquesne, 1998) p. 114 [hereinafter OBBE].
4. E. Levinas, 'Reflections on the Philosophy of Hitlerism,' *Critical Inquiry* 17 (Autumn 1990) 62–71, 69.
5. E. Levinas 'Humanism and Anarchy,' in *Collected Philosophical Papers*, trans. A. Lingis (Pittsburgh: Duquesne University Press, 1987) p. 131.
6. See 'The Rule of Law and its Shadow: Ambivalence, Procedure, and the Justice Beyond Legality,' *Journal of Law, Culture and the Humanities* 3 (2007) 225–243.
7. A. Herzog, 'Is Liberalism "All We Need"?: Levinas' Politics of the Surplus,' *Political Theory* 30 (2002) 204–227, 217 (emphasis in original).
8. E. Levinas 'Transcendence and Height,' in R. Bernasconi, S. Critchley and A. Peperzak (eds), *Basic Philosophical Writing* (Bloomington: Indiana University Press, 1996) p. 23.
9. Some Levinasian arguments seem to claim that the 'correct' view could be given to us by reading Levinas or behaving as altruists. That might be the case, for some persons some of the time. But I would point out that for Levinas the face of the other invites me simultaneously to ethics and to murder. He also states multiple times in *Otherwise Than Being* that his ethics is not altruism, that 'responsibility for others could never mean altruistic will' (111), because that would endow it with intentionality rather than passivity. It is often admirable when human beings are capable of adhering to an ethic for saints, but most human beings are not saints, and it is for these human beings that Levinas writes, with the hope that an ethics based in his vision of the subject would make genocide impossible to justify. It is important to remember that he makes this argument in a world in which mass violence and genocide recur, a world in which these violences are and have been justified by the work of rational thought as often they are and have been driven by belief in something beyond rationality.
10. K. Annan, *Report of the Secretary General, 54 GAOR, 4th Plenary Meeting*, 20 September 1999, A/54/PV.4 p. 2.
11. T. Franck. 'Interpretation and Change in the Law of Humanitarian Intervention,' in J. L. Holzgrefe and R. O. Keohane (eds), *Humanitarian Intervention: Ethical, Legal, and Political Dilemmas* (Cambridge: Cambridge University Press, 2003) p. 207.
12. M. Byers and S. Chesterman. 'Changing the Rule about Rules: Unilateral Humanitarian Intervention and the Future of International Law,' in J. L. Holzgrefe and R. O. Koehane (eds), *Humanitarian Intervention: Ethical, Legal, and Political Dilemmas* (Cambridge: Cambridge University Press, 2003) pp. 177–203, 184.
13. This point is also made by Michael Byers and Simon Chesterman in 'Changing the Rule about Rules?'
14. Levinas, OBBE, p. 159.
15. Ibid.
16. Ibid., p. 154.
17. Ibid.
18. Ibid.
19. Ibid., p. 158.
20. Ibid., p. 161.
21. Ibid.
22. Ibid., p. 162 (translation modified).

Part III

Leviticus

5

Verdict and Sentence: Cover and Levinas on the Robe of Justice

Robert Gibbs

Introduction

Few problems are as challenging to Levinas' ethics as the tension or even chasm that opens between ethics in relation to the face and the claims of the 'third'. Because of Levinas' focus on the face, and in his later work on nearness, we often regard the appearance of the third as some sort of interruption in my responsibility in face of the other. After many years of discussion, Levinasian texts have become almost rote: particularly those discussions in which infinite responsibilities are said to be betrayed by negotiated and finite ones. Of course, the relation to the face is itself an interruption, an interruption of some first-person stability captured in the notion of self-consciousness and even autonomy. We can tell a story, from one to two (the face) to three.

The language of two, particularly in *Otherwise Than Being*, is exorbitant: accusation, hostage, persecution, obsession, expiation – and the language of three is not only familiar but is itself measured: order, comparison, coexistence, institutions, the state, and so on. To offer a new angle on the relation of these two moments, and to see how they interact, let us focus on the courtroom as the scene for ethics. Much of the account of the face is captured in the notion of a trial of the accused (me), in which I am called to testify and to justify myself before the other who, like a judge or magistrate, rises above me. We may, however, gain an even richer insight into Levinas' ethics if we adopt the viewpoint of the judge – who seems to represent the third in the conflict between two parties to a suit.

The judge is responsible to the law, and to the state, or let us say the community, on whom the law is binding. There might be a judge who is only a mediator between two parties, but the judge in the courtroom must uphold the interest of the thirds, the community – and while this claim for justice might derive from infinite responsibility, we are not in the midst of an asymmetry of responsibility. The judge represents the equalization of responsibility, the betrayal of infinity, and so forth.

But the judge is not a bureaucrat – does not review your application according to guidelines and rules and make a purely administrative decision, of which you will be notified by mail. This is not the insurance company. Instead, the judge judges people in court. In the prisoner's dock, I am accused and so given not just the right but the responsibility to respond to the charge; so also as judge I am called to appear in the courtroom.

To appear, however, is to face, and even more radically to be faced. Who faces the judge? Why, the defendant! Or in a civil suit, the two parties. And if someone faces me, then I am put in question. The judge is not interrogated, but in the physical scene of the courtroom, she is also called to account, called with infinite responsibilities for the others, and particularly the other before her. The judge in the courtroom performs the complex relation of two and three, of infinite responsibilities *and* the claims of thirds and measured justice.

This was claimed by Levinas himself. 'Justice is impossible without the one who renders it finding himself in nearness.'[1] How does one do it? How can we hold together these two incongruous modes of interruption? I propose here to take a brief look at matters of law, in order to help frame this seemingly impossible role – the role that I would now identify as the appropriate focus for Levinas' ethics: the judge in robes. A leading American legal theorist, Robert Cover, explored the same problem, in his 1981 essay 'Violence and the Word'.[2] On the basis of his framing of the problem, we can approach a few comments about judges and sentencing in Levinas, and see how deeply entwined the second and the third are – always. Finally, I will turn to the question of how we are to describe and interpret ethics. What sort of methodology and what sort of interpretations can give us the best purchase on ethics? Here I believe that phenomenology is powerfully supplemented and transformed by our engagement with legal corpora.

Violence and the right to confront

Cover wrote in the context of the emergence of a hermeneutic vision of the law associated particularly with Ronald Dworkin. The process of considering precedent, examining legal code, developing and revising the interpretation of law was a step forward in recognizing the way that law changes over time through judicial interpretation. Lacking, however, were first the intrinsic role of application and second the sociality of the hermeneutic project. For the first, Cover explores the way that the judge is violent in the courtroom, violating the defendant, stripping the other of property, or freedom, of custody and legal rights, and even of life itself. For the second, Cover criticizes the individualism of an overly cognitive account of legal interpretation. Because the court exists to harm someone, it requires a series of institutional structures, and the right of appeal means that no judge is ever alone, never installed as the hermeneutic hero (whom Dworkin named Hercules). The *socializing* of the hermeneutic task parallels the differentiated roles of punishment: the bailiff, the warden, the executioner, and of course, the judge. What Cover explores is how the social practices of violence reflect our fundamental aversion to violating the other. The court is an institutional form for violating individuals, case by case, but the goal is not simply violation or cruelty. The court is not a group of thugs, any more than it is a nameless bureaucracy.

There is a certain parallel with respect to hermeneutics itself between our two authors. Levinas insisted that discourse was always addressed *to* an other person, that it was solicited and freighted with ethical responsibility even prior to any ability to interpret or to disclose the world. Cover also saw that hermeneutics (and particularly legal hermeneutics) requires a discourse *to* someone. 'I now pronounce you guilty and sentence you to two years in jail.' The address to the prisoner, to the defendant or to the parties to the action, this address *to,* reorients the task of legal interpretation. Of course, we cannot help but notice that Levinas' relation to the other is one of responsibility for her, while Cover's judge is violating the other.

But this is the point at which the relation in Levinas of two and three, and in Cover of the court as a differentiated setting, begins to overlap more significantly. Despite the emphasis in Levinas on speech acts like 'after you', or 'here I am', the judge, must also be able to pronounce verdicts and sentences in order to respond to the third, to respond on behalf of law. A society which did not punish criminal behaviour would be failing in its responsibility. Indeed, if the judge is a model for Levinas' ethics, than we will need to account for just the violence that Cover emphasizes. And on the other hand, because the judge is vulnerable, because she must also appear in the presence (within arms reach) of the prisoner, even in violating the other the judge is called into question, faced by the other. Neither Cover nor Levinas have the resources of the other. Cover manages merely a vague comment that there are various inhibitions on causing others pain.[3] Similarly, Levinas has little recourse to courtroom procedure, to the history of law, and to the material content of Cover's analysis. But we can draw them together, and in particular can draw them each back to legal texts they cite but fail properly to explore.

Thus Cover mentions a particularly troubling case when imagining the perspective of the defendant being sentenced:

> First, examine the event [sentencing] from the perspective of the defendant. The defendant's world is threatened. But he sits, usually quietly, as if engaged in a civil discourse. If convicted, the defendant customarily walks – escorted – to prolonged confinement, usually without significant disturbance to the civil appearance of the event. It is of course, grotesque to assume that the civil façade is 'voluntary' except in the sense that it represents the defendant's autonomous recognition of the overwhelming array of violence arranged against him, and of the hopelessness of resistance or outcry.[17[Cover],4]

This particular view shows us that the defendant seems both overpowered and acquiescent. For Cover, this is not unfortunate, and he is quick to comment that 'very often the balance of terror in this regard is just as I would want it. But I do not wish us to pretend that we talk our prisoners into jail'. So while the defendant is part of a civil discourse, the situation remains appropriately violent. I myself am far from presuming that the civil discourse is only a mask for the violence. On the contrary, I think the civil discourse (court procedure, etc.) itself recognizes the need to hear the defendant, to place the law in the position of being questioned.

Cover's footnote (slightly edited here) cites a particularly vexed case:

> [17] A few defendants who have reached their own understandings of the legal order have overtly attempted to deny the fiction that the trial is a joint or communal civil event where interpretations of facts and legal concepts are tested and refined. The playing out of such an overt course of action ends with the defendant physically bound and gagged... Our constitutional law, quite naturally enough, provides for the calibrated use of ascending degrees of overt violence to maintain the 'order' of the criminal trial. *See, e.g., Illinois v. Allen* 397 U.S. 337 (1970).[5]

Cover appears to lean even more heavily toward the defendant. There is an asymmetry here, not because the judge is not impartial, but because I cannot see a proceeding against me as symmetrical. As members of the society, we recognize the objection of the obstreperous defendant as an interruption, but that is just the immediacy of the defendant facing me as judge. We grant him the right to present his evidence, to question his accusers, to appear before the judge (and the jury), but not to question the whole process; not to contest the jurisdiction of the courts in general, or the even more anarchist denial of any court at all. The court threatens violence in order to maintain that limitation.

In August 1956, William Allen robbed a bartender of $200 at gunpoint, and he was tried in Chicago in 1957, and found guilty. The focus of the appeals was that he was disruptive, threatening, and obstreperous in court. After repeated warnings, he was removed from the courtroom, and although he was brought back several times, he was absent for almost all the proceedings. On appeal, the Illinois State Supreme Court upheld the conviction; the Federal District Court also; but the Federal Court of Appeals reversed the decision in 1969 arguing that the defendant has an absolute right to be present at his trial. In a split decision, the United States Supreme Court upheld the original conviction in 1970. There were three opinions: for the majority Justice Black, and concurring Justice Brennan, while Justice Douglas dissented.

The Sixth Amendment to the US Constitution secures the right to confront witnesses, and thus is directly related to the right to be present. There is an interesting connection to Levinas' discussion of the face, precisely because confrontation, facing, is regarded as legally protected. The right to a hearing (sometimes called 'natural justice') is a principle that extends beyond criminal procedure to many administrative contexts, too, but what is quite clear, is that the authority to question or to challenge someone is secured by facing them. Moreover, the courtroom is the place where people are subpoenaed, called to appear and to present themselves for questioning. The courtroom, then, is the place where society creates moments of facing, moments of being called to respond. None of these confrontations is symmetrical – even though the defendant is also subject to being questioned (and sitting in the dock, seems to be installed as the accused, as the one called to answer). But the right to be present and question others, to confront my accusers, arises from the same moral insight that Levinas interprets phenomenologically in relation to being faced by the other.

The question is whether there are limitations on what the Federal Circuit Court of Appeals referred to as the absolute right to be present. If the defendant challenges the court – 'there is going to be no proceeding' – the judge is left with three alternatives: (1) to bind and gag the defendant, keeping him in court; (2) to threaten and impose contempt penalties; and (3) to remove the defendant from the courtroom. Everyone agrees in the decisions that the second option is impossible (the accused would not have cared). The tension between (1) and (3) lies in the explicit or covert nature of the exercise of judicial violence (to which Cover referred). Brennan wrote:

> I also agree with the Court, that these three methods are not equally acceptable. In particular, shackling and gagging a defendant is surely the least acceptable of them. It offends not only judicial dignity and decorum, but also the respect for the individual, which is the lifeblood of the law.[6]

Black had been more pragmatic:

> But even to contemplate such a technique, much less see it, arouses a feeling that no person should be tried while shackled and gagged except as a last resort. Not only is it possible that the sight of shackles and gags might have a significant effect on the jury's feelings about the defendant, but the use of this technique is itself something of an affront to the very dignity and decorum of judicial proceedings that the judge is seeking to uphold. Moreover, one of the defendant's primary advantages of being present at the trial, his ability to communicate with his counsel, is greatly reduced when the defendant is in a condition of total physical restraint.[7]

Here it is a series of concerns: the dignity of the court, prejudice to the jury, and most ironically, the disruption of the defendant's ability to communicate (with counsel, but also, of course, to himself ask questions of his accusers). So, we are left to imagine a philosophical dispute: either there is rough justice, where the violence against the other (the accused) permits him no hearing, no situation to confront his accusers; or we provide a right to be present already contaminated by violence. Can a defendant waive the right to be present? And, indeed, the question of an involuntary waiver does arise in the opinions.

More importantly, Brennan's concurring opinion focused on the individual, and indeed was framed precisely to indicate how the court was needed to limit the violence of the state:

> History has known the breakdown of lawful penal authority – the feud, the vendetta, and the terror of penalties meted out by mobs or roving bands of vigilantes. It has known, too, the perversion of that authority. In some societies the penal arm of the state has reached individual men through secret denunciation followed by summary punishment. In others the solemn power of condemnation has been confided to the caprice of tyrants. Down the corridors of history have echoed the cries of innocent men convicted by other irrational or arbitrary procedures. These are some of the alternatives history offers to the procedure adopted by our Constitution. The right of a defendant to trial – to trial by jury – has long been cherished by our people as a vital restraint on the penal authority of government.[8]

Beyond the unnerving comparison of proper courts and their respect for the individual rights with the threat of violence, mobs, denunciation, and so forth, Brennan writes exactly of the court as the place where the state's violence is disrupted. The courts are a place where you can face your accuser, where violence is slowed down, and displaced from the mob to the procedure and attention to the other's questioning. The judge must protect the individual before her, must provide her the opportunity to question others. But if the defendant refuses to behave civilly, what can the judge do?

One last comment about this particular conflict depends on considering the dissent. Like Brennan, Douglas notes the risk of the state's violence. But the situation is made shockingly murky, because he questions the mental competence of the defendant. Allen had a record of mental illness, and had been found incompetent to stand trial in 1956, although the finding was overturned a year later. By 1970, there was no easy way to revisit that question. Douglas thus leaves us in a quandary, but proceeds to notice that the more profound issue is not about an armed robber, but about political trials. He himself accounts for a variety of such cases: from someone who protests their constitutional rights, to others who use the court to provoke repression. He distinguishes three situations: (1) an unruly defendant who can be properly disciplined, warned, and so on; (2) a defendant who may not be 'capable of understanding the nature and object of the proceedings against him, his own condition in reference to such proceedings, and have sufficient mind to conduct his defense in a rational and reasonable manner;' and (3) a political case, where the violent relation of the state and the individual is precisely in question.

While Cover is clearly drawn to this third situation (call it the conflict of the political with the judicial), the first is where Levinas' sense of the judge being near to the other and the defendant also being near her accusers are in tightest conflict. It is not that Levinas is oblivious to the problems of the political institutionalization of justice. But the first situation draws out the deeper conflict that constitutes all civil society – the tensions between the asymmetric responsibilities that require both the third and a continuing permeability of the third to the second. In the opinions offered in this case, the right to confront is held in suspense because of Allen's disruption of the opportunity for the prosecution – the third – to present their case. But in the process the right to be present ceases to be absolute – the chance to speak and to defend oneself becomes relative and contingent. The accused can effectively waive the opportunity to be present. But can the judge? Does not Cover ignore the fundamental ethical question? Must not the *judge* face the other, or, perhaps, more importantly, be faced by them?

Between verdict and sentence

Levinas discusses a quite remarkable passage in the Talmud, four times, that deals with the question of the judge facing the accused. He paraphrases the Talmudic text, which itself reconciles two biblical texts that seem in contradiction. Let me first present Levinas' comments, and then (as with Cover) we will consider a rather fuller version.

> At this point, I would like to cite for you a very beautiful portion of a Talmudic text. The rabbis brood over what seemed to them to be contradictions in the Scripture. One verse, Deuteronomy 1:17, says, 'Do not in justice, show partiality to someone' – which literally reads in Hebrew: 'do not look at his face when judging.' Another verse, Numbers 6:26, adds, 'May the Eternal One turn His face toward you.' A contradiction or close to it! The rabbis resolve it this way: 'Do not look at the face before the verdict. Once the verdict has been given, look at the face.' Charity can accomplish a lot, even after the passage of rigorous justice. Since justice constantly has a bad conscience, the demand of charity that precedes it remains and summons it. And justice, the justice that deserves its name, does not forget that the law

> is perfectible. It leaves open the possibility of a revision of a judgment once pronounced. And this is very important. Because justice – called by charity – nevertheless founds the State and its tyrannical component.[9]

The conceptual problem is the relation of justice and mercy. Justice is not captured by the strict rule of rigorous legality. Indeed, the law itself serves justice in recognizing that it is not itself perfect. There is, I would say, in the law a call to go beyond the law – and so the Talmud itself is that exploration of law's edge, which itself is neither against the law nor outside it, but within it. But what does the text focus upon?: the place of charity (in other texts also called mercy) within a judicial proceeding. In the first instance, the judge regards the others as thirds, and is similarly a third to their conflict. Justice is only justice if it is impartial. Such an impartiality is required by the face of the other – but what is required is *not* to regard the other's face, not to find oneself infinitely beholden to this specific person. This is a huge qualification, even a revocation of how we normally understand Levinas' ethics. But it is, I want to explore, central to that ethics, and *not* an objection to it.

Briefly, let me look at the Biblical text:

> In judging, do not regard the face; listen to the small as the great; do not fear the face of any man, because the judgment is God's. The matter that is too hard for you bring toward me and I will hear it.[10]

The text is from Deuteronomy, and it reflects part of Moses' instruction to the community. He is recounting the tale of the exodus and their wanderings to the edge of the Promised Land. Early on he was instructed to appoint a bureaucracy for governance, including judges to settle disputes and try criminals. But at the heart of this verse is a contrast between the relation to the face of another person and the task of judgment as it relates to God. In its context, one can see that the judge should not fear a vendetta, not fear the mob, nor the reach of the powerful. The judge is only acting for the sake of God, for a principle of justice that is beyond the reach of the powerful. Such is the encouragement given to a judge who fears retribution or even assassination.

But we also might read this warning in another direction. One must not face the defendant, for in facing one would encounter the infinite responsibility for this one before me. Do not fear to judge the other. The court represents a place where infinite responsibility is borne not exclusively by me, but by others. The anxiety of judgment, to which the readers of Levinas are especially sensitive, is calmed by the promise that God (or the institution, the society as instituted) can carry that burden. Again, the issue for this chapter is that the judge shall not face the defendant, or better, shall not be faced by him. This particular hiding from the face, which now appears at the core of Levinas' account of justice and of ethics, is clearly in utter opposition to the bystander or passer by who will not heed the beggar or the one in need. Here, in court, the responsibility to the others or third, as well as to the other, requires the impartiality that we normally associate with ethics, but which seems inconceivable to a more familiar reading of Levinas. The interrogation of this Biblical text alerts us to a key place for *not* being faced.

But then there is the second verse, one which comes from the Priestly Blessing, that is still recited in the Jewish community.

> THE LORD bless you and keep you.
> THE LORD make His face to shine upon you and be gracious to you.
> THE LORD lift His face upon you and grant you peace.[11]

In its context, the text is not about a judge in court. Rather the third petition (lift His face upon you) seems to be some sort of attention as falling under God's regard. To have that Face regard me is to be heard. What is at stake here is the most personal and most transcendent form of blessing (and of facing).

Levinas' comment about this verse, however, is to see that the judge must also face. And in facing, the judge acts from mercy. The tension between Justice and Mercy animates Jewish thought and Levinas renders it as a distinction between impartiality and the experience of the face. Again, it is not in the defendant's ethical situation that we see this tension, but rather in the judge's. And the two verses are equalized by considering both as addressing a human judge.

Let us now turn to the Talmudic text. And here, as we saw in Cover's use of *Illinois v. Allen*, there are real limitations to Levinas' treatment of it. The text comes from the tractate *Rosh Hashanah*, which deals with the New Year. In Jewish tradition New Year's Day is the day of judgment on which, based on last year's actions, one is sentenced to life or to death in the coming year. There follows a ten-day period for appealing the verdict. The judgment is of life and death, and God is the Judge. And so the days between New Year's Day and the Day of Atonement (the tenth day) are days of awe and fear. Indeed, this text links the courtroom to the divine throne-room, and imagines God as ascending to the throne of mercy to entertain pleas for leniency.

Levinas makes no reference to this mythic link of the judge in the human courtroom to God on high, nor does he pause to explore the whole story. He also excludes its frame and the *two* solutions it offers to the contradiction between the two verses.

> Come and hear: Bluria the proselyte put this question to Rabban Gamliel:
>
> It is written in your Torah, [she said] 'Who does not lift up his face' and it is also written, 'the Eternal shall lift up His face toward you'.
>
> Rabbi Yose the priest joined the conversation and said to her:
>
> 'I will give you a parable: what is this like? A man lent his neighbour a *maneh*, and fixed a time of payment in the presence of the king, while the other swore to pay him by the life of the king. When the time arrived he did not pay him, and he went to appease the king. The king, however, said to him: The wrong done to me I excuse, but go and appease your neighbour. So here one text speaks of offences committed by a person against God, the other of offences committed by a person against his companion.
>
> Until Rabbi Akiva came and taught:
>
> 'One before the sentence; the other after the sentence!' Here too the case is that of an individual.[12]

The rabbis' answers are fundamentally different in kind: a parable in the one case and a temporal distinction in the other. The first answer seems sufficient, until we hear the second. And Levinas only bothers with the second (and gives no hint that there was a first – much as Cover does not cite the dissent by Douglas in the case of *Illinois v. Allen*).

As for the problem, it seems that in the context of the New Year the question is whether God judges us with mercy or with strict justice, and in this section of the Talmud the question has been about the object of judgment: the people or an individual alone. In the parable the king cannot forgive the other's debt; although the king can waive his own rights in the case. The king does not withhold his face in relation to the wrong before the king, but he must be impartial and withhold mercy in relation to the loaner. The parable coordinates the relation between the two (loaner and borrower) through recourse to a third. The moral of the parable is straightforward enough: only the loaner can forgive the loan, can waive his right, and so the judge is not free to show his face, to be partial. To forgive the debt owed the other person would be to be partial to the one before the king.

And then Akiva changes the terrain: before and after the verdict: the human judge does not regard the face of the other before the verdict but does so after. Here mercy comes *after* strict justice is announced. My own title only fits roughly here because in this case the sentence itself is amended, or altered. But Akiva seems not to be describing a human courtroom at all – God as judge shows mercy after acting impartially. Even if we argue that the description of the divine is itself an allegory for the human courtroom, Akiva's explanation ignores any reflection on the messy relation between the two courts.

In terms of the problems of this chapter, however, we have a clear procedural solution: the judge impartially determines who is guilty, and then acts with a just mercy, taking heed of the particularities of the convict (and perhaps the victims, too), in determining the sentence. Verdict (without face), and sentence (with face). For Levinas this is the cornerstone of justice (and we would say of his ethics): a justice that neither ignores nor revokes the rule of law, but also that is not blind to the needs of the other for mercy. 'This is how the necessity of the state is able not to exclude charity'. 'This after-verdict, with its possibilities of mercy, still fully belongs – with full legitimacy – to the work of justice'.[13]

How complex is the overlap with Cover's argument about the courtroom, and particularly his point that judgment is never solely about a verdict, but always also about a sentence? A sentence that represents a specific mode of violence, not actually performed by the judge but only in the name of the court, by a jailer, a bailiff, an executioner, and so on. For Cover, responsibility for the enactment of the judgment is both shared and segmented, in part to overcome our own hesitation in inflicting a penalty on another. But Levinas insists that the moment of facing (in determining the sentence, or Talmudically, in adjusting the sentence) is bound to the courtroom, and not to the jail – that is, the judge who is faced by the convicted, now must respond to the singularity, to the uniqueness of other. Society constructs the courtroom in order to play out this particular sequence of moments.

What is philosophy of law?

I have reiterated often that the judge is the model for Levinas' ethics, for the responsibility for the other person and for the others. That the relation between second and the third appears most clearly here. To what extent is the philosophical account of judgment which this chapter has explored through Levinas and Cover dependent on the cases, on the texts which we have sought to examine and expand with some care here? In short, are the cases merely the pretence for a phenomenology that need not attend to the textuality of these citations?

Levinas seems to suggest so. He comments: 'I am very happy to have been able to give you an example of what an illustration by the verse can be. I did not start from this text; I discovered it after the fact'.[14] Here he is guarding against the criticism that he has been dogmatic or is operating on the basis of a Jewish text, so that his account would in some important way be limited to Jews only. This is not a rare issue in interpreting Levinas – the status of Jewish tradition in his philosophy. But I wish to accentuate here Levinas' claim that the idea of facing and not facing, the tension that governs courtroom justice, did not begin from his reading of the Talmudic text. That text was only found after the fact, after the process of having thought it through on the basis of thirds and justice and mercy, in a phenomenological manner that did not require the texts.

Yet the 'Jewish' character of these comments lies not in their explicit discussion of Jewish theology but instead in their Talmudic style and form. Levinas' telling obliterates the frame, eclipses the names, and occludes the sense that this teaching occurred as an historical event, or at least is said to have been an event. But he cannot eclipse the strange manner of its reasoning: to take two verses that appear to contradict each other and resolve the opposition. This choice of reasoning through texts and not through concepts or principles is the preferred manner of reasoning in Jewish sources. There is an intermingling of people in two pairs (Bluria and Rabban Gamliel; Yose and Akiva) with two verses. Levinas comments that 'the rabbis (who are considered terrible people setting minute and ridiculous problems – their manner of treating the most important questions)'.[15] Yet the smallness and the oddness of the problem *allows* them to address these important questions. Levinas compresses a full account of the question of the judge into a contradiction and resolution of two verses from scripture. It is not merely concision that is at stake, but an approach that in fact draws principles from the very specificity of texts (one legal, the other cultic). This is not uniquely Jewish, but the texts are Jewish and the manner of proceeding is quintessentially Jewish if not uniquely so.

The contrast with Cover is all the more interesting, then, because he too cites a case that has its own rich textual account. While he does mention the case by name, he does not refer to its history or its jurists.

You could say that, like most serious scholars, he has left plenty for his students and followers to write about. But what is more interesting in this case, is that like Levinas', there are multiple opinions. To bring this case as if it stood for only one point of view is a distortion. Not that we can agree with all three opinions – they are at variance with each other. But attending to the opinions requires an attention to the plurality of reasoners. Near the conclusion of his essay Cover pauses to emphasize again the interaction between the social reasoning of the judges and the violence in the system:

> If it seems a nasty thought that death and pain are at the center of legal interpretation, so be it. It would not be better were there only a community of argument, of readers and writers of texts, of interpreters. As long as death and pain are part of our political world, it is essential that they be at the center of the law. The alternative is truly unacceptable – that they be within our polity but outside the discipline of the *collective* decision rules and the individual efforts to achieve outcomes through those rules. The fact that we require many voices is not, then, an accident or peculiarity of our jurisdictional rules. It is intrinsic to whatever achievement is possible in the domesticating of violence.[16]

Thus in Cover's article, we find a serious justification for law as a social network of many voices. Not only do we segment law's violence, distinguishing the court from the prison and gallows, but in the court itself we require a multiplicity of voices – a jury and sometimes a panel of three or more judges. The task of judging, including the interpretation of the laws, is rendered social; case reports include dissenting, and even plural concurrent opinions. Cover explores this at a procedural level, discerning the deeper ethical and epistemological issues, but he does not respect it in his writing. Instead, we have a citation to the case without reference to the diversity of opinion that is relevant to the very arguments he is developing.

This chapter returns to the cases, Talmudic or legal, not just to set the record straight. On the contrary, in the diversity of opinions we find added depth to the general arguments advanced by the two thinkers. More, we recovered sources of insight into tension between the responsibility we bear for first-and-last named individuals and the responsibility we bear for society. While exploring philosophical resources in ethical or political theory also entails working on one person's name (Robert Cover, Emmanuel Levinas, etc.), both the Talmudic text and the report from the US Supreme Court are constituted by the *differences* of named opinions. The specifics of reasoning and of understanding thus intimately linked to the singularity of verses and names keeps breaking through any phenomenological or transcendental account. Better to say that this is a kind of philosophy of law that retains and even restores the centrality of individual names and texts to thought. And the result is that ethics at last finds its idiom.

Acknowledgement

This chapter was supported by a research grant from the Social Sciences and Humanities Research Council of Canada, and a different version appeared in *The Journal of Jewish Thought and Philosophy*, 14 (1–2), pp. 73–89. Thanks to Bettina Bergo and Lisa Austin for their help.

Notes

1. The texts of Levinas are cited, first to the French, and then to the standard translation, but all translations here are my own. *Autrement qu'être ou au-delà de l'Essence* (Dordrecht: Martinus Nijhoff, 1974), trans. by A. Lingis as *Otherwise Than Being or Beyond Essence* (The Hague: Martinus Nijhoff, 1981) p. 202/159. See also my commentary in *Why Ethics: Signs of Responsibilities* (Princeton: Princeton University Press, 2000) p. 153.
2. R. Cover, 'Violence and Word', in M. Minow, M. Ryan, and A. Sarat (eds), *Narrative, Violence, and the Law: The Essays of Robert Cover* (Ann Arbor: The University of Michigan Press, 1992) [1986] pp. 203–238.
3. Ibid., p. 218.
4. Ibid., pp. 210–211.
5. Ibid.
6. 397 U.S 337, pp. 350–351.
7. Ibid., p. 344
8. Ibid., pp. 347–348.
9. 'Levinas: au nom d'autrui' an interview with L. Ferry, R. Hadas-Lebel, and S. Pasquier in *L'Express*, 6 Juillet 1990, and translated in J. Robbins (ed.), *Is It Righteous To Be? Interviews with Emmanuel Levinas* (Stanford: Stanford University Press, 2001) p. 74/194. See 'L'Autre, Utopie et Justice', a conversation with the journal *Autrement*, in *Entre Nous: Essais sur le penser-à-l'autre* (Paris: Bernard Grasset, 1991), and in English in *Entre Nous: Thinking-of-the-Other* (New York: Columbia University Press, 1998) p. 261/230; interview with F. Poirié, *'Emmanuel Levinas: Qui êtes-vous?'* (Lyon: La Manufacture, 1987), in *Is It Righteous to Be?* p. 119/69; and interview with A. Ponzio, 'Responsabilité et Substitution' in *Sujet et Altérité sur Emmanuel Levinas* (Paris: L'Harmattan, 1996), in *Is It Righteous to Be?* pp. 145–146/231.
10. *Deuteronomy* 1: 17.

11. *Numbers* 6: 24–26.
12. *RH 17b.*
13. Levinas 'L'Autre, Utopie et Justice'.
14. Levinas, 'Interview with Françoise Poirié'.
15. Ibid.
16. Cover, *Narrative, Violence, and the Law: The Essays of Robert Cover*, p. 236.

6
'Current legal maxims in which the word neighbour occurs': Levinas and the Law of Torts

Desmond Manderson[1]

Introduction

Over the past hundred years, the law of negligence has transformed itself, and in the process transformed our sense of the obligations we owe to each other. Yet 'the duty of care' is an unusual obligation. It is not the outcome of an agreement founded on self-interest, like a contract. It is not a duty owed to the State, like criminal law. It describes a *personal* responsibility we owe to others to which we have not consented. It is a kind of debt we never consciously incurred. 'Am I my brother's keeper?' What does it mean to be responsible? These are not questions that are easier for us to answer than they were for Cain. Emmanuel Levinas offers a sustained meditation on them in language which will be uncannily familiar to any common lawyer. He writes about our duty of care to others; he seeks to understand the nature of a neighbourhood; he defends and articulates the idea of 'proximity'. Levinas writes, 'perhaps because of current moral maxims in which the word *neighbour* occurs, we have ceased to be surprised by all that is involved in proximity and approach'.[2] Here at last is a philosopher who speaks the language of torts.

Central to Levinas' meditations is an idea of *ethics* which implies a personal responsibility to another that is both involuntary and singular, and which is therefore peculiarly well fitted to articulate the common law duty of care. The demand of ethics comes from the intimacy of an experienced encounter, and its contours cannot therefore be codified or predicted in advance.[3] So, as opposed to most understandings of rules and law, ethics insists on the necessity of our response to others, and the unique circumstances of each such response, rather than attempting to reduce such responses to standard instances and norms of general application applicable to whole communities and capable of being settled in advance. Indeed, ethics constantly destabilizes and ruptures those rules and that settlement.[4]

The idea of responsibility offered by Levinas makes unique sense of the central insights of the duty of care: that we must put others first, and that this responsibility is not an unfortunate imposition on our naturally individual and autonomous subjectivity, but the *source* of that individuality. I develop this argument in Part 2. One consequence of such a view is to reclaim tort law as the expression of a distinct philosophical world-view, and to emphasize the importance of this perspective as foundational to our understanding of law itself, as I discuss in Part 3. A more pragmatic consequence is to transform our responsibility for omissions and the 'duty to rescue' from an anomaly into a core element of the duty of care, which is the theme of Part 4.

The curious resonance between Levinas and negligence is not coincidental. Levinas' work, and its translation into English – *Totality and Infinity*, 1967; *Otherwise Than Being*, 1981 – suggest the social and interdisciplinary relevance of a fresh approach to questions of duty and responsibility which was at the same time unsettling the law, first in the great English trilogy of the 1960s and then in a celebrated line of Australian cases from the 1980s and 1990s.[5] My purpose throughout this chapter is to bring these two redolent discourses, the legal and the ethical, into productive proximity and to introduce the contours of an argument which I have developed at greater less elsewhere, that such a proximity has the power to change our understanding of both the law and of Levinas.[6]

Responsibility

What does Levinas mean by 'assymetric' responsibility? In the first of Levinas' two major works, *Totality and Infinity* (1961, trans. 1967), Levinas asks us to think about experiences in our life which belie the assumptions of 'totality' – of the self as complete, as the origin of all knowledge and the justification for all morality. He treats these aspects as instances which point towards a new way of thinking about what it means to be a human subject – 'infinity' – in which our responsibility to another comes before our self-interest.[7] Accordingly experiences such as suffering, pain, and love are not secondary to his philosophical hypotheses any more than they are to our own: they are precisely why thinking and living matter. Emmanuel Levinas was a survivor of Holocaust, to whose victims his work was dedicated. And his purpose was this: to explain it, and explain above all why the suffering of others matters to us. Levinas is therefore not arguing that we *ought* to think more about ethics, or that we *ought* to care more about others.[8] Levinas wishes us to see that we *cannot* adequately explain our own experience and existence without reconfiguring our understanding of the relationship of selves to others.

For Levinas, we experience responsibility not as something rational and predictable, but on the contrary as an experience that just happens to us without our conscious will or consent being engaged. Any parent, of course, could tell you the same thing: responsibility, by its very nature, exceeds our expectations or our choices. There is a remarkable artwork by Antony Gormley that captures the ethical demand that the existence of others places on us. *Field* comprises almost 40,000 clay figurines in a vast room.[9] They are hand baked and of the crudest formulation. Nothing but a rough shape, elongated, and bulbous, with two indentations, probably fashioned by skewering them with a stick before they were baked. But it is enough. Just the presence of the two points makes eyes. Just the presence of the eyes makes a face. Just the presence of a face makes a figure. They are small beings, knee high, infinitely, though subtly distinct.

There is something overwhelming about entering a large room, crowded to overflowing with a city of little people, clumsy and naked. Forty thousand unique beings stare at you. And in that gaze there is already something else: an ethical entreaty, 'a field of gazes which looks at the observer making him or her its subject'.[10] The surprise and *assymetry* we experience at that moment – our capacity and their incapacity –which standard theories of the law of torts by and large fail to capture, seems to me precisely what the 'duty of care' expresses. It's not something you think about – the duty of care just *happens* to you. Before you know anything at all about another being, prior to language or any connection whatsoever, and indeed *in* the ineffable otherness and vulnerability of a face, there resides already a demand for care.[11] Responsibility is not a matter of a meeting of minds, then, not a question of *contract*. On the contrary, it starts from the shock that I am not a free and spontaneous being. I am being called to account, prior to my freedom of choice: asymmetrically, involuntarily. 'One calls this putting into question of my spontaneity by the [mere] presence of the Other, ethics.'[12]

Levinas makes the same point – that we find ourselves encumbered with responsibility before any content, any rules, any agreements – in relation to language. In order to explain this point, he distinguishes *le dire*, the act of 'saying', from *le dit*, the actual content of what is said. There can be no agreement on the meaning of a word without an initial trust – a trust that we mean well and that we mean what we say – and this initial trust cannot, by definition, be an exchange or a contract: it must be offered up *without* hope of an exchange.[13] Language is born out of a promise of responsibility and not the other way around.[14]

In *Otherwise Than Being* (1971, trans. 1981), Levinas investigates similar themes, but this time tinged with tragedy. But the recognition of the tragic in our lives is by no means a denial of truth. The shift can be observed in the theme of hospitality. In *Totality*, hospitality is the welcome we provide to the other's residence in us and the other's calls upon us.[15] It too is an obligation prior to all agreement, like the guest who knocks unbidden on the door. But of course not all guests are always welcome. Levinas recognizes the reality of the risk we run in being touched by the other. Our trust *might* be abused or betrayed. In the vulnerability of our interactions, we may find ourselves harmed or exploited. The host may at any moment become hostage. But Levinas' point is that the danger is nevertheless the very essence of responsibility. Ask a parent. Ask a child. Ask a friend. Ask a teacher.[16] Here we might have the definition of what is sometimes termed a 'calling': a relationship with the vulnerable that calls *us*, that cannot be circumscribed in advance, and that therefore inevitably places demands upon us that we may not wholly welcome and do not wholly expect.

So the whole premise of human responsibility is reversed. In Hobbes, responsibility is justified as an *exchange*: it comes into being as a *quid pro quo* that an autonomous and self-interested being decides upon. For Levinas, as for the law of torts, it does not. 'The inter-subjective relation is not symmetrical. I am responsible for the other without waiting for any reciprocity.'[17] Whether this proves a boon or a bane will depend upon the nature of our response, but here too we do not have an option to decline the burden. One way or the other, it cannot be ignored. We do not choose to be responsible: we (and here we see the influence of Levinas' Jewish theology on his philosophy) are the chosen ones.

We may summarize Levinas' position as follows. First, responsibility is inherent in the first encounter between persons. The obligation to respond is intrinsically prior to any specific response and therefore, any pre-existing rules of limitation.[18] Second, responsibility is not a choice. It 'precedes every free consent, every pact, every contract'.[19] Accordingly, I do not agree to it, but *find* myself responsible; it is not a way of advancing the ego's purposes, but rather disrupts them.[20] Thirdly, responsibility is not symmetrical.[21] It has nothing to do with some hypothetical 'social contract' between persons, still less with legal policies created by the State. My responsibility for another person is not dependent on any reciprocity of obligation. He may be responsible for me too, but as Levinas curtly remarks, 'that's *his* business'.[22] Fourthly, it follows that in the challenge with which responsibility confronts us, we are singled out as the one or ones who can most make a difference. This is what Levinas means when he says that the relationship with another 'is not a species of consciousness whose ray emanates from the I; it puts the I in question. This putting in question emanates from the other'.[23] In stark opposition to the standard view, responsibility is not derived from our individual autonomy. It inaugurates it.

Finally, the exercise of responsibility is always changing, always deepening. This, too, describes very well both the actual experience of responsibility and the actual development of the law. Since we are continually being constituted and re-constituted through our responsibilities, no formula of words, system, or rules could entirely determine the conditions of its future exercise. We always remain open to future and as yet undiscovered obligations of responsibility. The necessarily *responsive* and developing nature of responsibility is a problem for law, which after all seeks to fix and finalize these things. But at the same time this approach provides a serious justification which other models do not address for the flexibility and change that imbues the common law of negligence. As Levinas suggests, fluidity and openness are intrinsic to the very idea of responsibility. The uncertainty of the common law, its constant transformation, reassessment and modification under the pressure of new cases and new circumstances is a failure if what you want from law is certainty, but a success if what you want from it is responsibility.

The origin of responsibility in torts

From within the orthodox common law tradition of negligence, responsibility must be justified by something within me: my conduct, my consent. But for Levinas, responsibility comes from something outside of me: her gaze, his vulnerability. On this view, negligence law reflects not some artificial limitation on our imagined natural freedom, but our initial indebtedness to 'a neighbour'. This provides us with an attractive justification for the nature and concerns of tortious obligation, and particularly of the duty of care. It suggests the philosophical origin of these obligations in terms which speak persuasively to our instincts and emotions, and which draw on vital elements of human experience that matter to us and about which many contemporary theories of law are oddly silent. Levinas' theory of responsibility connects law to ourselves, our feelings, and our relationships.

Neither is the question of law's origins of only theoretical interest. Consider negligent acts committed in the course of illegal conduct. No doubt 'there is no rule denying to a person who is doing an unlawful thing the protection of the general law imposing upon others duties of care for his safety'.[24] You cannot run over a burglar in the street. But the court has had more difficulty with what is called 'joint illegality', that is, where one party is negligent towards the other in the course of shared criminal conduct. In the High Court of Australia, with which I will later compare the approach of the Supreme Court of Canada, the problem came to a head in *Gala v Preston*.[25] Some young men stole a car after an extended bout of drinking. They headed off up the Queensland coast around 8:00 in the evening. Some hours later, while the plaintiff was asleep in the back seat, the car crashed into a tree. One of the passengers, Ray Simms, was killed, and Preston was injured. 'If it were not for the joint criminal activity of the four young men who were unlawfully using the vehicle, there would be no doubt but that the first defendant as driver owed a duty of care to the plaintiff as passenger.'[26] Yet the court held unanimously that the boy could not sue. The majority of the court focused on the extent to which the illegal context affected the court's ability to determine the relationship between the parties.[27] A getaway driver can hardly be sued for driving dangerously when that's what he's there for.[28] Yet the boys were not 'on the run' in circumstances in which dangerous driving was only to be expected.[29] On the contrary, the driving took place under no pressure and while the plaintiff was asleep. Nevertheless, the majority concluded that there was no duty owed by the driver to the passenger because 'it would not be possible or feasible for a court to determine what was an appropriate standard of care to be expected' without reference to the criminal elements of their relationship.[30] Accordingly, 'there was no relationship of proximity' between the parties.[31]

Merely to express the argument in these terms exposes the fragility of its logic. It is simply bizarre to try and claim that there was no 'proximate relationship' between the parties. On the contrary, the relationship of two people in a car is 'a textbook example' of a duty of care.[32] The concurring judgments of Brennan and Dawson JJ get to the heart of the matter more clearly. Both indicate that the duty of care founders not just because the boys were behaving illegally but because to allow the plaintiff to recover for his injuries would 'condone a breach of the criminal law'.[33] Brennan J distinguishes between *Gala v Preston* and cases involving less serious criminality, such as if the drivers, for example, had been unlicensed.[34]

> It is only where the admission of a duty of care impairs the normative influence of the law creating an offence that the civil law can be said to condone a breach of that law. In such cases, it would be contrary to public policy to admit a duty of care.[35]

Justice Dawson's argument is similar. The recognition of a duty of care 'gives validity to the criminal enterprise by using it as the foundation for erecting a standard of care'.[36]

So for the Court, the normative value of the criminal law takes priority over the purely instrumental value of acknowledging a duty of care. Crime trumps tort. In support of these ideas the courts are prepared effectively to outlaw certain persons, or at least to withdraw from them the support of the law of torts. In this case a 19-year-old boy with serious injuries was denied any compensation or support.

Levinas helps us start from a different perspective. There are *two* relevant relationships in a situation like *Gala v Preston:* that between the boys and the State was breached by criminal conduct (and will, we imagine, be punished accordingly); and that between the two boys themselves was breached by negligent conduct and is no less important. The High Court of Australia suggests that to give respect to the relationship between the parties would amount to 'condoning a breach of the criminal law'. In what sense, *condoning*? Each action is independent of the other. Should we continue to be blind to the actual suffering and needs of the plaintiff, and to the actual relationship which gave rise to it? The Court seems to think here that it must make a choice between 'real' law – crime – and the expendable superstructure of civil compensation. But for Levinas, the relationship between neighbours at the heart of the legal maxim of the duty of care is much more important for our law and our society than that.

In *Hall v Hebert,* the Supreme Court of Canada was faced with a broadly similar situation involving 'a souped-up muscle car' that exuded, in the ironic commentary of Cory J, 'a compelling seductive charm that would attract young men of all ages'.[37] An accident took place when the defendant allowed the plaintiff to drive while drunk. Yet the court in that case rejected the idea that to recognize a duty of care in such circumstances would somehow undermine the criminal law. Justice

McLachlin distinguished those situations involving attempts to enforce illegal contracts or secret trusts,[38] or as in the celebrated US case of *Riggs v Palmer,* to probate a testament having disposed of the testator.[39] In those cases, the 'fabric of the law' is compromised because it is being used to allow someone to profit from their illegal conduct. The hypothetical burglar who negligently puts too much gelignite in the safe and blows up his partner might be placed within this category. Above all, we ought to be wary of requiring the courts, in effect, to lay down rules defining standards of 'reasonable criminal conduct', where the duty of care 'would require modification by reference to the criminal aspects of the venture',[40] as in situations 'necessitating secrecy, subterfuge, or haste'.[41]

There is a difference between asking the court to define standards *of* illegal conduct, and standards of general conduct that happen to take place illegally. The court in *Gala v Preston* was not being asked to lay down standards of 'reasonable joy riding'; just to apply the normal standard of care for driving. To sustain the action would not have 'condoned' the boys' criminal conduct. It would merely have recognized that there was also, and Levinas would insist, in no way derivatively, a personal relationship between them that did not disappear the moment they transgressed the margins of the state. Our responsibility to one another is not conditional on good conduct, or posited by the State only as a reward for law-abiding behaviour.[42] The duty of care expresses our recognition of a kind of ethical relationship between two persons that exists prior to any substantive law and is of the utmost and foundational importance to it. This personal relationship, says Levinas, is not a legal fiction or convenience which the State giveth and the State taketh away, but the foundation of our ethics and our society. *Gala v Preston,* by creating outlaws, did not withhold from them an instrumental convenience invented by the State, but an ethical principle – care, trust, our personal responsibility for others – that *sustains* it.

Ironically, the joint majority judgment in *Gala v Preston* might be thought to have known what was at stake. In a celebrated series of cases over several years, the Australian courts had recognized the importance to be attached to the independent normative edifice of negligence principles. Under of the rubric of 'proximity' the Court had insistently (though not always successfully) sought to define what it was about particular relationships that necessarily attracted a duty of care – not just because the law said so but because our ethical instincts demanded it. Unfortunately in *Gala v Preston* the court concluded that 'the requirement of proximity... will include policy considerations'.[43] These policy considerations, foremost among them the primacy of the criminal law, proved so determinative that 'the parties were not', by judgment's end, 'in a relationship of proximity to each other' after all.[44]

This is a nonsense which has been subject to much deserved criticism.[45] Not, however, because the idea of proximity is itself meaningless, as some have argued,[46] but on the contrary because the court did not give sufficient weight to the ethical principle it expresses. Proximity was for Levinas, too, the key word to describe our ethical responsibility for others.

> The relationship of proximity cannot be reduced to any modality of distance or geometrical contiguity, or to the simple 'representation' of a neighbour; it is already an assignation, an extremely urgent assignation – an obligation, anachronously prior to any commitment.[47]

The notion of proximity was a radical and controversial jurisprudential development that led to innovation after innovation in the High Court's judgments. When I first read these judgments it seemed to me that the court was groping towards a new idea of the nature and the legitimacy of our ideas of responsibility. Then when I read Levinas some years later, I came to appreciate much more clearly what they might have wanted to say and why it mattered. But in *Gala* and like cases, the majority did not follow through on its insights. Firstly, rather than a 'conceptual determinant',[48] proximity, that is to say the closeness between persons, is a fact: a relationship of vulnerability and response ability. The *event* of proximity, not the concept or 'truth' of proximity,[49] is what determines its parameters. It is clear enough that this relationship actually existed between the driver in the front seat and the passenger asleep behind him. Secondly, rather than smuggling public policy in, the court could have decided that, except in the very limited circumstances recognized by the Canadian Supreme Court in *Hall v Hebert,* it had no part to play at all. The effect of these two approaches, which are implicit in the majority judgment's own underlying reasoning, would have been to give added weight to the ethical cornerstone that alone makes sense of the duty of care.

Applying asymmetric responsibility

One strength of an ethical approach is that it explains and legitimates the *a*symmetry inherent in tortious obligation. The law of negligence is therefore worthy of our respect because it recognizes that we emerge, as responsible individuals, from this structure of asymmetry rather than from a contractual realm of freedom and equivalence. On the one hand, in line with orthodox corrective justice models of the duty of care, the personal nature of the relationship remains crucial. No system of social security could adequately express our personal and unique obligation to care for those around us. The common law's symbolic and detailed discourse around responsibility is therefore of enduring importance.

On the other hand, most corrective justice models agree that the law ought strongly distinguish actions from omissions in deciding whether or not to recognize a duty of care.[50] As Deane J noted, 'It is an incident of human society that action or inaction by one person may have a direct or indirect effect on another. Unless there be more involved than mere cause and effect however, the common law remains indifferent'.[51] Law's commitment to the autonomy of the self demands nothing less. To be responsible for an omission is to be responsible for what one *hasn't done*. If I come across a child drowning through no fault or action of my own, why on earth should I find myself foisted with a responsibility to him?

> The law casts no duty upon a man to go to the aid of another who is in peril or distress, not caused by him. The call of common humanity may lead him to the rescue. This the law recognizes, for it gives the rescuer its protection when he answers that call. But it does not require that he do so.[52]

In this way, the notion of consent is preserved as a recognition of autonomy that alone justifies the imposition of a responsibility.[53] The question in every case will be, what responsibilities of positive conduct were voluntarily assumed, consented to, or undertaken by the defendant?[54] Absent such a prior relationship or choice, an omission will not be culpable.[55]

What if Levinas were right and the duty of care is not something we choose but something that chooses us? If it is the need of the other person, coupled with the capacity of the defendant to respond, that determines the ambit of the relationship, then the duty to rescue is no longer an anomaly or an embarrassment; it is on the contrary the very paradigm for the duty of care. The reason that we owe a duty of care on the roads, for example, is just the same as the reason that we owe a duty to rescue someone in trouble if we can help. The real practical *asymmetry* of the relationship, the vulnerability of the one to the actions of the other, and not their purely theoretical equality or their purely hypothetical agreement, draws forth that duty in each case. The *closer* we are, conceptually speaking, to the paradigm case of that drowning baby or that house on fire, the stronger the call of the duty of care. If we do not recognize the abiding ethical significance of that asymmetry,[56] we will never see the underlying truth about the nature of responsibility which the so-called 'duty to rescue' actually directs us towards.

Indeed, under the influence of the notion of proximity, in the 1980s and 1990s the High Court of Australia significantly moved away from the language of consent as the hallmark of responsibility and towards an emphasis on elements of the defendant's 'control' over a situation – which is to say, their response-ability – and the plaintiff's 'vulnerability' to it – which is to say, the call or gaze of the other.[57] The Court itself came to recognize that responsibility cannot be understood in terms of the autonomous decision of the defendant alone, but the situation in which they find themselves.

This begins to reflect a significant ethical shift in the law. Responsibility-as-autonomy decrees that I have no obligation to help a neighbour whose house is on fire because *I* have done nothing to establish the relationship. The situation is not 'mine'. But responsibility-as-ethics declares that proximity is the description of an event, not an intention; asymmetry is its nature and its justification, not its problem. 'We do not conceive of relation,' says Levinas, 'We *are* in relation.'[58] It is not choice but predicament that generates a responsibility.

A case from the New South Wales Court of Appeal provides, I think, a salutary example of the difference between these two registers of duty.[59] An 11-year-old boy named Patrick had an epileptic seizure. By the time his mother discovered him, his condition was serious. She sent her 14-year-old daughter, Joanna, to get Dr Lowns, whose practice was nearby. But the doctor refused to come.[60] As a result, Patrick suffered irreparable brain damage. Did Dr Lowns owe him a duty of care? The majority held that he did but conceded that the main barrier to the action was the principle of non-liability for mere omissions. Dr Lowns was not the family physician. He had never even met Patrick. Kirby P (and Cole JA agreed) held that a relationship had been established between them 'notwithstanding their lack of previous professional or personal association'.[61] Referring to the NSW *Medical Practitioners Act*, which imposes a statutory obligation on doctors to come to the aid of 'persons…in need of urgent attention',[62] his Honour held that 'the noble profession of medicine' imposed special obligations to which, by becoming a doctor, the defendant had impliedly consented.[63] It was on just this point that Mahoney JA dissented. He noted that the professional obligations created under the *Medical Practitioners Act* were not tortious. There is no duty of care owed by a doctor, argued Justice Mahoney, 'if that person is one to whom the doctor has not and never has been in a professional relationship of doctor and patient'.[64] Both judges, therefore, agreed that the issue was one of an omission in the absence of any prior relationship. They disagreed as to whether some prior consent could somehow be implied.

Starting from the idea of autonomy, the doctor's lack of agreement to act is a thorny problem. Starting from the idea of ethics, the lack of prior contact is hardly relevant. Contact now, at this very moment, *is* responsibility.[65] What matters is the *fact* of proximity that Joanna, by asking for his help, had established; the extent of the emergency, which was readily apparent; and the doctor's response-ability. Understood in this way, the majority's reasoning fails not because the duty they propose is too wide but because it is too narrow! Rather than singling doctors out as the subject of special obligations, the court would have done better to think of responsibility as an event that might single any one of us out at some moment. Someday, we might all be called on to render such a service.

The difficulty with this case is that the notion of a duty to rescue was treated, by both the majority and the minority, as entirely irreconcilable with standard negligence principles. Both sides sought to shoehorn the doctor's predicament into established notions of autonomy and agreement. But Levinas points us to an alternative theory in which the duty to rescue is central to the duty of care. Responsibility is always a surprise, never entirely chosen, and never – indeed by its very nature – a symmetrical exchange. That Dr Lowns did not want this responsibility, did not choose it or expect it, was perhaps bad luck. But that is the way of responsibility. Its always singular demands often arrive unexpectedly; arriving unexpectedly or with unexpected dimensions or aspects, they cannot therefore be completely consented to; not being consented to, they may sometimes prove burdensome. Responsibility, in short, is never entirely predictable and never entirely convenient. I venture to say that we would not be truly responsible otherwise. Yes, responsibility is a kind of intrusion on our solipsism: that's the point. And the duty to rescue is *not* alone in possessing these features; it shares them will all aspects of the duty to care, though in sharpened form.

Responsibility and judgment: Levinasian ethics and the common law

The notion of ethics and responsibility advanced by Levinas is marked by uncertainty, surprise, and the constant questioning of our relationship to others. This is really not such a strange way of thinking about law. The common law, for all its admitted imprecision, has always been a vehicle for a dialogue on these terms. The efforts of the Australian High Court to characterize the duty of care by reference to 'proximity', to take one particularly noteworthy example, suggested precisely the operations of a judgment that cannot be entirely determined in advance and that remain sensitive to the particular and the experiential – the place of the ethical *in* law. Certainly, this made 'proximity', as is its critics never tired of pointing out, 'a legal rule without specific content, resistant to precise definition and therefore inadequate as a tool...'[66] But this misses the point: such indeterminacy is inevitable.[67] To which Derrida adds that it is more than inevitable: it is a stroke of luck. 'This moment of suspense... is always full of anxiety, but who pretends to be just by economizing on anxiety?'[68]

In the law of torts, the duty of care is the *structural* site in which responsiveness to the experience of others has been purposely kept open, an institutionalized and unstable force for reflection and change. It is the part of the 'third' or social realm that witnesses our rendezvous with the other, providing a space for a 'never-ending oscillation' between ethics and politics.[69] Despite its admittedly sloppy use over the years, the legal notion of proximity developed by the High Court of Australia did not merely 'mask... policy preferences'.[70] On the contrary, it was also the site of an ethics, an anti-law, in Levinasian terms.

How is such co-existence even possible when the instability that remains so important to ethics and justice is always trying to be eliminated by law?[71] Levinas rather helpfully provides us with a metaphor of knots, which 'interrupt the [seamless or dogmatic] discourse' of law.[72] Levinas criticizes the State as attempting to cut out these knots of discourse, and thus to repress the interstices of ethics. But judicial decision-making is different. Precedent, like a rosary, remembers and continues to worry over that knotty problem of the past. It builds knots upon knots, imperfections upon imperfections. Certainly the High Court, faced with such interruptions in its supposedly seamless thread of rules, will always attempt to gather up the loose ends and retie the thread over and over again. That is how our institutions work.

But the knots thus formed conserve the *memory* of that disruption and authorize the possibility of new ones to further unsettle a purely internal and conceptual system of order.[73]

On one level, the discourse of the duty of care attempts to describe citizens' responsibilities for each other and the dimensions that such a response ought to take. And as we have seen, the articulation of such responsibilities is necessarily – ethically – imperfect and subject to constant reassessment. Sometimes, the call of others will put the responsible citizen on the spot *without* any prior rules to guide him. On another level, the swirling conversation around the duty of care has also been the forum for the common law's recognition of its *own* response – ability. Judges too are forced to remind themselves that a responsible judgment cannot simply be mailed in advance; Courts must always be open to acknowledge the approximation of their doctrines. Sometimes the call of others will put the responsible *judge* on the spot and force them to reconsider the meanings and purposes of law's rules and relationships. As a legal principle, then, the word proximity, with all its overtones, provided a meditation on the ethical attentiveness that connects persons – while as a legal discourse, it provided the occasion for an ethical attentiveness between those who declare the law and those who come before it asking to be heard.

For these reasons we should be concerned that the High Court of Australia has, over the past few years, moved steadily away from the language of proximity and towards what we might describe as a more rule-based and narrow conception of the duty of care.[74] The imaginative leaps in both substance and methodology with which proximity was associated have largely been recanted, even forgotten. But this retreat from ethics to law encompasses both misunderstanding and danger. Should the eclipse of proximity continue to be accompanied by a loss of the ideals of asymmetric response ability with which it has been associated, the law will have settled down. In such a world, we will have rules, we will have obedience, and we will all, including the law, *know who we are*. But this is just the attitude for which Levinas chides us. One is accustomed to think of 'settled law' as an ideal, but Levinas suggests that ethics means never being entirely settled, never at home in our world, always in movement and in question.[75] It is not of course that law should abandon rules altogether; but ethics asks that we also find a place from which to recognize and give effect to the *necessary* unsettlement of our obligations, since that unsettlement and openness makes responsibility possible. The duty of care is one such place.

Notes

1. This article incorporates aspects of chapters 3, 4 and 7 of D. Manderson, *Proximity: Levinas and the Soul of Law* (McGill-Queen's University Press, Montreal, 2006). Parts of it were originally published as 'Emmanuel Levinas and the Philosophy of Negligence', *Tort Law Review* 14 (2006) 1–18. Publishers' permission is granted and gratefully acknowledged.
2. E. Levinas, *Totalité et infini: essai sur l'extériorité* (Paris: Kluwer, 1961); *Totality and Infinity*, trans A Lingis (Pittsburgh: Duquesne University Press, 1968) p. 5 [hereinafter TI].
3. Z. Bauman, *Postmodern Ethics* (Oxford: Blackwell, 1993); M. Diamantides, *Ethics of Suffering The Ethics of Suffering* (Aldershot: Ashgate, 2000) 2 et seq.
4. R. Bernasconi, 'Deconstruction and the Possibility of Ethics', in J. Sallis (ed.), *Deconstruction and Philosophy: The Texts of Jacques Derrida* (Chicago: University of Chicago Press, 1987) p. 131; M. Diamantides, 'Ethics in Law: Death Marks on a Still Life', *Law and Critique* 6 (1995) 209–228, 224–225.
5. *Hedley, Byrne & Co. Ltd v Heller & Partners Ltd* [1964] AC 465; *Dorset Yacht Co. Ltd v Home Office* [1970] AC 1004; *Anns v London Borough of Merton* [1978] AC 728; *Jaensch v Coffey* (1984) 155 CLR 549; *Sutherland Shire Council v Heyman* (1985) 157 CLR 424; *Caltex Oil (Australia) Pty Ltd v The Dredge 'Willemstad'* (1976) 136 CLR 529.
6. See Manderson, *Proximity*.
7. Levinas, TI, p. 28: 'a deduction – necessary yet non-analytical'.
8. E. Levinas, *Théorie de l'intuition dans la phénoménologie de Husserl* (Paris, Vrin, 1930, 1963); *En découvrant l'existence avec Husserl et Heidegger* (Paris, Vrin, 1949, 1967).
9. A. Gormley, *Field for the British Isles* (1993).
10. Reported, *inter alia,* in http://www.sbc.org.uk/home/newsroom/sub_newsroom/main/archive/9746637.
11. A. Lingis, 'Translator's Introduction' in E. Levinas, *Otherwise Than Being, or Beyond Essence,* trans. A Lingis (Pittsburgh: Duquesne University Press, 1981) xxxiii [hereinafter OBBE].
12. See E. Levinas, *Le visage de l'autre,* dessins de Martin tom Dieck (Paris: Editions Seuil, 2001). For a recent discussion, D. M. Duncan, *The Pre-Text of Ethics: On Derrida and Levinas* (New York: Peter Lang, 2001) 41.
13. Levinas, OBBE, p. 49.
14. E. Levinas, *Éthique et Infini: Dialogues avec Philippe Nemo* (Paris: Fayard/Radio-France, 1982) 83–84. I have attempted to replicate the casualness of the conversation in my translation.
15. Levinas, TI, p. 27.
16. Ibid., p. 101.
17. Levinas, *Éthique et Infini*, p. 93–94.
18. On this point, see particularly Levinas, OBBE, pp. 45–48.
19. Ibid.
20. Ibid., p. 86.
21. Amongst other places, see ibid., p. 85.
22. Levinas, *Éthique et Infini*, p. 94.

23. Levinas, TI, p. 195. Translation mine.
24. *Henwood v Municipal Tramways Trust* (1938) 60 CLR 438, 462 per Dixon and McTiernan JJ.
25. *Gala v Preston* (1991) 172 CLR 243.
26. Ibid., p. 263 per Brennan J.
27. *Progress and Properties v Craft* (1976) 135 CLR 651, 668 per Jacobs J.
28. *Hall v Hebert* (1993) 101 DLR (4th) 129; 2 SCR 159 per Sopinka J (SC Canada).
29. *Smith v Jenkins* (1970) 119 CLR 397.
30. *Gala v Preston* pp. 254–255.
31. Ibid., p. 254.
32. Ibid., p. 277 per Dawson J.
33. Ibid., p. 273. See in identical terms p. 279 per Dawson J.
34. *Jackson v Harrison* [1978] 138 CLR 438.
35. *Gala v Preston* p. 271 per Brennan J.
36. Ibid., p. 279.
37. Ibid.
38. *Nelson v Nelson* (1995) 184 CLR 538.
39. *Riggs v Palmer* 22 NE 188 (1889) (New York Court of Appeals).
40. *Gala v Preston* p. 279 per Dawson J.
41. Ibid., p. 269 per Brennan J.
42. *Hall v Hebert* 182 per McLachlin J.
43. *Gala v Preston* p. 253.
44. Ibid., p. 254.
45. R. Kostal, 'Currents in the Counter-Reformation', *Tort Law Review* 3 (1995) 100.
46. See M. McHugh, 'Neighbourhood, Proximity and Reliance', in P. Finn (ed.), *Essays on Torts* (Sydney: Law Book, 1989); A. Kramer, 'Proximity as Principles: Directness, Community Norms and the Tort of Negligence', *Tort Law Review* 11 (2) (2003) 70–103; P. Vines, 'The Needle in the Haystack: Principle in the Duty of Care in Negligence', *University of New South Wales Law Journal* 23(2) (2000) 35–57; S. Yeo, 'Rethinking Proximity: a Paper Tiger?', *Tort Law Review* 5 (3) (1997) 174; P. Vines, 'Fault, Responsibility and Negligence in the High Court of Australia', *Tort Law Review* 8 (2000) 130–145.
47. Levinas, OBBE, pp. 100–101.
48. *Stevens v Brodribb Sawmilling Co Pty Ltd* (1986)160 CLR 16, 52–53 per Deane J; *Cook v Cook* (1986) 162 CLR 376.
49. E. Levinas, *The Levinas Reader,* trans. S. Hand (Oxford: Blackwell, 1989) p. 120.
50. P. Atiyah, *Accidents, Compensation and the Law*, 4th ed. (London: Weidenfeld and Nicholson, 1987) 63–72; M. Shapo, *The Duty to Act* (Dallas: University of Texas Press, 1978); E. Weinrib, 'The Case for a Duty to Rescue', *Yale Law Journal* 90 (1980) 247–293.
51. *Jaensch v Coffey* (1984) 155 CLR 549, 578 per Deane J.
52. *Hargrave v Goldman* (1963) 110 CLR 40.
53. T. Honoré, 'Are Omissions Less Culpable?' in *Responsibility and Fault* (Oxford: Portland, 1999) p. 44.
54. *Geyer v Downs* (1977) 138 CLR 91.
55. *Sutherland Shire Council v Heyman* (1985) 157 CLR 424.

56. See the discussion of responsibility as death and as gift in R. Burggraeve, 'Violence and the Vulnerable Face of the Other: The Vision of Emmanuel Levinas on Moral Evil and Our Responsibility', *Journal of Social Philosophy* 30 (1999) 29–45; J. Derrida, *The Gift of Death*, trans. D. Wills (Chicago: University of Chicago Press, 1995).
57. See in particular *Perre v Apand Pty Ltd* (1999) 198 CLR 180 per Gleeson CJ and McHugh J.
58. E. Levinas, *Difficult Freedom: Essays on Judaism*, trans. S. Hand (London: Athlone, 1990) 140.
59. *Lowns v Wood* [1996] *Australian Torts Reporter* 81–376; and see L. Haberfield, '*Lowns v Woods* and the Duty to Rescue', *Tort Law Review* 6 (1998) 56–80.
60. *Lowns v Wood* 63,172 per Cole JA. The doctor told a different story but it was not accepted by the Court.
61. Ibid., 63,155 per Kirby P.
62. *Medical Practitioners Act* 1938 (NSW), s 27(2).
63. *Lowns v Wood* 63,155 per Kirby P.
64. Ibid., per Mahoney JA.
65. E. Levinas, 'Language and Proximity' in OBBE, p. 116.
66. *Pyrenees Shire Council v Day; Eskimo Amber Pty Ltd v Pyrenees Shire Council* (1998) 192 C.L.R. 330, 414 per Kirby J.
67. K. Llewellyn, *Jurisprudence: Realism in Theory and Practice* (Chicago: University of Chicago Press, 1962).
68. J. Derrida, 'Force of Law: The Mystical Foundation of Authority', *Cardozo L. Rev.* 11 (1990) 920–1045, 955.
69. W. Simmons, 'The Third', *Philosophy and Social Criticism* 25 (1999) 83–104, 84; see also S. Roberts, 'Rethinking Justice: Levinas and Assymetrical Responsibility', *Philosophy & the Contemporary World* 7 (2000) 5–12, 7–8.
70. *Hill v Van Erp* (1997) 188 CLR 159, per Gummow J quoting McHugh, 'Neighbourhood, Proximity, and Reliance'.
71. Levinas, OBBE, pp. 165–171.
72. Ibid., p. 170.
73. 'The discourse that suppresses the interruptions of discourse by relating them maintain the discontinuity under the knots with which the thread is tied again': ibid.
74. *Perre v. Apand* pp. 209–210, per McHugh J; 'It is tolerably clear that proximity's reign . . . has come to an end': *Pyrenees Shire Council v. Day* 414 per Kirby J.
75. Thus see Levinas, OBBE, p. 108; Levinas, TI, pp. 268–70; and see J. Derrida, 'Bois', in S. Critchley (ed.), *The Ethics of Deconstruction* (Oxford: Blackwell, 1999) pp. 107–109. See also H. Caygill, *Levinas and the Political* (New York: Routledge, 2002) pp. 85–86, Bernasconi 'Deconstruction and the Possibility of Ethics' p. 131.

7

To Judge a Vegetable: Levinasian Ethics and the 'morality of law'

Marinos Diamantides

For over three years in the early 1990s a man called Anthony Bland lay on a hospital bed in the condition that medicine used to call 'persistent vegetative state' and now calls 'permanent vegetative state' (hereafter PVS).[1] The responsible physicians provided him with nutrition through a nasogastric tube, antibiotics whenever an infection arose and other basic care. As far as one could tell Bland was aware of nothing. There he was, without relation to an exteriority; food and oxygen being of relevance to him only once they had been absorbed into his body. In *Airedale NHS Trust v Bland* [1993] 1 All E.R. 821 his doctors sought declarations from the English High Court that it would not be unlawful for them to let him die through starvation and dehydration. The case proceeded to the Court of Appeal and finally the House of Lords.

Unable to identify (with) Bland either positively as a living-something *or* negatively as a dead-nothing, one would have feared that perhaps life and death are not alternatives but, horrifyingly, aspects of an absolutely bland *there is* from which there is no escape. In 'Humanism and An-Archy' Levinas posited such a condition as being's most intimate relation to itself. He spoke of a basic 'inwardness'[2] of being which is neither anonymous nor yet has a name: neither a nothing nor a becoming. His inaugural essay 'On Escape'[3] helps us relate to this more directly: *dasein*, or being-there, was analysed in the mode of 'self-shame' and 'nausea' that come with the pre-reflective feeling that one is always inescapably implicated in the *there is*, of which being and nothingness are just different phases. Elsewhere he wrote of the dread weariness of the insomniac: even when daylight breaks and 'becoming' recommences one still remains enchained to the *there is* of anonymous and shapeless existence, which at night one feels more directly and from which daylight only temporarily distracts us. In other words, the nausea and horror of the *there is*, of *being there*, attach to us notwithstanding our verbality, our capacity to become which death measures.

This innermost pre-reflexive relationship to ourselves is absolute (death won't end it) and yet we are incapable of experiencing it neutrally. Instead, like the feeling of nausea, it is endured as a riveting, an enchainment which was never preceded by freedom. It comes, Levinas wrote, with all the force of a contract even if we never entered into it. Being a self, that is a singular human existent, does not allow us to overcome this riveting. Unable to escape the *there is* and yet unable to experience it neutrally, a singular existent exists in so far as s/he desires an otherwise than being *or* not being. In other essays of his, for instance in 'Reflections on the Philosophy of Hitlerism', Levinas analysed this in terms of the experience of pain where the spirit's opposition to pain is described as a 'rebellion, a refusal to remain within it and consequently an attempt to go beyond it'.[4]

The final stage of this rebellion against the nausea and blandness of existence is accomplished when we experience ourselves as 'otherwise than ego', a subject 'hostage' to the absolute other expressed in the face of the particular Other, the subject of responsibility-as-responsiveness that emerges between persecution and obsession by the Other, answerable before it is asked.[5] 'Infinite' and 'gratuitous' responsibility for the Other, therefore, are not abstract duties. They correspond to a being which *anticipates* an Other to which it is hostage. This, I think, is the basis of Levinas's 'infinite' and 'anarchic' responsibility for an Other whose disincarnate, vulnerable Face, a mask hiding no secrets, signifies the otherwise than being. To put it otherwise, being a singular existent is the empirical side effect of this impossible desire to escape *there is* by feeling responsible *for* a particular Other.

Exposure to Bland's situation must have intensified the feeling of nausea in those around him. But did it also result in a greater expression of their an-archic responsibility for him as per Levinas? To think of someone like Bland as either still alive or already dead is to deny the horror of the *there is* and, *ipso facto*, the desire for an infinite responsibility for the Other *otherwise than* either as a being which persists in being or as nothing.

The medical definition of death coincides with the cessation of electrical activity in the entire brain.[6] Insensate patients like Bland, a common metaphor for whom is 'vegetable',[7] are therefore medically alive. English law has adopted this definition as a matter of course. Consequently when a PVS patient is brought before the common law, the courts deal with it as if it is still living, that is as the immortal phantasm of the conscious, self-possessed subject of law that it was previously. This requires an inventive and imaginative restoration to the patient of a phantasmatic will capable of harmonisation with the rule of some authority or other. In the United States this process takes the form of litigation between the past wishes of the patient, if any (the so called 'living will'), and their construction according to the constitution. It becomes a right-to-die issue.[8]

In England *Bland* was a first – it has since been followed routinely[9] and its principles have now become part of statute.[10] In the first place, the courts focused on the vegetating patient's right to self-determination. A patient must always consent to medical treatment and if he cannot the latter is only lawful if it is in their 'best interests'; once the doctors find that no interests are served then the doctor has no right to interfere with the patient's bodily integrity. Hence, the judges sought to present a-conscious Bland as a living object of law or a still-life given to the extant law: a persevering existent, lacking exteriority but 'naturally' endowed with freedom, rights and autonomy. The point of departure was the near-sacred status of individual self-determination and autonomy which liberal law has extended over time to the most obviously dependent persons such as children and patients. The proposed action – the withdrawal of all care – was therefore constructed not as violence but as a decision to desist from violating the patient. In view of this it was possible to deny any judicial activism and reinstate the myth of submission to existing law. In *Bland*, there was no legislation on the subject, and the only existing law to which the judges could turn took the form of precedent framed in terms of the paramountcy of a conscious patients' autonomy and best interests. The Court insisted that its action would not in any way render the proposed conduct an exception to the criminal law, but instead would:

> simply apply the law as it now stands... [T]he declarations will therefore achieve no more in the present case than the useful but limited function of reassuring the doctors that what they wish to do was lawful when proposed and will be lawful when carried out, and will as a by-product ensure that in practice if the proposed conduct goes ahead no prosecution will ensue. (at 888)

Yet, at the same time, the courts in these cases treat the vegetating patient as if dying, if not already dead. Indeed, undermining their formal presentation of such a patient as living the courts go out of their way to present him/her as someone whose time has come, who is only 'artificially kept alive', a corpse in all but medical definition; not quite a still-life but, as the French call it, *nature morte*. Thus, for the American judge in the seminal *Cruzan* case

> highly invasive treatment may perpetuate human existence through a merge of body and machine that some might reasonably regard as an insult to life rather than as its continuation... there is a serious question as to whether the mere persistence of [the PVS patients'] bodies is 'life' as that word is commonly understood. The State's... unflagging determination to perpetuate... physical existence is comprehensible only as an effort to define life's meaning, not as an attempt to preserve its sanctity. Absent some theological abstraction, the idea of life is not conceived separately from the idea of a living person.[11]

Likewise in *Bland* we were told that the 'mere persistence' of Bland's body was not life 'as that word is commonly understood' (at 832). Bland's '... body is alive, but he has no life in the sense that even the most pitifully handicapped but conscious human being has a life' (at 850). The judge wondered '[W]hy do we think it would be a tragedy to allow Anthony Bland to die? It could be said that the entire tragedy took place at [the place where the accident which caused Bland's injuries] and that the curtain was brought down when [he] passed into persistent vegetative state' (at 851). '[T]he mere fact that he is still a living organism' (at 851) was not enough to call him alive since 'life' required a minimum self-consciousness and self-possession. And in case any doubt remained: '... the very concept of having a life has no meaning in relation to [Bland]. He is [artificially] alive but *has no life at all...*' (at 853, my emphasis). At the House of Lords, Lord Keith of Kinkel emphasised that Bland 'cannot see, hear or feel anything. He cannot communicate in any way. The consciousness which is the essential feature of individual personality has departed for ever' (at 859) and it was 'permissible to say that to an individual with no cognitive capacity whatever, and no prospect of ever recovering any such capacity in this world, it must be a matter of complete indifference whether he lives or dies' (at 861). Lord Mustill said that '... the time has come when Anthony Bland has no further interest in being kept alive' (at 895) and 'I... believe that the proposed conduct is ethically justified, since the continued treatment of Anthony Bland can no longer serve to maintain that combination of manifold characteristics which we call a personality' (at 896).

Presenting Bland as effectively already dead and in need of a dignified burial was essential to an argumentative strategy aimed at morally/politically justifying their decision to withdraw nutrition and basic care which, paradoxically, ran in parallel with the arguments from the legality of such course of action that wanted him alive. Now, Bland was not a living object of law but the dead subject of morality. The paradox is that by presenting him as dead in all but name the judges were undermining their reliance on the extant law examined above which relies on the notion of the incompetent patients' medically defined best interests. It was indeed admitted that the case of the completely insensate Bland (at 826) was very dissimilar to all the available precedent cases which involved the assessment of the interests of sentient beings such as minors and mental patients (at 829). Why, then, turn to medicine to find out Bland's interests if medical science and technology were never intended to be used to prolong 'biological life in patients bereft of the prospect of returning to an even limited exercise of human life' (at 837)? Why focus on Bland's interests at all if Bland 'has... no consciousness of his life and it could be said to be a matter of indifference to him whether he lives or dies' (at 851). There was:

> ...no question of [Bland's] life being worth living or not worth living because the stark reality is that [he] is not living a life at all. None of the things that one says about the way people live their lives – well or ill, with courage or fortitude, happily or sadly – have any meaning in relation to him. (at 855)

Alongside discrediting the best interests approach came a sense of difficult freedom. The doctor's assessment 'may well be influenced by his own attitude to the sanctity of human life' (at 875). The judicial development of law too 'would of necessity reflect the judge's views on the underlying ethical questions' (at 879).

> If the criteria for the legitimacy of the proposed... contain an element of ethical judgement... the judge is no better equipped, though no worse, than anyone else. In the end, it is a matter of personal choice dictated by his or her background. Legal expertise gives no special advantage to her. (at 886)

This freedom was no doubt unwelcome and the judges found themselves at a loss since Parliament no longer authorises them to simply decide on behalf of incompetent patients, as it used under the jurisdiction of *parens patriae*.[12]

In sum, Bland was represented as both a still living object of law and as the dead subject of morality. The function of the former representation was to legitimate the withdrawal of nutrition and basic care as ordinary medical conduct while the latter served to justify it as a form of non-state violence that was morally acceptable.[13] Both versions required a lot of inventiveness on behalf of the judges. But to the extent that their construction implicated their judgment in extant law such inventiveness passed for merely 'applying' the law. By contrast resolving to also see Bland as a corpse in need of a proper burial is an obvious case of judicial activism given that the definition of death is a parliamentary (or in this case a medical) matter and not within the scope of judicial authority. By what authority, then, could the judges effectively redefine death in such an *ad hoc* manner?

While modern judiciaries operate within a positivistic understanding of the law they have never entirely given up the option of appealing to a normativity above and beyond positive sovereign law: be it natural law, God's law or, in the case of the common law, customary law handed down from our dead ancestors. Thus, in *Bland*, Judge Hoffman could say that this case was not '... an area in which any difference can be allowed to exist between what is legal and what is morally right' (at 850) and then referred to moral principles which relate the living to the dead:

> Most people would like an honourable and dignified death and we think it wrong to dishonour their deaths, even when they are unconscious that this is happening. We pay respect to their dead bodies and to their memories because we think it an offence against the dead themselves if we do not. ... [I] am not concerned to analyse the rationality of these feelings. It is enough that they are deeply rooted and the law cannot possibly ignore them. (pp. 853–854)

And:

> The mere fact that he is still a living organism means that there remains an epilogue of the tragedy which is being played out. This is because *we* have a strong feeling that there is an intrinsic value in human life... *we* should not try to analyse the rationality of such feelings. What matter is that, in one form or another, they form part of almost everyone's intuitive values. No law that ignores them can possibly hope to be acceptable. (855, my italics)

Among these values the judge emphasised the principle of respect for the dignity of the individual human being which transcends death:

> [W]e pay respect to the dead and to their memory because we think it an offence against the dead themselves if we do not. Once again I am not concerned with the rationality of these feelings. It is enough that they are deeply rooted in our ways of thinking and that the law cannot possibly ignore them. (at 854)

In saying that 'the mere fact that he is still a living organism means that there remains an epilogue of the tragedy which is being played out' the judge has unintentionally described the fate of natural law: it now haunts the absolute self-referentiality of positive law, as the epilogue to the tragedy of its own irrelevance. An epilogue is a short speech addressed directly to the audience by an actor at the end of a play or a short passage added at the end of a literary work. It does not add to the story but it does have empirical effects in that it affects how we relate to it. Here, the story is that of the living object of law, of bare life included in a totality of law as closed system. The epilogue does not change this but casts it in a light of doubt. In so far as Bland was presented as dying/dead subject of morality the judges doubted – without exceeding – their bureaucratic role and alluded to their historical function as the voice of morality, dictated to the living by the dead, speaking from the past immemorial of the common law and beyond. In this sense the courts are a crucial link between society as the sovereign community of those of us living now and as immortal corporation that includes the living, the dead and the unborn.

The alternate judicial reanimation and mortification of Bland exemplify two things. First, a judicial allergy towards the resistance of that being to all our prior established categories; which is to say, in Levinasian terms, an indifference towards alterity. This is understandable since obvious indeterminacy made the fundamental judicial task of declaring the proposed medical action either lawful conduct or unlawful violence extremely difficult. Indicative of this allergy, the judge asked 'why do we think it would be a tragedy to allow Bland to die, if it could be said to be a matter of indifference to him whether he lives or dies?' (851). He then answered his question by noting that one can have interests in things one is unconscious of and therefore Bland could be said to be interested in having a dignified death. In sum, his chosen starting point was that Bland was either indifferent or interested in his fate. What is lost here is any sense of the judges' *own* responsibility, which confronted them whether or not Mr Bland remained in some sense 'interested' in it. Secondly, the alternate judicial reanimation and mortification of Bland exemplify the two sides of the paradoxical manner in which the legal discourse structures the relationship of modern judges to sovereign power. Modern judges are expected both to apply the will of the community of the living and to bestow on it a semblance of transcendence as if this will was not blind to past and future generations of humans but was informed by them.

Taken together, the above two points suggest that modern judges have at their disposal two, paradoxically linked, methods for dissimulating their individuated responsibility before the unique human Other they confront in each case. In order to avoid the immediate affective responsibility they faced, the judges wanted Bland dead *and* alive, albeit at different moments of the judgment. At once he was a still living subject of law characterised by the 'radical will that makes us want to live' that Foucault has noted must be assumed for sovereignty to exist.[14] And a dead human nature – the aftermath of post-humanist man – which is still in communion with those who lived in less uncertain times. Both these versions were necessary for rendering judicial responsibility in accordance with either the extant law or the principles of morality and, therefore, in either case, less than infinite and somehow authorised. By the same token we can say that Bland was unwanted as vegetating, that is as a unique and peculiarly uncategorisable modern being who would command from each of the judges an individuated responsibility in excess of any *arche*. In this respect, Levinas could not have been more relevant to the case of *Bland*:

> Responsibility for the unique, shattering the totality: responsibility before the unique that rebels against every category, a signifier outside the concept, free, for an instant, from all graspable form in the *nakedness* of his exposure to death ... in his or her supreme precariousness and in the imperative that calls out to me. Behold vision turning back into non-vision, into insinuation of a face, into the refutation of vision within sight's centre, into that of which vision, already assuming a plastic form, is but forgetfulness and re-presentation.[15]

Bland's existence threatened to shatter the totality, to rebel against every category and to signify his exposure and his vulnerability. Totality was reinstated in so far as the judges managed to 'mirror' themselves in such a being (now a pure biological life captured by the necessary law; now a dead subject of a morality that transcends the positive law) and to see in him what they imagine themselves to be: either living cogs in law's closed circuit, an indifferent, self-same body which produces its own meaning; or 'dead meat', useless to the law. The activation of this mimetic desire was a precondition for the imaginative capture (*catalepsis*) of the vegetable-man and constitutes a *sine qua non* for the project of modern law, in which personal judgment and responsibility is ruthlessly expunged from a system part positive rules and part moral norms.

But if Levinas is right, proximity with the Other as unthematisable other, that is as obsession, delirium, shame and culpability, does not stop having empirical effects just because we don't want them to.[16] In sum, one remains hostage to the Other even if only in a warped sense. And indeed *Bland*'s bizarre *ratio* seems ultimately to highlight rather than mask the individual responsibility of each judge for the patient who was neither alive nor dead. What the doctors were proposing to do was at once legitimate, ordinary, peaceful action *and* justifiable extraordinary violent action. As it was characteristically 'held' by the editor of the *All England Law Reports* the decision to withdraw life support from the insensate Bland would be lawful '... provided responsible and competent medical opinion was of the view that it would be in the patient's best interests not to prolong his life ... because such treatment was futile and would not confer any benefit to him' (*Bland* at 822). The death of a vegetable-man with no capacity for therapeutic interests is thus 'based' on his therapeutic interests! The contradictory basis of the *ratio* also meant that the judges' personal responsibility was not exhausted despite – indeed because – their successful parallel efforts to re-represent him as both alive and dead.

For Finnis, who argues that the point of law is to provide certainty, the decision suffers from a 'fatal flaw'.[17] Since hospitals need a declaration before they can withdraw treatment, he reasoned, the current position is that they are required to obtain a declaration that it is not a crime for them to stop committing a tort. Yet, for Fitzpatrick, the ability of the courts to provide any answer to a case is crucial to the survival of law irrespective of its ability to provide certainty: 'The ability or the aspiration of the rule of law to provide certainty, an assured stability, cannot mark an achieved completeness for law, *if law itself is to survive*'.[18] Does not this ability of modern formal law to survive as a system pass through the judges embodying a paradoxical social role that entails the promise but never the delivery of legal certainty? Are they not trying to address both present litigants and those who came before them and will come in their stead? This position is difficult to embody and, arguably, renders the experience of judging close to that of the 'shameful' and nauseous Self in the pre-reflective, lived, Levinasian sense explained at the beginning of this chapter. If Levinas was right – and *Bland* would only exemplify this – the Other is always already inside the Same but can only be ill-fitting; to be just to the Other can only mean to experience this ill-fitting. In 'Transcendence and Height', among many other texts, Levinas wrote that the movement whereby the Same welcomes the Other by 'putting itself into question' (BPW, 16) is *not* controlled by the self-same subject who, thus, is always caught unawares, radically passive. Justice, then, cannot be a project, the work of overcoming a difficulty, but the undergoing of a fracas. 'The just person who knows himself to be just is no longer just' said Levinas[19] which leaves the possibility open that one can be just unknowingly.

The court's fundamental confusion lay in its failure to recognise that it was their consciousness and not Bland's that was ultimately called in question by the decision. Self-questioning is neither an act of introspection and reflexivity (like discovering a moral norm) nor of entering a 'supra-personal, coherent and universal discourse'[20] (like applying a legal rule) – but an event of individuating 'election' *by* the Other human who affects me. This occurs when confronted with an Other who has nothing in common with me (who is wholly other than myself) but calls on me independently of 'who' and 'what' I am to myself. Not 'I am who I am'; nor 'I am what I am'; but 'I am for my Other'. For Levinas, this is what happens in every encounter with every human Other who 'through the nakedness and destitution of his defenceless eyes... forbids murder and paralyses my impetuous freedom'.[21] It is the result of the Other's epiphany as a face that commands my responsibility in excess of who/what the Other shows himself to be and without the excuse that what remains opaque does not concern me. The absolutely Other 'resists the indiscretion of intentionality... to the point where its very resistance does not become converted into a content of consciousness'. This means that the Other is not reflected in my consciousness either positively, as an object of my representation, or negatively as something which resists my intentionality. Hence, the 'putting into question does not amount to a being conscious of this putting into question.... What is at stake is putting consciousness in question and not the consciousness of putting into question' (ibid.). In 'Substitution' the relationship between the shamed me and the Other, 'proximity', is once again proclaimed to be irreducible to consciousness and thematisation. It is an anachronistic relationship of obligation since the self only exists in so far as it is summoned by the Other, and 'anarchic', without the mediation of any principle, since the Other signifies as a singularity before being bestowed with sense.[22] This responsibility is an 'obsession', 'disequilibrium', 'delirium' or 'passion' whose active source is irreducibly exterior, 'extra-ordinary', leaving me speechless. And because every self is, according to Levinas's premise, caught up in such proximity, my identity is never settled but always undergoing an unrest, an 'irritability'.[23] 'The ego is in itself like one is in one's skin, that is to say, cramped, ill at ease in one's skin'.[24]

The modern judiciary is inherently prone to such irritability. A modern judge has to relate to her body, the body of the Other before her, and the body of laws, at once as immortal 'living thing', systemic closure, self-referentiality *and* as dead weight, a system crushed by exteriority, heteronomy. This is a painful condition to be in – and perhaps for the better. Unable to be either one thing or the other but having to be both a judge is ill at ease with his/her self and speaks contradictory words (and nothing but...) and thus, perhaps, lets us get a glimpse of her Self as neither autonomous nor heteronomous but in-between, as affectivity for-the-Other. Could we say that a judge – or her critics – can seize on this to go beyond autonomy and heteronomy? Could judges turn justice from an irritable condition to an identity?

Because Levinasian responsibility is rooted in the 'irritability' of the singular body left to itself, his ethics-as-first-philosophy is further distinguished from Giorgio Agamben's ontology. For the latter any discourse on ethics begins not in one's skin, as in Levinas, but with the knowledge of the fact that:

> ...there is no essence, no historical or spiritual vocation, no biological destiny that humans must realize. This is the only reason why something like an ethics can exist, because it is clear that if humans were or had to be this or that substance, this or that destiny, no ethical experience would be possible – there would be only tasks to be done.[25]

Ethics relates to the manner in which humans experience necessity and contingency as impotence and, at the same time, as potentiality (to-be and not-be).[26] Of these two only the potential to not-be has no determinate object (some activity or *energeia*) and is, therefore, aimed at potentiality itself (*potentia potentiae*), an altogether 'majestic potentiality' that Agamben equates with the thought that includes the power not to think.[27] Thus the ethical commences with the experience of the impossibility of escaping the necessary and the contingent, but ends with the sovereignty of a thought that thinks nothing but itself: namely, in pure reflexivity.[28] By contrast, Levinas suggest that any such pure sovereignty is still illusionary:

> The idea of being is an idea adequate in itself.... the adequation is so rigorous that the entire gravity of being can resolve itself in the play of consciousness, in illusion... Being is easily reflected and confounds itself with reflection.... Descartes thought that by myself I could account for the sky and the sun despite all their magnificence... For the claim of realism – the recognition of another than I – to be possible, it is necessary that I myself am not originally what I remain even in my explorations of the obscure or the unknown: the peaceful and sovereign identification of the self with itself and the source of adequate ideas.[29]

Agamben's majestic reflexivity is a sufficient basis for the human to have an ethical experience, without requiring bodily malaise nor exposure to a concrete Other human.[30] Consequently, his ethics is not about repentance but will.

> Ethics has no room for repentance;... the only ethical experience (which, as such, cannot be a task or a subjective decision) is the experience of being (one's own) potentiality, of being (one's own) possibility – exposing, that is, in every form one's own amorphousness and in every act one's own inactuality.[31]

The will necessary to turn me into an individuated ethical subject is directed to myself as a singular instance of what, in reality, is common to all through accident and necessity.[32] In sum, Agamben conflates the ethical self, through reflexivity and will, with self-love. Individuating involves the identification of the self with its habits which constitute its 'second nature' and which constitutes 'the only happiness possible for humans'.[33] Quite a contrast to Levinas's ethics of obsession for and persecution by an Other who remains always an asymmetric other. Here it is not the happiness of ethos but the shame of ethics that individuates:

> [I]t is not that the I becomes conscious of its non-justification and the powerlessness of its power such that it, looking down on itself, already settles down in its good conscience, in its non-culpability, to

> take refuge in itself where there would remain a fragment of the world untouched by the original sin. The event of putting into question *is* the shame of the I for its naïve spontaneity, for its sovereign coincidence with itself... this shame is a movement in a direction opposed to that of consciousness, which returns triumphantly to itself and rests upon itself.[34]

One might say that justice too can only be done if those who participate in it remain shameful of the obligations upon them and the lack of foundation for their actions.

In connection with the *Bland* case, of the three competing modes of contemporary ethics – Levinas's ethics of obsession, Heideggerian ethics of 'authenticity' and Agambian ethics of the 'irreparable' – the first is the odd man out. Only Levinas would not be prepared to join the court in splitting the vegetating man into two in order to comprehend him. Heideggerian existentialists would be drawn to Bland as *nature morte*, death as annihilation, a being without existence equating zero, the impossibility of meaning which, however, could occasion the anxiety in the living necessary for them to produce meaning. Perhaps they would also wish to evaluate whether the judges did or did not turn their anxiety into the will to apply extant norms of law and morality to Bland, instead of 'inauthentically' pretending to be bound to apply them. Agambians would be interested in Bland as still-life, as a biological organism colonised by the law, without essence but also without reference to an otherwise than being, and therefore amenable to any meaning the law gives it.[35] For Agamben, critique would centre on whether or not there were any happy self-reflective moments in which the judges might have abandoned the differentiation between correct and false representations and admit that these were neither necessary nor contingent, neither objective nor subjective, but speech acts through which a world of meaning manifests itself and with it a the potential for a different meaning becomes possible.

Should we agree that by accepting that neither law nor morality authorises us to speak, we distance ourselves sufficiently from evil? Such reflexivity, arguably, is precisely the situation of good conscience in which, Levinas warned, the 'I' settles when it 'becomes conscious of its non-justification and the powerlessness of its power'.[36] For Levinas, the good requires more of us than this. It requires our exposure as culpable, shameful; and to feel shame is to expel one from consciousness and knowledge and '... not simply to be conscious of this already glorious exile' (ibid., my emphasis). In *Bland* the judges unintentionally expelled themselves from their sovereign authority, to which reflexivity would have restored them, by shamefully presenting Bland as dead and alive and by over-authorising their decision. Their success in hiding their responsibility is their shame. Read together, the parallel judicial efforts to legitimate *and* justify their stance render the overall decision – that which was 'held' as the editors of the law journals put it – absurd. It is true that judicial labour always aims at diminishing the Other's alterity and, by the same token, presenting judicial responsibility as authorised and determinate. Yet this labour does not manage to remove the empirical effects of an infinite responsibility owed to the Other which the judges in *Bland* revealed – perhaps despite themselves – nor the voice of an ethical critique in law to which the decision irritably opens itself.

> What is at stake is putting consciousness in question and not the consciousness of putting into question. At stake is a movement oriented in a way that is wholly otherwise than the grasp of consciousness and at every instant unravels, like Penelope at night, everything that was so gloriously woven during the day.[37]

Notes

1. PVS arises from the destruction of the 'cerebral cortex', the part of the human brain which shows most electric activity when cognitive and sensory tasks are performed, while the 'brain stem', the part of the brain that is considered to be the seat of the reflexive functions of the body, in particular heartbeat, breathing and digestion, continues to operate.
2. In being 'the beginning is preceded' but does not become present or a representation. 'Something has already come to pass "over the head" of the present, something that precedes the beginning and the principle, that is an-archically despite being, reverses or precedes being. Is it then a something? A something remains in being, assumable and exterior. Here it is a question of an un-assumable passivity, which is not named, or is named only by an abuse of language, with the pro-noun of subjectivity. The obverse of being involves a reverse that cannot be turned over. This formula does not result from some complacency for the ineffable and the incommunicable. What is ineffable or incommunicable in inwardness and cannot adhere in the said is a responsibility, prior to freedom. The un-speak-ability of the ineffable is described by the pre-original element of responsibility for others, by a responsibility prior to every commitment, before being described by its inability to appear in the said'. E. Levinas, 'Humanism and An-archy' in *Collected Philosophical Papers*, trans. A. Lingis (Pittsburgh: Duquesne University Press, 1987) pp. 132–133.
3. E. Levinas, *On Escape*, trans. B. Bergo (Stanford: Stanford University Press, 2003) p. 4. In his preface, Jacques Rolland approaches that piece from the philosopher's youthful work not as an object of historical enquiry but as

'philosophically alive'. This means that the text is read 'in the introductory spirit in which it sees itself' and therefore its central question – over the need for escape from being – is taken to 'open the path of a thought that is one and whole (p. 6), a thought that is not only premised on the distinction between Being, or existence, and beings, or existents', like all existential philosophy, but which developed into a protestation against the boredom, or claustrophobia, of ontological thought that is content to accept as absolute and definitive the character of being. In this section, I, too, assume Roland's attitude because it seems to me that the ethical term 'hostage', which the older Levinas uses for 'ethical subjectivity', must be read alongside the younger philosopher's existential analytic of being as suffering its plenitude to the point of nausea signalling the desire for an escape – which stands, within Levinas's phenomenology, for being's need 'to get out' of itself without, crucially, desiring to go anywhere in particular. In a more analytically rigorous sense, I am convinced by Rolland's argument, first, that the meaning of the word being developed in Levinas's youthful text *On Escape* remains unchanged into the most mature works, and, second, that behind the choice of the obscure metaphor of 'escape' lies the requirement of thinking beyond being and non-being which found more adequate philosophical expression in the analysis of the there is – namely the 'presence of nothing' to which the darkness of night rivets us – in *Existence and Existents*, and in the notion of essence – as the indefinite, in the seminal *Otherwise than Being or Beyond Essence* (cf. Rolland's preface to *On Escape*, pp. 27–29). Cf. M. Diamantides, 'From Escape to Hostage' in A. Horowitz and G. Horowitz (eds), *Difficult Justice – Commentaries on Levinas and Politics* (Toronto: Toronto University Press, 2006) pp. 191–220.

4. E. Levinas, 'Reflections on the Philosophy of Hitlerism', reproduced in G. Horowitz and A. Horowitz (eds), *Difficult Justice – Commentaries on Levinas and Politics* (Toronto: Toronto University Press, 2006) p. 8.
5. '... [T]he ego can be called into question by the other in an exceptional way – not as an obstacle which it can measure, nor by the death which it can also give itself. The ego can be brought to accusation, despite its innocence, by violence, to be sure, but also, despite the separation in which the exclusiveness and insularity of the psychic leave it, by the other. The other, as other... obsesses it, and, nearby or far off, imputes to it a responsibility... for which it had not taken any decision, but which, closed up in itself it cannot escape. Reduced to silence it still gives a response beneath the logos... Prior to the amphibology of being and entities and to the state of being a nature, the subject is undeclinable precisely as hostage irreplaceable with others:' Levinas, 'Humanism and An-archy', pp. 132–133.
6. For more on the modern history of medical definitions of death, see P. Singer, *Rethinking Life and Death – The Collapse of Our Traditional Ethics* (Oxford: Oxford University Press, 1995) pp. 20–37 and *Causing Death and Saving Lives* (London: Penguin, 1990) pp. 43–44.
7. Specifically a 'cabbage' for Lord Donaldson in *Re J* (a minor) (wardship: medical treatment) [1990] 3 All ER 930 at 938.
8. If no 'living will' exists one will be invented as the court will appoint a person who will substitute his or her judgment for that of the vegetating-ward. In one infamous instance such was the American court's zeal to see

the autonomous legal subject for the vegetating-man that a substituted judgment was called for even though the patient had been legally incompetent prior to becoming insensate: *Superintendent of Belchertown State School et al v. Joseph Saikewicz*, 370 N.E.2d 417 (Mass., 1977).

9. Recently followed by: *Re D (Adult: Medical Treatment)* [1998] 1 F.L.R. 411, *Re G (Adult Incompetent: Withdrawal of Treatment)* (2002) 65 B.M.L.R. 6, *Re H (a patient)* [1998] 2 F.L.R. 36, and *NHS Trust A v M* [2001] 1 All E.R. 801 whereby Bland was found compatible with *European Convention on Human Rights 1950* Art. 2(1) because the state had no obligation to prolong the life of PVS patients where that treatment would be futile; and Art. 3 because PVS patients are insensate and would be unaware of the withdrawal of their treatment and their subsequent starvation whereas the prohibition of torture and degrading treatment was inapplicable as it required the victim to be aware of said inhumane treatment.
10. *Mental Capacity Act 2005*.
11. *Cruzan v Director, Missouri Dept of Health* (1990) 110 S Ct 2841, 2883.
12. 'Although no one has been able to explain why Parliament chose to take this course (indeed it has been suggested that it was an accident) no step has been taken to restore to the courts the parens patriae jurisdiction over the body of a mentally disabled adult' (at 882).
13. I am here using Arendt's distinction between legitimating power with reference to the past and justifying violence with reference to the future. According to Arendt, power, being inherent in the very existence of political communities, needs no justification in relation to its consequences, but it does need legitimating by appeal to the past. Violence, by contrast, can never be legitimate although it can be justified. H. Arendt, *On Violence* (San Diego, New York, London: Harvest, 1970) p. 52.
14. M. Foucault, *Society Must Be Defended* (New York, Picador, 2003) p. 96.
15. E. Levinas, *Outside the Subject* (London: The Athlone Press, 1993) p. 115.
16. Ibid., p. 115, my emphasis.
17. J. M. Finnis, 'Bland: Crossing the Rubicon', *Law Quarterly Review* 109 (1993) 329–337, 329.
18. P. Fitzpatrick, 'Death as the Horizon of Law', in D. Manderson (ed.), *Courting Death* (London: Pluto Press, 1999) p. 20.
19. Supra.
20. Levinas, *Basic Philosophical Writings*, p. 18.
21. Ibid., p. 16, my emphasis.
22. Ibid., p. 81.
23. Ibid., p. 86.
24. Ibid.
25. G. Agamben, *The Coming Community*, trans. M. Hardt (University of Minnesota Press, 1993) p. xi, my emphasis.
26. Ibid., p. ix.
27. Ibid., pp. 36–37.
28. Ibid.
29. Levinas, *Basic Philosophical Writings*, p. 15.
30. G. Agamben, *The Coming Community*, p. xi.
31. On the other hand, and with the same sovereignty, man can decide to side with evil. Agamben tells us that this is possible in two ways. First '[I]n the

decision to remain in a deficit of existence, to appropriate the power to not-be as substance and a foundation of existence; or rather (and this is the destiny of morality), to regard potentiality itself . . . as a fault that must always be repressed:' G. Agamben, *The Coming Community*, p. xi. Evil is exemplified by Eichmann's claim that he was following orders, an 'absolutely banal man who was tempted to evil by the powers of right and law:' ibid., p. viii.

32. Ibid., pp. vii, 28–29.
33. Ibid.
34. Ibid., my emphasis.
35. Ibid., pp. iv, 14–15.
36. Levinas, *Basic Philosophical Writings*, p. 17.
37. Ibid., p. 16.

Part IV
Numbers

8
Subjecthood and Alterity in International Law

Sébastien Jodoin

Introduction

The primacy of the State permeates the whole of the international legal system and shapes its basic structures, doctrines and norms, such that the very existence of international law is made dependent on the will of the State.[1] As one classical account describes it:

> International law, being the embodiment of state practice, might, it is clear, date from the birth time of states, or from the time when one state, become aware of its own corporate existence, found itself by the necessities of international intercourse obliged to accord recognition to the same quality in other communities.[2]

Territory, jurisdiction and responsibility are all concepts that rest on state sovereignty and even human rights and environmental protection norms are tied to the State either as originator, offender or guardian. At a more fundamental level, statehood has profound implications for the nature of the international legal system. The very notion of international law implies the existence of a national space or of autonomous actors organized as states. Answering the question 'what is international law?' invariably involves the State through conventional understandings of the relationship between international law and municipal law, sources doctrine and the basis of international legal obligation. This leads Simpson to conclude that most of the topics in international law 'could simply be reconfigured as aspects of "The State" (what it controls, what it is, what it can do and what it is again)'.[3]

Even in matters which appear are ostensibly ethical or normative in character, analytical priority is still accorded to statehood as a guarantee of legitimacy, peace or order. International lawyers display a largely unarticulated, abstract and normative commitment to formal statehood as something which is inherently valuable.[4] The state remains the starting point and the frame of reference for ethical arguments in international law. As Koskenniemi puts it, in international law, the State 'is the professional *a priori*, the transcendental condition from which discourse proceeds and which is not itself subject to discussion'.[5]

In this chapter, I argue that the primacy of the state as a category of thought in international law has led to the violent suppression of difference. The underlying premise of my argument is that international law is predicated on the belief that the State preceded the international community and its law and that this belief is essentially ontological in the sense that it is concerned with knowledge of the existence of States, with knowledge of Being. In order to critique international law's commitment to the State and ontology, I draw upon the philosophy of Emmanuel Levinas, whose main contribution to Continental philosophy was to criticize Western thought for its emphasis upon Being[6] at the expense of what is otherwise than Being, the Other. Just as Levinas shows us that on a personal level the 'self' amounts to Being, within the realm of international law, the State amounts to Being. Non-state actors whose ways of being or acting are different from and not reducible to the State constitute the Other.[7]

I will first discuss how sovereign statehood shaped and continues to shape the concept of subjecthood in international law and thus defines the way in which international law apprehends non-state actors. I will then argue that the denial of subjecthood to non-state actors had resulted and continues to result in epistemic violence, in that the State forms the medium of truth through which difference is encountered, as well as actual violence, by the exclusion of non-State actors from processes, rights and mechanisms tied to international legal subjecthood. I will conclude by considering how applying some of Levinas' ideas might lead us to rethink international legal subjecthood on the basis of the Other rather than Being.

Subjecthood and alterity

Emmanuel Levinas is critical of the priority accorded to ontology in the Greek tradition of philosophy because of its totalitarian and totalizing tendencies.[8] He posits that ontology is marked by the anterior existence of a transcendental Being or a living being. Such a Being forms a totality and exists as if it defined existence itself and lay at the very origins of existence.[9] The living being is oblivious to a reality which lies outside of itself and only ever encounters exteriority from within its own interiority:

> The living being per se, then, is not without consciousness, but has a consciousness without problems, that is, without exteriority, an interior world whose center it occupies, a consciousness not concerned with situating itself in relation to an exteriority, which does not comprehend itself as part of a whole (for it precedes all comprehension), consciousness without consciousness to which the term unconscious (which hides no fewer contradictions) or instinct corresponds.[10]

I argue that the sovereign State is the equivalent in international law to this Being which precedes exteriority and understands others only by reference to its own consciousness and conditions. One of the most significant consequences of the State's existence as Being has been the way in which it has occupied centre stage in international law, in other words, the way in which it has defined the notion of international legal subjecthood.

State sovereignty and international legal subjecthood were equated with each other from the very beginning of the European state system. Sovereign statehood developed during this period in response to important changes in social epistemology regarding the way in which individuals conceived of political community and its organizational basis.[11] As Spruyt explains, 'sovereign states preferred similar modes of organization in their environment. Actors intentionally created a system of sovereign, territorial states. They preferred a system that divided the sphere of cultural and economic integration into territorial parcels with clear hierarchical authorities'.[12] This preference was reinforced by the mimicry displayed by elites which sought to become the equals of the sovereigns,[13] a process later to be repeated at the time of decolonization.

This focus on the Same – the autonomous, hierarchical, independent, territorial, State – at the expense of the Other coincided with a foundational moment of exclusion, the Peace of Westphalia.[14] At the Peace of Westphalia, the Hanseatic League was denied standing, most notably by the German principalities, who argued that:

1. The Hanseatic cities are either intermediate cities, who are represented by their lords, or imperial cities, and in that capacity naturally

represented at the conference. 2. The Hansa cities were not mentioned in the religious treaty of Augsburg of 1555. 3. One does not really know what the Hansa in essence is.[15]

This line of argument was premised on the notion that states naturally possessed subjecthood and that the League did not and that the essence of the State was known, while the essence of the League was not. Meanwhile, the German principalities and the Italian city-states were allowed to participate in the Peace of Westphalia as 'the result of their empowerment as equivalent actors on the international scene, because of their external similarity to sovereign, territorial states'.[16] At the Peace of Westphalia, international law developed on the basis of knowledge of the Same (states, the German principalities and the Italian city-states) and incomprehension of the Other (the Hanseatic League).

State sovereignty also developed in response to increased contact with – and, inevitably, further incomprehension of – non-European peoples. According to Antony Anghie, the doctrine of sovereignty was 'forged out of the attempt to create a legal system that could account for relations between the European and non-European worlds in the colonial confrontation'.[17] Sovereignty was thus an assertion of power, authority and legitimacy which the Same (European states) possessed and which the Other (non-European peoples) lacked.[18] These two moments of exclusion resulted in international legal subjecthood acquiring the primary characteristics of the European State, which itself was defined by what other competing and contrasting forms of organization in Europe and abroad were lacking.

In the nineteenth century, the international legal system's knowledge of the Same evolved and led to the development of objective criteria for the acquisition of international legal subjecthood. International law resulted from the participation of states in a body of positive law which had originated in Europe and was only applicable to European states.[19] As a result, sovereign statehood was no longer a sufficient condition for the attainment of international legal subjecthood – only those States which had achieved a significant degree of civilization, approximating that of Western Europe, were proper subjects of international law. Simpson describes this form of exclusion of non-European states in these terms: 'They were like the European powers in a functional sense (effective government, territory) but dissimilar in a cultural sense (lack of democracy/civilization/Christianity).'[20]

The endpoint of this process of blindness lay in the doctrine of recognition: 'the act through which it becomes apparent that an old State is ready to deal with a new State as an International Person and a Member of the Family of Nations'.[21] Before it could be admitted into the law of nations, the Other had to not only adopt a European form of political organization, the State, it had to be *recognized* by European states. Recognition had three relevant meanings in this context. First, European states acknowledged the existence of the Other and approved of its organization and degree of civilization. Second, they identified it as something that had been perceived before – they *remembered* the Other as familiar and knowable because the Other had transformed itself in accordance with the precepts of Western civilization.[22] Third, through the act of granting recognition, states endowed the Same with international legal subjecthood while denying it to the Other. International legal subjecthood, in its equation with sovereign statehood, formed an ostensibly neutral and universal concept through which states came to understand the Other. However, the Other was always apprehended by reference to the prior existence of the State and of certain states in particular, thereby ensuring that the Other was understood in contrast to the Same. This reflects what Levinas terms the totalitarian tendencies characteristic of Western thought: 'Western philosophy has most often been an ontology: a reduction of the Other to the Same by interposition of a middle and neutral terms that ensures the comprehension of being.'[23]

This form of ontological imperialism continues to inform international law's approach to the Other. Of course, doctrine today acknowledges the existence and relevance of non-state actors in the international legal system.[24] And the system has, over the course of the twentieth century, accorded them an enhanced legal status. However, the fact remains that non-state actors, still less the citizens within States, are not full or complete subjects of international law because whatever particular form of legal personality they may have pales in comparison to that of an anterior Being: the State. For instance, the recognition of the existence of the legal personality of international organizations is dependent on state consent: it must be enshrined in a treaty or must be deduced from the powers and the functions attributed to the organization.[25] As well, the rights granted to individuals and the privileges accorded to NGOs all flow from inter-state treaties or decisions made within inter-state organizations. As Noortmann concludes: 'As opposed to the original and comprehensive legal personality of states, all other forms of international legal personality are considered to be limited by definition and are functionally defined.'[26]

The legal personality of non-state actors is indirectly derived from the one belonging to states in the sense that international legal subjecthood continues to be equated with the traditional indicia of statehood. Malanczuk identifies the following as the characteristics of international legal personality: the capacity to bring claims arising from the violation of international law; to enter into relations with other subjects of international law and conclude valid international agreements; and to enjoy privileges of and immunities from national jurisdiction.[27] However, this attempt at decoupling the prerogatives of statehood from international subjecthood 'only reinforces the position of states and the notion that states are the only original subjects of international law'.[28]Accordingly, international law continues to rest on the fundamental distinction first drawn at Westphalia between the State and the Other. In a Levinasian frame of analysis, international law essentially amounts to 'knowledge of being and the Same'.[29]

Subjecthood and violence

As a self-absorbed and exclusionary epistemology, international legal subjecthood is a fundamentally violent concept. For Levinas, the process whereby the Same understands the Other through its own consciousness necessarily does violence to the Other by suppressing its difference:

> By relating to beings in the openness of being, understanding finds a meaning for them in terms of being. In this sense, understanding does not invoke them, but only names them. And thus, with regard to beings, understanding carries out an act of violence and negation. A partial negation, which is violence. And this partialness can be described by the fact that, without disappearing, beings are in my power. The partial negation which is violence denies the independence of beings: they are mine. Possession is the mode by which a being, while existing, is partially denied. It is not merely the fact that the being is an instrument and a tool – that is to say, a means; it is also an end – consumable, it is food, and, in enjoyment, offers itself, gives itself, is mine.[30]

Athough the violence wrought by the State at the expense of the Other may appear removed, abstract and intellectual, it has very concrete and physical aspects. International law does violence to non-state actors by subordinating them to the State. One consequence of this subordination is that the procedural and participatory rights open to non-state actors remain severely limited. For instance, no matter what position one takes on the status of individuals under international law, one cannot help but agree with Higgins that:

> [...] individuals are extremely handicapped in international law from the procedural point of view. They have little access to international arenas; and are dependent upon the nationality-of-claims rules, whereby an individual must, generally speaking, pursue a claim at the international level by getting his government to take it up on his behalf. There is, of course, a close relationship between the notion of nationality of claims and the unavailability of most international tribunals to the individual.[31]

The lack of capacity of individuals and other non-state actors results from their inclusion within the sphere of the State. Non-state actors are of domestic concern – they exist within the State and any claim they may have to independent personality is subsumed by it. They are moreover elements of the very Being of the State and injury to them is an injury to the State. There is in fact something quite concretely violent in the act of delegitimating the Other's claim to an independent existence and subjecthood.

Abstract violence becomes more concrete as well when non-state actors are denied the justice, status, standing, rights and recourses they seek; when they are prevented from participation in law-making, law-applying and law-interpreting mechanisms; when they are (sometimes physically) turned away from the doors of international courts and tribunals, policy-making conferences and decision-making forums; and when they are told or made to realize that their views and existence do not matter – that they are in fact subsumed within the State.

The international norm of non-intervention provides an example. In cases where the safety or security of individuals or populations is at risk, such individuals are still apprehended as nationals of a given State and with a view to preserving that State's sovereignty. The discourse of humanitarian intervention is essentially a rebuttal of the 'sovereignty presumption' – the need to prove the 'the existence of a humanitarian catastrophe or emergency capable of outweighing a commitment to the sovereignty principle'.[32] The problem with the 'sovereignty presumption' is that the ethics of the situation calling for action are not directly balanced against the ethics supporting the maintenance of sovereignty in the given case, but rather are opposed to the desirability of adhering to a principle, the ethical basis of which is presumed to exist in the abstract and closed off from direct reconsideration.

Furthermore, the discourse of subjecthood made possible the colonial project and the very real violence involved in conquering non-European communities who were constructed as non-sovereign objects to be appropriated.[33] What is not a Being is simply a thing; what is not a subject is necessarily a mere object. Indeed, the communities colonized by European powers were considered to be lacking sovereignty and thus to be lying outside the scope of international law. Consequently, colonies or protectorates were subject to the domestic law or, worse, the will of the colonizing power: 'Colonial States have no international position whatever; they are, from the standpoint of the Law of Nations, nothing else than colonial portions of the mother country, although they enjoy perfect self-government, and may therefore in a sense be called States.'[34] Although this prevented local rulers from obtaining international legal personality, this did not prevent European powers from concluding unequal treaties with them whereby they ceded their right to participate in the international legal system.[35] Consequently, through the notion of subjecthood, international law became integral to the colonial project: 'the European states created a "ruler's law" for its relations with the extra-European world. Of this law, non-European, colonized people were the object rather than the subject'.[36]

International law's knowledge of the Same and the Other continues to evolve through more recent discourses of human rights, modernity, democracy, liberalism and development.[37] Such projects have the potential to redefine the notion of subjecthood and thereby continue to exclude the Other from its purview, with the consequence of legitimating violence and exclusion. The Other – pirate states, criminal states and failed states – is conceived as having lost a measure of sovereignty and is thereby subject to varying forms of intervention.[38]

For example, the right to use force and the status of combatant is essentially reserved for states. To use force, non-state actors must be pre-states in the exercise of their right to self-determination as part of a Protocol I war of national liberation[39] or fight like states, possessing a structure, territory and military capabilities similar to those of a state as part of a Protocol II internal armed conflict.[40] As a result, certain rights and privileges are reserved to some and not to others and the act of killing is made legitimate for some and not for others.[41] Thus, the law of armed conflict is as much about ensuring that armed conflicts are fought according to a state-centric model of belligerency as it is about humanitarianism. This view is encapsulated in the famous words of Al-Qadhafi: 'Those who use missiles or fighter planes and rockets are legitimate. Those who use explosives or small bombs are considered terrorists.'[42]

The monopoly over subjecthood is thus essentially a monopoly over the legitimacy of violence. State sovereignty finds itself doubly strengthened as the right to use force is conceived as a prerogative of the sovereign while sovereignty is invariably defended as bringing about a certain measure of peace, order and security.[43] Both international law and the sovereign State have an interest in restricting the use of violence for the sake of their preservation, as Benjamin explains: 'violence, when not in the hands of the law, threatens it not by the ends that it may pursue but by its mere existence outside the law'.[44] The current problématique in regard to violence is undoubtedly the question of the terrorist whose acts of violence pose a threat to the very structure of the international legal system: 'By construing all citizens as co-agents of the state, equally responsible for the latter's actions and policies, terrorists not only blame individuals for actions for which they are only indirectly, if at all, responsible, they also obliterate any distinction between the state and its nationals on the international stage.'[45] To paraphrase Benjamin, this is why the terrorist forms the 'great criminal' of today. His 'violence confronts the law with the threat of declaring new law'.[46]

International law, by subordinating the Other to the Same in its conception of international legal subjecthood, is thus primarily an ontological rather than ethical enterprise. Its focus on ontology – knowledge of the State – thus results in epistemic violence through the suppression of difference and legitimates violence done to the Other. The Other constitutes an object to be reduced to, or subsumed within, the Same through the act of knowledge.[47] This amounts to a subordination of ethics to ontology, or in other words, a subordination of 'the relations between beings to the structures of being'.[48]

Conclusion

Levinas impels us to move away from ontology as first philosophy to ethics as first philosophy. Levinasian ethics, or the ethics of alterity, result from an encounter of the Same with the Other, through which the Same fails to understand the Other and realizes that it must share the world with the Other.[49] Rather than focusing on its own existence, the Same is constituted by its relationship to the Other:

> Conscience welcomes the Other. It is the revelation of a resistance to my powers that does not counter them as a greater force, but calls in question the naive right of my powers, my glorious spontaneity as a

living being. Morality begins when freedom, instead of being justified by itself, feels itself to be arbitrary and violent.[50]

The ethics of alterity thus amounts to a calling into question of the Same by the Other: 'The strangeness of the Other, his irreducibility to the I, to my thoughts and my possessions, is precisely accomplished as a calling into question of my spontaneity, as ethics.'[51]

The pursuit of the ethics of alterity in international law requires us to rethink the notion of international legal subjecthood on primarily ethical grounds. In doing so, we may reconceptualize international law less an instrument for understanding the world than as a way of ensuring that we do right by those who inhabit it.

Within the formal structures of international law, we must work towards establishing legal doctrines which can effectively remove individuals and peoples from the state-centric boxes in which they have been placed for the sake of convenience but in which they do not, either exclusively or by and large, understand their lives. In the context of humanitarian intervention, we cannot deny the Other assistance simply because we have construed him as falling under the sovereign jurisdiction of another state.[52] In the context of human rights, we must expand the field of application of protections afforded to individuals, irrespective of their status or the status of their abusers.[53] If ethics are our first priority, then we need to reflect upon the ethical basis of sovereign statehood on an *ad hoc* basis. In some cases, there may be good reasons to respect sovereignty and in other cases, there may be reasons not to. If one seeks to view the world from a primarily ethical point of view, one cannot stop at the general, but must instead attend to the particular, for each Other is totally Other.

We must also be more open to diversity in our juridical and jurisdictional arrangements and to ever-greater participation and inclusiveness in international law as well as self-awareness of the inherent exclusionary character of any arrangement to this end. We must work towards the elaboration of a decentred principle of sovereignty open to constant reconsideration.[54] We must conceive of international legal personality as plural, involving many different actors and entities with separate and distinct forms of existence. We must improve the level and the modalities of participation of different entities in the various mechanisms and processes of international law.[55] It is surely not too controversial to suggest at this stage that any genuine resolution of many of the endemic problems of the Middle East will require us to move towards more flexible and contemporary notions of overlapping and partial sovereignty and away from the unitary and centralized concept of the State which is hardly serving us well.

These are worthwhile projects so long as they are accompanied by a healthy dose of scepticism about the level of justice they ultimately provide to the Other. Our ability to pursue an ethics of alterity within a formal, positivistic system of international law is necessarily limited. This system is not the whole of international law – it is only one aspect of it or more appropriately one conception of it. There is therefore a need to work towards reconceptualizing the discipline of international law itself, a need to redefine both the modes and sites of what counts as law within the system: bringing in new voices and discourses into the formal, as well as imagining new ways and places in which we can be international lawyers.

Within the informal structures of international law, we must pursue strategies and projects of interpretive counter-violence.[56] At the most basic level, ethical subjecthood requires the calling into question of the State. We must pursue projects which celebrate dissimilarity, decentredness and difference. This can involve consideration of international law through social movements,[57] gender[58] and cultural politics.[59] Another way this may take place is through an uncoupling of subjecthood from statehood and the location of subjecthood elsewhere, nowhere or everywhere. Most of all, we must pursue projects which make international law aware of the violence which it does to the Other.[60] Such counter-strategies 'give the law pause and, in that hesitation, in the minute space between the law's violence and the violence of the other – a space in which the law sees the terror of its own force – lies the space for justice'.[61]

Another set of strategies must be aimed more directly at the ontology of statehood. Therefore, we must continue to engage in the task of decentring the Self of the State by putting into doubt its sovereignty and majesty in relation to sub-national and trans-national actors, movements, regimes and forces. We must explain the way in which the State is socially, culturally and legally inscribed, bound by or in interaction with its environment and incapable of escaping this form of inscription or interaction. Most notably, we must reveal to the State the way in which it is in fact constituted by the Other, transcended by the Other and incapable of understanding the Other. One might readily imagine the difference that such a perspective might make, for example, to Western policies of international aid and development mired as they are in narrow conceptions of State autonomy and even narrower conceptions of State responsibility. This has obvious implications for conceiving of international aid not as a form of charity, flowing from a sense of *noblesse oblige*, but as an obligation, flowing from the demands of justice. This is surely an object lesson in international relations. In sum, we need to destabilize the idea that the State forms a Self.[62]

This chapter argues that the Other, rather than the State, should become the pre-eminent concern of the discipline of international law. It is not suggested, however, that it might be possible to completely do away with statehood or ontology. Levinas' writing itself rests upon a constant tension between the Same and the Other wherein he seeks to preserve both.[63] Likewise, the pursuit of the ethics of alterity in international law requires a constant negotiation of the tension which exists between statehood and alterity.[64]

The point is not so much that ontology or statehood are irrelevant to ethical reflection, but rather that they must be apprehended from a primarily ethical perspective. States most assuredly matter at a number of levels, but they are not at all that matters. As international lawyers, we must contend with the existing ontology and epistemology of statehood, but they need not be the primary schemes through which we view the world. Ultimately, before we are in a position to move away from the primacy of statehood and move towards fulfilling our responsibility to the Other, we must revisit our most basic emotional, ideological, ontological and epistemological commitments. By doing so through Levinas, we may then discover that the pervasiveness of the State as a category of thought in international law has as much to do with the tension between ontology and ethics as with the sociological realities of the modern world.

Notes

1. R. Jennings and A. Watts, *Oppenheim's International Law 9th ed* (London: Longmans, 1993) p. 14 (International law depends on 'the existence of an international community the common consent of whose members is that there shall be a body of rules of law').
2. T. Walker, *A History of the Law of Nations* (Cambridge: CUP, 1899) p. 31.
3. G. Simpson, 'The Guises of Sovereignty', paper presented at SAID workshop (London: January 2006) p. 7.
4. Ibid., p. 1.
5. M. Koskenniemi, *From Apology to Utopia* (Cambridge: CUP, 2006) p. 132.
6. In this chapter, I have used the terms 'Being', 'Self' and 'Same' interchangeably. The term 'being' refers to the state of existence itself.
7. The use of the term non-state actors to refer to that which is not the State illustrates the way in which the language of international law and international relations is wedded to the State as a primary category of thought.

The most common non-state actors include individuals, NGOs, IGOs, TNCs, peoples, sub-federal entities, nations and armed groups.

8. E. Levinas, *Totality and Infinity*, trans. A. Lingis (Pittsburgh: Duquesne University Press, 1969) p. 33 [hereinafter TI].
9. E. Levinas, 'The *I* and the Totality', in Levinas, *Entre Nous: Thinking-of-the-Other*, trans. by M. Smith and B. Harshav (London: Continuum, 2006) p. 11.
10. Ibid., p. 12.
11. H. Spruyt, *The Sovereign State and its Competitors* (Princeton: Princeton University Press, 1994) p. 103; J. Ruggie, 'Territoriality and Beyond: Problematizing Modernity in International Relations', *International Organization* 47 (1993) 139–174, 157.
12. Ruggie, 'Territoriality and Beyond: Problematizing Modernity in International Relations', 179–180.
13. Ibid., pp. 171–172.
14. International law is generally held to have originated, whether in myth or reality, at the Peace of Westphalia: S. Beaulac, 'The Westphalian Legal Orthodoxy – Myth or Reality?' *Journal of the History of International Law* 2 (2000) 148–177.
15. Spruyt, *The Sovereign State and its Competitors*, p. 170 (translation of quote from Hand-Bernd Spies, 'Lübeck, die Hanse und der Westfälische Frieden', *Hansische Geshichtsblätter* 100 (1982) 110, p. 114).
16. Ibid., p. 176.
17. A. Anghie, *Imperialism, Sovereignty and the Making of International Law* (Cambridge: CUP, 2005) p. 3.
18. Ibid., pp. 29, 104.
19. P. Fauchille, *Traité de droit international public* (Paris: Rousseau, 1922) pp. 28–29; W. Hall, *A Treatise on International Law* (Oxford: Clarendon, 1909) p. 39.
20. G. Simpson, *Great Powers and Outlaw States* (Cambridge: CUP, 2004) p. 238.
21. L. Oppenheim, *International Law* (London: Longmans, 1905) p. 110.
22. See, for example, T. Walker, *A Manual of Public International Law* (Cambridge: CUP, 1895) p. 7: 'International law, if it is to be at once definite and reasonably progressive, must cut adrift from the practice of laggard nations. A community becomes a state when it becomes possessed of some clearly marked characteristics: it becomes an international person when, possessing those characteristics, it makes known its ability and its intention to reasonably approximate its international conduct to the demands of the highest civilisation.'
23. Levinas, TI, pp. 33–34.
24. See, for example, Jennings and Watts, *Oppenheim's International Law*, pp. 16–22.
25. Ibid., p. 47.
26. M. Noortmann, 'Non-State Actors in International Law' in B. Arts, M. Noortmann and B. Reinalda (eds), *Non-State Actors in International Relations* (Aldershot: Ashgate, 2001) 59, p. 64.
27. P. Malanczuk, *Akehurst's Modern Introduction to International Law* (London: Routledge, 1997) p. 99.
28. Noortman, 'Non-State Actors in International Law', p. 69.

29. E. Levinas, 'Philosophy and Awakening' in Levinas (ed.), *Entre Nous: Thinking-of-the-Other* 66, p. 72.
30. E. Levinas, 'Is Ontology Fundamental?' in Levinas (ed.), *Entre Nous: Thinking-of-the-Other* 1, p. 8.
31. R. Higgins, *Problems & Process: International Law and How We Use It* (Oxford: Clarendon, 1994) p. 51.
32. Simpson, 'The Guises of Sovereignty', p. 7.
33. See Anghie, *Imperialism, Sovereignty and the Making of International Law*, chapters 1–2.
34. Ibid., pp. 102–103.
35. T. O. Elias, *Africa and the Development of International Law* 2nd ed., revised by R. Akinjide (Boston: Martinus Nijhoff, 1988) pp. 19–20.
36. B. V. A. Röling, *International Law in an Expanded World* (Amsterdam: Djambatan, 1960) p. 47.
37. B. Bowden, 'In the Name of Progress and Peace: The "Standard of Civilization" and the Universalizing Project', *Alternatives* 29 (2004) 43–68, 53–61.
38. Simpson, *Great Powers and Outlaw States*; Simpson, 'The Guises of Sovereignty', pp. 13–14; G. Simpson, 'Piracy and the Origins of Enmity' in M. Craven, M. Fitzmaurice and M. Vogiatzi (eds), *Time, History and International Law* (Leiden: Martinus Nijhoff Publishers, 2006) p. 219.
39. *Protocol Additional to the Geneva Convention of 12 August 1949 and Relating to the Protection of Victims of Non-International Armed Conflict*, June 8, 1977, 1125 U.N.T.S. 609, article 1(4).
40. *Protocol Additional to the Geneva Convention of 12 August 1949 and Relating to the Protection of Victims of Internal Armed Conflict*, June 8, 1977, 1125 U.N.T.S. 3, article 1(1).
41. C. af Jochnick and R. Normand, 'The Legitimation of Violence', *Harvard International Law Journal* 35 (1994) 49–95.
42. M. Viorst, 'The Colonel in His Labyrinth', *Foreign Affairs* 78 (1999) 60–75, 68.
43. B. Roth, 'The Enduring Significance of State Sovereignty', *Florida Law Review* 56 (2004) 1017–1050, 1019; A. James, 'The Practice of Sovereign Statehood in Contemporary International Society', *Political Studies* XL:VII (1999) 457–473, 471.
44. W. Benjamin, 'Critique of Violence' in M. Bullock and M. Jennings (eds), *Walter Benjamin: Selected Writings*, vol. 1 (Cambridge: Harvard University Press, 1996) 236, 239.
45. See S. Jodoin, 'Terrorism as a War Crime', *International Criminal Law Review* 7 (2007) 77–115.
46. Benjamin, 'Critique of Violence', p. 241.
47. Ibid., p. 6.
48. Levinas, 'Is Ontology Fundamental?' p. 5.
49. Levinas, TI, p. 27.
50. Ibid., p. 84.
51. Ibid., p. 33.
52. Simpson, 'The Guises of Sovereignty', p. 7 (discussing 'the sovereignty presumption' in the context of humanitarian interventions).
53. See, for example, J. Moore, 'From Nation State to Failed State: International Protection from Human Rights Abuses by Non-state Actors', *Columbia*

Human Rights Law Review 31 (1999) 81–121; I. Gunning, 'Expanding the International Definition of Refugee: A Multicultural View', *Fordham International Law Journal* 13 (1989–1990) 35–85.

54. C. Taylor, 'A Modest Proposal: Statehood and Sovereignty in a Global Age', *University of Pennsylvania Journal of International Economic Law* 18 (1997) 745–809, 753; F. Snyder, 'Sharing Sovereignty: Non State Associations and the Limits of State Power', *American University Law Review* 54 (2004) 365–399.
55. See, for example, I. Gunning, 'Modernizing Customary International Law: The Challenge of Human Rights', *Vanderbilt Journal of International Law* 31 (1991) 211; D. Rubinton, 'Towards a Recognition of the Rights of Non-States in International Environmental Law', *Pace Environmental Law Review* 9 (1992) 475–494; J. Mertus, 'Considering Non-state Actors in the New Millennium: Toward Expanded Participation in Norm Generation and Norm Application', *NYU Journal of International Law & Politics* 32 (2000) 537–566.
56. P. Tuitt, *Race, Law, Resistance* (London: Glasshouse, 2004) p. 97.
57. B. Rajagopal, *International Law from Below: Development, Social Movements and Third World Resistance* (Cambridge: CUP, 2003).
58. See, for example, H. Charlesworth and C. Chinkin, *The Boundaries of International law: A Feminist Analysis* (Manchester: Manchester University Press, 2000) pp. 88–95.
59. D. Otto, 'Subalternity and International Law: The Problems of Global Community and the Incommensurability of Difference', *Social & Legal Studies* 5 (1996) 337–364.
60. Tuitt, *Race, Law, Resistance*, p. 101.
61. Ibid., p. 114.
62. See, for example, J. Elshtain, 'Sovereign God, Sovereign State, Sovereign Self', *Notre Dame Law Review* 66 (1991) 1355–1378; T. Biersteker and C. Weber eds., *State Sovereignty as Social Construct* (Cambridge: CUP, 1996).
63. E. Levinas and R. Kearney, 'Dialogue with Emmanuel Levinas', in R. Cohen (ed.), *Face to Face with Levinas* (Albany: SUNY, 1986) 13, p. 20.
64. Koskenniemi, *From Apology to Utopia*, pp. 224–302 (on the tension between different conceptions of sovereignty).

9

The Lesser Violence Than Murder and the Face-to-Face: 'Illegal' Immigrants Stand Over American Law

Marie A. Failinger

The appearance

Arizona desert near Tucson, July 2005

Neticia, a 23-year-old mother of two boys, aged 3 and 5, has been left behind by her group crossing the US border from Mexico. She is stranded in the harsh Arizona desert. On the 14th of July, the 'cruel temperatures of that cloudless sky reach 116 degrees, an intensity of heat that forces all life into survival mode,' according to the young humanitarians who volunteer to bring food, water, and medical care to desert migrants under the banner of the nonprofit group No More Deaths find Neticia. They remark on

> [t]he cruel current of maternal desperation and the promise of the American dollar [that] pulled her from her home in Oaxaca and from her two young boys . . . She could not bear the thought of turning back empty-handed, because her youngest child needs expensive medical treatment. Yet she fell during the night and hurt her knee, and then found herself alone, immobile, lost, and without food or water. To abandon her would surely have meant inevitable death.

Neticia is a face among faces.

Arizona desert near Nogales, June 2005

Cesario Dominguez searches among the cold, dead masks in the desert for the face of his daughter, Lucresia, who crossed the American border so her children could see their father in Texas. Cesario's grandson,

Jesus, is permitted a day's visa to show Cesario where he saw his mother dying. Cesario searches for days, stopping occasionally to provide water to other border-crossers. Each time he finds another body in the desert, he muses, 'I wonder... did she die like this? Face down in the middle of a dirt road?' Finally, he comes upon '[a] skull. Ribs. Everything bleached white, except three fingers on an otherwise skeletal hand... [with] three rings... a pearl, another a rose, and on the pinkie, an image of the Virgin of Guadalupe. "God saved us that hand," Dominguez said. "He wanted me to find my daughter."'[1] Lucresia is de-faced, and with her, Cesario and Jesus.

Chicago, 1914

Moy Wing Sun is laid bare to the United States Government. From the rack in the laundry where he works, coworkers steal intimate letters written by a Chinese wife to her husband and accuse him before his employer and the Government of sneaking into the United States illegally. Though Moy Wing Sun swears he is a native-born American, and five (white!) witnesses testify that he has gone to Sunday School in Chicago, the United States government declares that he crossed the border illegally in 1913, and prepares to deport him. Moy Wing Sun must deny this Chinese wife who writes lovingly of their last parting in order to hold on to his home. He is rescued from a slow ship ride to China – a country he may have never seen – by a legal technicality, a statute of limitations, a rule of evidence.[2]

San Francisco, 1917

Chin Shee is not so lucky. She waits, probably at the Angel Island immigration station, with her four-year-old daughter Yee Tuk Oy and three-year-old son, Yee Yuk Hing, for her husband, Yee Won to plead unsuccessfully with the US courts to free her.[3] At Angel Island, she is likely 'penned up like a flock of sheep' in a 'cheap, two-story wooden building... where the odors of sewage and bilge are most offensive; unclean, at times overrun with vermin....'[4] There, even today, the walls give testimony of the wives of Chinese laborers, of those who hanged themselves in shower stalls so they would not have to wait, to live imprisoned or to be deported. Their plaintive poetry keeps saying.[5]

Yee Won is a free man: he wangled an immigration certificate on his way from America to China to marry Chin Shee; a legal document admits him back to the Gold Mountain when he returns. But Chin Shee, the wife of a Chinese laborer in the eyes of the law, is barred with her children from entering the United States.[6]

The turning away and the truth

The faces are innumerable; they press upon us. But the United States Supreme Court will not look into the faces of Neticia or Lucresia, nor give more than a glance toward Moy Wing Sun, or Chin Shee, or the innocent eyes of Yee Tuk Oy or Yee Yung Hing. The only faces this Court will see in more than a century of looking are the faces of criminals, those who sneak across the border like thieves or spies, their faces threatening a civilization. This Court refuses the 'saying' for the 'said,' bowing before the majestic, cold language of the United States Code, the 'absolutely prohibited' coming of Chinese laborers to the United States in the nineteenth century, the declaration that Mexican and Central American immigrants who risk their lives crossing the borders in the twenty-first are federal criminals.[7]

Emmanuel Levinas reiterates, reframes, revises, rehearses, as if we are too thick to grasp his words – lovingly as if we who live out the law are his dim-witted children who misunderstand the stakes involved in what is real: The 'face,' he insists, is our precedent: it precedes any code, any court decision. Before there is the idea of a Code or a court order, before there is the idea of legal or illegal, right or wrong, there is the face. 'The face' is the primordial that orders the universe, thought and experienced and touched. What is *really* real are the faces of Yee Tuk Oy, this little girl, and Yee Yuk Hing, this little boy, standing over the officials of the United States of America, standing over all of us. The face is that surprise that gives authority to the authoritative. The face is the law of Law.

Levinas tells us not what we should do, not the 'said' of law but its 'saying' – who we are, how we find ourselves before we are awake enough to find or say *anything*. And still, the bureaucrats and black-robed justices and Americans go about their daily life undisturbed by their suffocation of these faces, applauding the powerful totality of American borders, natural and barbed-wired, not realizing that in the long run they suffocate their own authority.

The accusation

> The metaphysical desire tends toward something else entirely, toward the absolutely other... The metaphysical desire does not long to return, for it is desire for a land not of our birth, for a land foreign

to every nature, which has not been our fatherland and to which we shall never betake ourselves.[8]

The story of immigration begins with desire, the desire to take the other into the same, to convert the inconvertible, to absorb the indigestible. But as the story unfolds, as we desire, so are we threatened: the face, standing above us, threatens in its height and in its need. We demand the shriveling of the face, the shrinking of its stature, first employing violence that the law will not see; then defining the face through discrimination; then practicing the highest and harshest word of property: I exclude.

In the beginning of totality, there is desire. In the history of immigration law, we witness that sometimes frenzied, sometimes languid tango of desire between the immigrant and the New World, each beckoning and longing toward the other until the domestic lover abruptly turns away. The new nation thirsts greedily for those whose vibrant spirit and determined labor is necessary to forge its destiny. Immigrants are drawn, inexorably as a Greek tragedy, to that absolutely other country dreamed as freedom and dignity, the voyage to the Gold Mountain in the nineteenth century, the journey to *El Norte* in the twentieth century. As if ravenous, they undertake the dangerous journey toward a future that promises work or death – smuggled across the border into invisibility in Chinatowns, or trekking hundreds of miles in desperate conditions to reach a barren stretch of border where they can quickly slip into the trunks of cars or railroad containers.[9]

Yet, the nation's desire for the immigrant is not metaphysical; it is not desire which 'The desired does not fulfill ... but deepens ... '[10] We confront the hard truth that '[t]he absolutely other is the Other ... Neither possession nor the unity of number nor the unity of concept link me to the stranger [*l'Etranger*], the stranger who disturbs the being at home with oneself [*chez soi*].'[11]

Levinas predicts it: we Americans are disturbed by the stranger's threat to our *chez soi* dream-world of Fourth of July picnics spread under majestic oaks and blond-haired, blue-eyed children who pledge a thoughtless allegiance. The Other is too immense; too high above us. Unseemly as it is for a whole nation to admit that we fear the young caregiver or the aging farmworker standing vulnerably above us, we must admit that we are willing to go only so far: we will recognize the height but not the need.

The dance with the immigrant desired is indeed a tango back and forth, first pushing away, then holding close. As we push away, difference becomes subversive. Seeking to justify how we see their height and the violence of our response, we place grotesque masks over the face of the others looking down at us. For us to be at home, Mexican children must become drug smugglers, and Salvadoran pregnant women al-Quaeda operatives and dirty bombmakers. Then we comfort ourselves with visions of fences and National Guardsmen who will save us from these nightmares. And the law affirms both the nightmare and the disguise: 'the presence of foreigners of a different race in this country, who will not assimilate with us, [is] dangerous to its peace and security.'[12]

In those brief moments when we have the courage to take off the monstrous masks we have imposed, we see that the greatest threat of the other is from its demands to 'impose itself... precisely by appealing to me with its destitution and nudity – its hunger – without my being able to be deaf to that appeal.' [13] We are most threatened by the most needy because they demand not just our lives, as a monster swallows us bodily, but ourselves, our souls – our goodness.

If we are not to give up our very selves at the sheer size of the other's need, unmasked, the Other must be either be rejected, shut away, or else confined and held close, 'smothered into our own lives.'[14] Desire, momentarily blinking at the true need of the other, seeks a safe freedom by reducing him to 'a mere means,' instrumentalizing the one who is beyond grasp, 'cannibalizing' living persons into the same.[15] Our irrepressible drive to make an undisturbed *chez soi*, a manageable economy, by absorbing the other into the self transmutes the 'spontaneous, natural consideration of others' into a reductive reciprocity.[16] As Levinas predicts, trying to 'possess [ourselves],' to 'extend [our] identity to what of [ourselves] comes to refute this identity,' we practice 'the imperialism of the same' in the name of freedom and opportunity,[17] demanding that those whose otherness challenges us must either assimilate or become invisible in our midst. As the price of bringing his wife and children to the Gold Mountain, Yee Won must assume the identity of a 'capitalist and a property owner,' a merchant whose family may enter the United States.[18] As the price of working in our fields and our factories, Americans demand that Central Americans' mother tongue be cut out, that they assume the identity of English-speakers and natives, that all that is exotic about the immigrant worker be domesticated. We can control our own terror only if we 'kill only [this] existent absolutely independent, which exceeds my powers infinitely, and therefore does not oppose them but paralyzes the very power of power.' [19]

In the nineteenth and the twentieth centuries, the murder of the other, either by assimilation or by exclusion, is premeditated in the very same way, aided and abetted by American law: when we Americans fail in our impossible erasure of them through assimilation or invisibility, we resort first to mob violence against the body, then the violence of discrimination, then exclusion. In its allergic reaction to the need of the other, one antibody launched by the self is to accuse them of infection. In the nineteenth century, Chinese women are refused admission because they are surely prostitutes, moral viruses; and Chinese enclaves are, in William Randolph Hearst's newspapers, breeding grounds for depravity and disease, opium-smoking and gambling as much as cholera and the bubonic plague.[20] In the next scene, discrimination: the face becomes literal, the other becomes simply skin color, eyes, nose, tongue. In our desire to reduce the other to the same, as Burggraeve claims, they become 'not only "slaves" but... also "enslaved spirits"' who lose 'the experience of... [their] autonomy and... of [their] obedience.'[21]

But in the back and forth dance, the face once again resists the obliteration of its unique visage, its shrinkage into a mass of features. Its insistent demand to be seen hammers at the conscience of one determined not to recognize. The only way to still that voice is to push them further away so that the face cannot be seen, the voice not heard. In the late nineteenth century, when the national thirst for workers is quenched, Americans rise up against the 'horde of [Mongolian] invaders' and demand their exclusion.[22] In the late twentieth and early twenty-first centuries, those devoured into the deep American workforce are spit out, rounded up, and disappeared in meatpacking and manufacturing raids by federal agents.

The accomplice

Law is our justification and our accomplice. At first, Law simply abets by standing by and watching our violence against the other – the mob beatings of 'Chinamen' in the nineteenth century, the Minutemen strapping handguns and nightscopes to patrol the Mexican border for crossers in the twenty-first.[23] It has nothing to say about *our* brutality, either by using its own brute force to stop our erasure of the other or by encircling them in safety. In the next moment, law authorizes our totalization of the other: just as violence restrains the freedom of the other physically, legal discrimination – segregation in housing, schools, employment, the denial of property rights[24] – restrains their freedom.

Finally, law conspires with us to authorize the way we push the other out of proximity, miniaturizing his need into a tiny image. In the American law's rejection of the other's need for respect and for hospitality, Levinas' language of property becomes absolutely literal – as I identify and occupy my site, as I find a place to be at home with myself (*chez soi*), as I seek to maintain myself, to sojourn[25] and to absent myself from the vicinity of the Neighbor, I practice the very meaning of property: I exclude. In the name of my freedom, I speak property as force to the infinite other. Property legitimized in law denies the responsibilities and rights of citizenship, stripping the foreigner of the protection of the police and courts, refusing him the dignity of witnessing and taxing him for the privilege of being in my vicinity.[26] We bar from this vast country, as a threat, any beggar, 'convict, lunatic, idiot or any person unable to take care of himself or herself without becoming a public charge.'[27] Becoming my accomplice, the law gives up its freedom in favor of a 'universal order which maintains itself and justifies itself all by itself.'[28] So immigration law seeks legitimacy through just principles and efficient 'themes' that diminish the height of the Other. The 'saying' becomes the 'said': the excluded become identical to 'objective' criteria – 'illiterate' or 'public charge' or mere numbers in a quota system.

Law, ethics, and responding to the 'one more'

Even if I turn away from the law, and prepare to offer a response, law quietly enters a hall of mirrors. There is never just one person for whom I am responsible, but a vast array of conflicting demands on me. Not just the Other but always 'one more' confronts me, face-to-face with the face of the other, and with me. Levinas' words return: 'Justice is this very presence of the third party' – as justice, our address is always 'to the other in the presence of a third party.'[29]

Law enters into this dilemma: In responding to the accusation of the other, offering myself as hostage and immolating myself in hospitality to the other, I begin. Yet between the accusation and the offering is the pause that cheats ethics. For looming over me, higher than the face is high, more infinite than the face is infinite, is the face of 'the one more.' Levinas describes this moment of recognition as 'the birth of thought, of consciousness, of justice, and of philosophy.'[30]

With the introduction of the one more, Levinas appears to stagger back. Louis Wolcher describes this moment of distress at the apparently inevitable violence I must inflict upon the other or the 'third' as

> a form of suffering, a kind of making-present of the actual and possible suffering of others. In distress . . . the Other and other Others are bound tightly together in a care that stands immobilized before a decision. The impending decision . . . will sunder care into a living portion and a dead remainder, cutting its superabundance of generosity in two . . . [like] a fateful cutting-off of possibilities . . . .[31]

Will this distress that 'precedes the de-facing and violence of justice' result in a rescue of justice from its own harsh results by taking the quest for justice back to its source, 'my obligation to other men;' or will we 'escape from the torment of a decision between others by means of a collapse into foundationalism?'[32]

Perhaps the awful truth of our ethical situation means that we can and will forget our responsibility to the other. More likely, the dilemma of the other and the one more remains a paradox; at one and the same time 'my responsibility for everyone can manifest itself while also limiting itself' and 'the ego may be called, in the name of this unlimited responsibility, to be concerned also with itself.'[33] In that moment of paradox and pause before our response to the other *and* the one more, the Law tempts us, like the devil in our wilderness, to resolve this tension in the immigration cases by adjudicating the priority of the other *against* the one more. Law tempts us with its traditional seductions. We are tempted by its plausible insistence that it must choose those who will come in and those who will not, and that the choice must be hard, because hard choices are the essence of making law. We are wooed by law's methodology, its keenness to compare incomparables, its promise of equal treatment and thus equal dignity. We are tempted by law's passion for efficiency, prioritizing skilled workers over family reunification.[34]

Indeed, we find ourselves falling under the spell of the law's insistence on categorizing, on making a clean line between legal and illegal, deserving and undeserving. We are tempted by law's hunger for regularization, for taking things in order, that produces waiting lists, queues of the needy. These adjudicatory priorities are ordered by legal binaries: the retroactive and the prospective, the supererogatory and the obligatory, private and public, the violence of the person and the violence of legal regulation. These legal binaries are the lies we concoct in that moment between the accusation and our response, a response that would have emptied itself on behalf of the other but for the opportunity we seize to lie about his otherness.

Retroactive and prospective

One geography mapped by the law in the immigration cases (as with others) is a landscape of legal time, the retrospective and the prospective. As any lawyer knows, timing is everything: statutes of limitations and rules against retroactivity magically transform past legal obligations into present nullities and confer immunities for the past that cannot be pleaded in the present or future. The geography of legal time mimics the split between real and unreal that Levinas rejects, that is, the constitution of the self as a separate subject prior to relationship instead of the unfolding of self as a predicate responding to the command of the other. In the legal landscape of time, Yee Won and his father precede and thus are immune from the law of Chinese exclusion, while his wife Chin Shee and his children postdate the law of exclusion and are imprisoned.[35] Neticia is a criminal because she comes to the United States too soon: if she had put herself on the immigration list and years later crossed into the United States when her 'legal time' came, she might not be a criminal; if she had come years earlier, she might already be granted amnesty. Never mind that to put oneself on an immigration list is to put oneself into a no-man's land of time and space: one begins to leave behind one's own past, own community and yet cannot enter one's future.

Chin Shee and Neticia are suspended in time on Robert Cover's bridge. For Cover, law is the bridge between the real and that alterity, that country of justice we might hope or wish for, but one that does not accurately account for our current experience.[36] Chin Shee and Neticia cannot go backward because their condition is hopeless: if they are deported, Chin Shee and her two infant children will return to China with neither family and nor husband to protect them, and Neticia will go back to one child dying and another who is invisible to the immigration law. At the same time, neither Chin Shee nor Neticia can go forward: one is imprisoned literally, the other by her undocumented status.

Supererogatory and obligatory

A second legal landscape is the height, or unbridgeable distance, that separates law and ethics: in that landscape, law is described as 'minimalist' (and obligatory) duty and justice or ethics as 'supererogatory' (and optional) rectitude. In this account, law responds to and orders what is real; justice or ethics orders what is above the real – that to which we look up in hope, that goodness with no face or form or even specification yet clearly at a far distance from proximity. Law is ontological and present-oriented, the self gazing on the real, threatened with destruction by the alien other and the one more rather than *constituted* by him or her. Ethics is desired, desirable, above; but never here, compelled, existent. Alterity is not the present pull of the face but a fantasy of masks that we look on passively, without feeling.

Law's creation of an impossible distance between ethics and the real earth where we stand, between supererogatory justice and minimalist law, denies the identity of compulsion and desire, the inexorable pull of the one who desires justice. As Wolters suggests, desire unhinged from the command of the other, abstracted and becoming only a wish, enervates us into a state of guilty malaise.[37] It presses us into lassitude and powerlessness, leeches out our hospitality on behalf of another. We are ashamed when we think about Chin Shee or Leticia, but absent the *compulsion* of the face, our paralysis causes us either to look away or angrily to re-victimize. Perhaps Immigration Commissioner White is impervious to the faces of Chin Shee and her children. Or perhaps they do tug upon his conscience, but instead of responding to their need, he pushes them beneath him in an attempt to transfer the shame he is feeling to them. So the law makes it possible for Chin Shee or Leticia to be at fault for pleading for justice,[38] and we are washed clean of responsibility.

Private and public

The third attempt of law to resolve the tension created by 'the one more' acknowledges the call of the other as private, and that of the one more as public. My relationship with the proximate 'private' other that I absorb into myself as husband or wife, parent or child, demolishes the space for hospitality and makes the private other my property. The stranger – the one more – is too far away, and public. He has no claim on me in his need. His legal claim is only the law of 'don't touch' and 'don't intrude.' Law recognizes this 'negative freedom' but pushes him beyond my sight. It pushes him out into the public world, the world that, paradoxically, belongs to everybody and because it belongs to everybody, belongs to nobody. Bereft of any responsible one, the stranger stands exposed in his public nudity as every single one turns an embarrassed gaze away. If we do not look, we cannot see; if we cannot see, we are not responsible. Even the immigration bureaucrat, the designated onlooker, turns his face away when the stranger speaks, confusing responsibility with voyeurism.[39] Of course, Levinas exposes the double lie in the privatization of ethics: not only does the stranger stand over me in all his otherness, but so does the intimate, who escapes my attempt to 'know' and totalize him in all of his otherness.

At the same time, a privatized ethics mistakenly assumes that the mask of the stranger's face is all we know, that the wholly otherness of the stranger is all we encounter when we come upon him. In the geography of public law and private ethics, we may be willing to acknowledge, with Levinas, that the face of the intimate precedes our existence but we reject the possibility that the call of Neticia or Chin Shee comes before us. It is not for us to look upon their desperation, and speak. And so, Americans get angry at the newspaper photos of bleached bones and desperate border-crossers in the Arizona desert. As they insist it must, immigration law binds 'We the People' in a web of care to each American at home within our borders constructed by our law; but the border marks where we can *refuse* to see other faces. Separated literally by mere inches and moments, a pregnant Mexican woman who staggers over the border to deliver births one with an indubitable claim upon my life, whereas the mother who falls to her knees just before the barbed wire creates one whose very life is 'illegal.'

Personal violence and legal regulation

A final legal landscape recognizes the violence of the face, its sheer capture of our attention, but in a way that denies that any freedom issues from the face to face. The impossible height of ethics standing over law, of faceless alterity standing high over the visage we see, may cause us to disguise the face of the other as *only* a threat to us.

In the moment of our fear before the Face, law becomes the armor we pull over ourselves, compelled to defend our misunderstood freedom. Law becomes the electronic fence that we interpose quickly between ourselves and the other to keep the other at bay, to contain the other, forsaking his height. As we interpose this fence, law is the way we each reason with ourselves, 'in the name of the freedom of the ego – as though [we] had witnessed the creation of the world, and as though [we] could only have been in charge of a world that would have issued out of [our] free will.' [40] Instead of visionaries – people with clear vision – we become cowardly voyeurs of the other's need, and will not raise our voices to offer ourselves as hostages.

The story we tell ourselves in the *Chinese Exclusion Acts*, and in modern American legislative attempts to contain Mexicans behind a wall, is that we are using contained and ordered violence to prevent uncontained, disordered violence. If we can put up the wall, we can prevent the overrunning of our landscape by the 'coolie hordes' or the 'swarm of locusts'[41] that are the immigrant other, the 'one more' and the 'still one more.' If we can put up a wall, we can protect ourselves in our obsession that the other will trick our authorities into believing that he is a refugee escaping persecution,[42] or concoct a false identity to stay in the country. We can rid our *chez soi* of the threat of the stealthy intruder, a 'paper son' or 'paper daughter' who forges his identity[43] to become our brother, our obligation. We can protect not only our own lives and those whom we have absorbed, our property, but the very relational ground in which our lives are planted, our communities, our children's lives, indeed, the very civilization on which our hopes rest.[44] To be tricked into giving ourselves as a sacrifice threatens just as much as force threatens, requiring our cooperation and our complicity in the act of surrender.

Law gives us a wall, to be sure. But it is mirrored, allowing us to see ourselves but letting us believe that there is no other side, and thus no Other standing there. It allows us to claim that the violence precedes the wall, that the true violence lies beyond the wall, that the wall forestalls the violence instead of creating it.[45] Because we look at ourselves in this mirror, we want to accuse Levinas of eliding the hard questions that conservatives pose about whether a nation or system of laws can ever be coherent if, by it, we open ourselves and every other to the fraud and the oppressive demand of the one more. It is one thing, they claim, to choose to sacrifice myself to the oppression or fraud of the other, heeding the traditional call of ethics. It is another to stand passively by, while the one more employs the law to oppress us all. The rancher may bear an occasional thief, but the frontier town cannot bear a gang of outlaws.

But using the call of the other as a basis to suspect the need of the one more totalizes them both. To legally pronounce that the silent migration of Mexicans and Central Americans into the United States is immigration fraud implies that the one more is unjustly elevating his similar need above the other, in violation of our paraded norms of equality. The current immigration debates over giving 'amnesty' to illegal immigrants living in the United States reflect a vision of the law as a comparison of abstractions: Congressmen claim that those who have entered illegally should not fairly 'cut into the citizenship line' where those equally needy and deserving who have respected our law patiently queue up for years.

This claim that there is justice in the immigration queue, of course, obscures Levinas' whole understanding of what is at stake. The face defies comparison. Most ironically, this claim fails to notice that American lawmakers who complain about immigrants 'jumping the queue' have themselves demanded the advantage of height. They assume that everyone will and should respect their priority as native-born Americans against the need of the other *and* the one more. Indeed, they assume the authority to adjudicate the relative worthiness of the other versus the one more.

At the bottom of this demand for a queue, however, is perhaps a darker explanation for the allure of law over Levinasian justice: the law of quotas acknowledges that we are inclined to commit the ultimate violence against *both* the other and the one more when we fear that they are swarming our borders. Law is the means by which we hold ourselves back, if ever so slightly, from committing this violence. In this account, standing before the demand of the other and the one more and the still one more, we have only the alternatives of uncabined interpersonal violence or cabined legal violence. Then the abstract priorities of the law become a necessity. The literal and complete erasure of the other and the one more, and the still one more, and each of their demands, can be constrained by the law to a 'practical' size that is not so literal and overpowering.

This argument makes the claim that we segregated and discriminated against nineteenth century Chinese immigrants not to reinforce the severe private physical violence leveled against them, but to contain it. It argues that the conservative push to build a wall against Mexico is an attempt to forestall the violence of starvation and dehydration, of bandits and coyotes, of civilian 'patriot patrols' that may turn from vigilance to assault to keep out illegal intruders, and of course, of al-Qaida and its friends. Law is a proper form of violence because it is constituted by the self pulling back from the ultimate act of murder, sating its desire to draw the other into the same for its own safety. In this account, law finds contentment in battery instead of in homicide. In this lesser-violence-than-murder, Abraham stops himself in mid-air, his hand dangling the knife over Isaac's prostrate body, and contents himself with a son's exile.

This lesser-violence-than-murder may seem to be simply self-justification, and it is that. But, realistically, it does permit the other a future not possible in the absolute negation of the Thou Shall Not Kill. The lesser-violence-than-murder imagines that the other is not simply a passive object of our actions, but a responsive agent, capable of reacting to our attempts to totalize her and take her into the same. It imagines the other not only as an infinite demand but as one who can respond powerfully to our attempts to crush the infinitude of her demand.

The lesser-violence-than-murder of law, insofar as it embraces an imagination of the other larger than her demand, is also part of American immigration history. It is not just the story of the self's attempt to preserve his property by assimilating the other into the same, or pushing the contagious other out of proximity with discrimination, isolation, and finally exclusion. It is also the story of the other's response to the self: though the Chinaman advances into proximity, he also recedes of his own accord, accepting his invisibility and exclusion in order to give the self a reason not to violate him. The other does not simply demand of the self, but practices tolerance and compassion for the self struggling with the temptation to murder. She forgives even before the self is willing to ask for forgiveness for defining the world only as the alternative of violence or lesser-violence. If that is not part of this story, then it is hard to explain, exactly, why some of these same pushed-away Chinese would demand that their children take pride in being American, or why Japanese Americans would forgive their internment during World War II. Indeed, it is difficult to explain why Muslim Americans and Mexican Americans would exercise such grace in the face of their own identification as contagious diseases on the body politic.

If we accept at face value the law's proposal that we can only choose among forms of violence as the law confronts the height of the other and the one more, then abstract and seemingly neutral rules, monocular categories such as 'public charge,' and numerical quotas may seem inevitably required to select the admitted from the excluded. Yet, to concede the necessity of comparison, to demand objectivity in place of justice, seems to defeat the Levinasian project in any but the most intimate encounters of the self with the other.

Turning our faces back toward the other

Yet it is possible to take responsibility, even for our own violence and oppression of one more by the other, without conceding the necessity to objectify, reduce, enumerate – to totalize. First, we are obliged to take off the deformed mask of illegality that we have placed over that face, and acknowledge how we have obscured the hope it engenders. For the face brings not just nightmares but our future. It brings the hope that proximity will not decimate us but show us the truth of our situation and transform who we are. If the beauty of the other's face is hidden by our contorted claim that the call upon us is much too high, we will be thrown back into despair. Despite us, the face, still demanding yet responding to our desperation, reaches out with promise.

Second, we must acknowledge that in offering ourselves as sacrifice to the need of the other in the fullness of his height, we may inadvertently ignore the need of the one more. To acknowledge our finitude as we stand before the other and the one more is to acknowledge the legal pretenses with which we deny it. The honesty that allows us to recognize that abstractions like 'illiterate' and 'skilled worker' and the numbers of the queue simply lie to us about justice is critical to the enterprise of adjudicating an overwhelming need. If we claim that it is not our choice, we claim that it is not our responsibility, and we claim our doom.[46] If we claim that our choice is bound up in rules, we too easily claim that we must serve as hostage to only one, and thereby found our citizenship on a sterile responsibility. On the other hand, if we claim that we have a choice, then we claim an alterity, a possibility.

Third, we must never waiver from telling and living out of the first truth: that '[the concern for justice] always starts from the face, and [it is] from the responsibility for the other that justice appears.'[47] The name for that face-to-face in our common law system is equity. The other, in his vulnerability, stands before a real person and not a legal abstraction in pleading his case, and that official is authorized to up-end the law for the sake of justice.

Even the encounter of immigrants with equity is not without its violence, for some will not be admitted, though surely more will be offered hospitality than quotas and criteria presently bring. But at least in acknowledging our *difficulties* as we behold the face of the other and the one more, we can refuse to allow ourselves to be comforted by the so-called justice of totalization. Even if we agree with Levinas that '[i]f there were no order of Justice, there would be no limit to my responsibility,' we can reject his conclusion that 'justice... takes precedence over the taking upon oneself of the fate of the Other.'[48] Even if we concede that 'there is always a third party in the world: [who] is also my other, my fellow' and that in some senses 'I must judge, where before I was to assume responsibilities,'[49] we can deny that '[i]n that necessity of being concerned with justice... there is a necessity for [an objective] "weighing," a comparison, a pondering....'[50]

That is, we can reject the rejection of the face-to-face. For justice always interrogates the law by confronting it with the face. Admittedly, equity is not a perfect hearing of the other; it recognizes only the other's plea, and does not always accede to her demand. It concedes too much to the fear of the other, and is too self-conscious that the power of its vague boundaries will be misused by the judge. But, it is at least a faint shadow of philosophy that is not simply the weighing of abstractions, and thus 'the appearance of wisdom from the depths of that initial charity... the wisdom of love.' [51] And at least equity begins where Levinas insists we *must* begin: from priority and the precedent reality of the face-to-face, the seeing and hearing of the plight of the other that equity demands. Equity takes risks on behalf of the face, the only risk worth taking in the law.

Notes

1. This report and quotations are from *No More Deaths 2005 Year End Report*, http://www.nomoredeaths.org/Endof SummerReport 2005.html, at 2 [herein after 'NMD website,' available from author] and C. Lo Monaco, 'Child, hundreds of photos lead pair to dead daughter,' *Tucson Citizen* (Friday, July 29, 2005).
2. *Moy Wing Sun v. Prentis* 234 F.2d 24, 25–26 (7th Cir. 1916).
3. *See Yee Won v. White* 258 F. 972, 974 (1919).
4. See R. Cole and G. Chin, 'Emerging from the Margins of Historical Consciousness: Chinese Immigrants and the History of American Law,' *Law & History Review* 17 (1999) 325–364, 329 (quoting Rev. Ira Condit and reformer Mary Roberts Coolidge who visited the site); Angel Island Immigration Station Foundation, http://www.aiisf.org/history? [hereinafter Immigration Station]; V. Natale, 'Angel Island: "Guardian of the Western Gate,"' *Modern American Poetry, http://www.english.uiuc.edu/maps/poets/a_f/angel.natale.htm*, pp. 5–6.
5. Immigration Station; Natale, 'Angel Island,' p. 31.
6. *Yee Won v. White* 256 U.S. 399–400, 402 (1921).
7. Ibid., at 400–401 (citing 28 Stat. 1210 (prohibiting the entrance of all Chinese laborers except those with a wife, child or parent in the United States or $1000 in property); *Illegal Immigrant Reform and Immigrant Responsibility Act* 1996, 8 U.S.C.A. 1252 (1996).
8. E. Levinas, *Totality and Infinity: An Essay on Exteriority* (Pittsburgh: Duquesne University Press, 1961) pp. 33–34 [hereinafter TI].
9. See Separate Lives, Broken Dreams Introduction at http://www.asianamericanmedia.org/separatelivesbrokendreams.intro2. html at 1 (describing entrance of Chinese immigrants in the nineteenth century); 'Photographer Recounts Crossing U.S. Border with Mexican Illegal Immigrants,' *National Geographic Adventure*, January 23, 2003, available at http://nws.nationalgeographic.com/news/2003/01/0123_030123_border.html (describing border crossing of Mexican and Central American immigrants).
10. See Levinas, TI, p. 34.
11. Ibid., p. 39.
12. *Chae Chan Ping v. United State* 130 U.S. 581, 606 (1889) (recognizing Congress' right to exclude Chinese immigrants).
13. Levinas, TI, p. 200.
14. *Nishimura Ekiu v. U.S.* 142 U.S. 651, 661 (1892) describes the way in which nineteenth century immigration law rejects the 'imperfect.'
15. R. Burggraeve, 'Violence and the Vulnerable Face of the Other: The Vision of Emmanuel Levinas on Moral Evil and Our Responsibility,' *Journal of Social Philosophy* 30 (1999) 29–45, 37–38.
16. Ibid., p. 36.
17. Levinas, TI, p. 87.
18. See *Yee Won v. White* 258 F. 792, 794 (1919).
19. Levinas, TI, p. 198.
20. K. Aoki, '"Foreign-ness" & Asian American Identities: Yellowface, World War II Propaganda, and Bifurcated Racial Stereotypes,' *Asian Pacific American Law Journal* 4 (1996) 1–74, 29–31, at 29–31; Cole and Chin, 'Emerging from the

Margins of Historical Consciousness: Chinese Immigrants and the History of American Law,' p. 362.
21. Burggraeve, 'Violence and the Vulnerable Face of the Other,' pp. 37–38.
22. See Aoki, ' "Foreign-ness" & Asian American Identities,' p. 31.
23. See, e.g., Cole and Chin, 'Emerging from the Margins of Historical Consciousness: Chinese Immigrants and the History of American Law,' p. 327; 'Civilian Militia Patrol U.S.-Mexico Border,' *NewsHour Extra,* April 6, 2005, available at www.pbs.org/newshour/extra/features/jan-june05/minuteman_4-06.html; L. Saturno, *Borderland Photos* accessed at http://www.jmc.kent.edu/kpa/stories3/ls_borderland/content/borderland_14_large.html.
24. Aoki, ' "Foreign-ness" & Asian American Identities,' p. 20; P. Price, 'Alien Land Restrictions in the American Common Law: Exploring the Relative Autonomy Paradigm,' *American Journal of Legal History* 43 (1999) 152–208, 153, 167–168, 172–174.
25. See Levinas, TI, pp. 37–38.
26. Cole and Chin, 'Emerging from the Margins of Historical Consciousness: Chinese Immigrants and the History of American Law,' pp. 326–327.
27. *Nishimura Ekiu v. U.S.* 142 U.S. 651, 661 (1892) (quoting the Former Act of 3 August 1882, c 376, s.2, 22 Stat. 214).
28. Levinas, TI, p. 87.
29. E. Levinas, 'Substitution,' *Otherwise than Being or Beyond Essence,* trans. A. Lingis (Pittsburgh: Duquesne University Press, 1998) p. 191, note 2.
30. See E. Levinas, 'Substitution,' in A. Peperzak, S. Critchey, and R. Bernasconi (eds), *Basic Philosophical Writings* (Bloomington: Indiana University Press 1996) p. 95.
31. See L. Wolcher, 'The Tragic Foundation of Human Rights,' *Wisconsin International Law Journal* 24 (2006) 523–556, 545–546.
32. Ibid.
33. Levinas, Substitution, p. 95; OBBE, p. 128.
34. C. Lochhead, 'Immigration deal already appears to be unraveling: Immigration bill has something for all to oppose,' *San Francisco Chronicle* (May 22, 2007).
35. *Yee Won v. White* 258 F. 792, 793 (1919).
36. R. Cover, 'Nomos and Narrative,' *Harvard Law Review* 97(1983) 4–68, 9.
37. See Levinas, TI, p. 84; Wolcher, 'The Tragic Foundation of Human Rights,' pp. 547–548.
38. See Wolcher, 'The Tragic Foundation of Human Rights,' p. 549 (discussing reason's turn to the concept of 'just' or 'necessary' suffering).
39. I owe this insight to correspondence with Desmond Manderson, who noted: 'Levinas does, in a way, "privatize" ethics in the sense of making it ALL of our duties and not just an institutional one. And on an institutional level, the kind of process [addressed in the article] purposely pushes applicants into the public realm and – at the same time – into a realm of invisibility (at least as individuals, but also more generally), thus removing both our own ability to be responsible and our ability to see what happens in that public realm, too.'
40. Ibid., p. 122.

41. See Aoki, '"Foreign-ness" & Asian American Identities,' pp. 31, 33 and note 141.
42. See B. Bezdek, 'Religious Outlaws: Narratives of Legality and the Politics of Citizen Interpretation,' *Tennessee Law Review* 62 (1995) 899–996, 939–941.
43. See Natale, 'Angel Island: "Guardian of the Western Gate,"' pp. 6–7.
44. See M. Crowley, *'Border War,' New Republic Online*, 24 March 2005, available at http://www.tnr.com/doc.mhtml?i=20050328&s=crowley032805 (describing the threat to Western civilization from illegal immigration).
45. Desmond Manderson provided this insight, commenting 'the "border" places violence…beyond the border, at the very moment of the border (Derrida's parergon or frame, neither inside nor out) – and thus allows our legal system to claim that the violence is not being done by us, by law; but only before the law.'
46. Again, Desmond Manderson has helped reinforce this point, noting 'the point [of Levinas' demand for the law] is about knowledge and choice being made and acknowledged, rather than the invisibility, rules, and ignorance that numbers and abstractions provide. We "can" allow ourselves to see what we do, and to recognize our capacity to do otherwise, either in this particular case, or in all cases – but instead, we choose not to contemplate the possibility of our choices and our complicities in what is happening, so we might feel that the violence will take place elsewhere (in another country, on a border) and by others, not us. But (perhaps) it is this distancing and abstraction, this protection mechanism of law against its own complicity, which is one of the reasons that we come to "see" the other {but of course we see no specific other at all} as insatiable, a menace, a threat. The legal structure seems to have let loose our imagination while denying our connection.'
47. E. Levinas, *Entre Nous: Thinking-of-The-Other*, trans. M. Smith and B. Harshav (New York: Columbia University Press, 1991) p. 104.
48. Ibid., pp. 104, 105.
49. Ibid., p. 104.
50. Ibid.
51. Ibid.

10
Negative Witnessing and the Perplexities of Forgiveness: Polish Jewish Contexts After the *Shoah*

Dorota Glowacka

> *The transgressions of man toward God are forgiven him by the Day of Atonement;*
> *The transgressions against other people are not forgiven him by the Day of Atonement if he has not first appeased the other person.*
> – *Mishna Torah*, quoted by Levinas in 'Toward the Other'[1]

'We must not relinquish responsibility for this crime': Kielce, July 4, 1946

After the war, the surviving remnants of Polish Jewry were coming 'home,' often in the hope that they might find family members still alive. Returning from the death camps, from places of hiding and from exile in the Soviet Union, they were, in the words of a witness, a sad, incredible spectacle: 'gloomy, quiet, like after the funeral.'[2]

On July 4, 1946, an estimated 42 Holocaust survivors were murdered in the Polish city of Kielce. They were beaten or shot to death by an angry mob, aided by militia, security forces and army units that had been called in to restore order. What directly provoked the attack was the accusation that Jews had kidnapped a Christian child for the purpose of ritual murder. An eight-year-old boy, Henryk Błaszczyk, who had disappeared from his home the day before, was instigated by his father to tell a story of abduction and imprisonment in the basement of the house on 7/9 Planty Street, where over 100 Holocaust survivors were temporarily residing. It did not matter to the enraged crowd that the 'Jewish' house did not even have a basement. The medieval superstition of blood libel was now embellished with the belief that Jews needed

Christian blood for transfusions for the returning death camps survivors. Amidst the turbulent events of communist takeover in Poland, the pogrom in Kielce followed closely the events of the national referendum held on June 30, 1946, the results of which were falsified by the communists in order to secure their hold on power in the country. That political context was instrumental in the unfolding tragedy of the Polish Jews, since widespread accusations that Polish Jews collaborated *en masse* with the Soviet regime and were largely responsible for inflicting communism on Poland, fuelled hostility toward Holocaust survivors. In the eyes of 'Kielczanie' (the people of Kielce), the temporary inhabitants of Planty 7/9 were hostile strangers, affiliated with those in power or themselves holding key positions in the hated Security Forces (Urząd Bezpieczeństwa).

In *Fear: Anti-Semitism in Poland After Auschwitz* (2006), Jan Tomasz Gross describes the pogrom in Kielce, as well as a number of other violent anti-Semitic incidents that took place immediately after the war, in which an estimated 500–1500 Jews died at the hands of their former Polish neighbors.[3] The facts about the murders in Kielce were not unknown in Poland prior to the publication of *Fear*. In addition to publications by historians, in 1987, Polish director Marcel Lozinski produced a documentary about Kielce poignantly entitled *Świadkowie* [Witnesses], which consisted of a series of interviews with 'Kielczanie.' Gross' book appeared in the United States roughly at the same time as the publication by Instytut Pamieci Narodowej [The Institute for National Memory] of the volume *Wokół pogromu kieleckiego* [Around the Kielce Pogrom], which contained interpretative essays by historians and sociologists, as well as documentary materials, including the protocols from the trials of the perpetrators. The novelty of Gross's interpretation of the events and the reason for the outrage it provoked in Poland stem from the Princeton historian's insistence that violence against the Jews after the war was a widely tolerated social behavior, and that it was precipitated by Poles' earlier widespread complicity in the 'Nazi-driven plunder, spoliation, and eventual murder of the Jews.'[4] Rather than being a culmination of long centuries of Christian anti-Semitism, Gross argues, the murderous frenzy in Kielce arose from its inhabitants' repressed guilt of having profited both economically and socially from the destruction of their former neighbors. Further, argues Gross, since during the war and immediately after, Poles had moved into positions and occupations formerly held by Jews, the Jewish civic presence in Poland could not be tolerated. The violent acts appear even more shocking if we consider that they occurred in a deeply Roman-Catholic country, in contravention of the basic Christian precept of loving one's neighbor. As such, the post-war violence against Holocaust survivors signaled 'a moral failure that touched some core of collective being.'[5] According to Gross, the violence against Jewish survivors was largely condoned by the authorities, reluctant to pursue and prosecute complaints of theft of Jewish property and assaults on the Jews.

Fear arrived as a sequel to Gross' 2000 book *Neighbors*, in which he described the burning in a barn, in July 1941, of the Jewish inhabitants of Jedwabne by their Polish neighbors.[6] At the unveiling of the monument at Jedwabne in 2001, at the ceremony commemorating the 60th anniversary of the pogrom, former Polish President Aleksander Kwaśniewski apologized for 'the wrongs that Poles have done to others' and asked 'the shadows of the dead and their families for forgiveness.'[7] As the political climate in Poland shifted to the right in 2005, with the conservative party Prawo i Sprawiedliwosc [Law and Justice] coming into power, there were no official requests for forgiveness at the unveiling of the new monument in Kielce (commemorating the 60th anniversary of the pogrom) on July 4, 2006. The Polish President, Lech Kaczyński, did not attend the ceremony for reasons of health, although his deputy read a letter conveying his sincere regret for 'the crime that occurred 60 years ago…for which there can be no excuses.'[8] To Jewish ears worldwide, however, this official rhetoric may have sounded as hollow as did the words pronounced at the funeral of the victims of the pogrom in 1946: 'We must not relinquish responsibility for this crime, which cast a shadow over the good name of Poland.'[9]

Five years ago, the revelations about Jedwabne divided Polish society, revealing a profound rift in the nation's historical and social imaginary. The right-wing, ethno-nationalist camp, the defenders of Polish honor, condemned Gross and his sympathizers for attempting to corrode national unity and for catering to 'foreign interests.' Similar accusations surfaced when the news of Gross' new book reached Poland. In fact, the right-wing press alleged that Gross had been commissioned to write it by the Jewish movement to reclaim lost property. On the other hand, a large number of predominantly left-wing politicians, academics and members of the clergy saw the crisis as an opportunity to wrestle with the painful legacy of Polish anti-Semitism.

As Joanna Michlic argues, in her book *Poland's Threatening Other: The Image of the Jew from 1880 to the Present*, Jews have always been perceived in Poland not only as the pre-eminent historical and political menace but equally as an ontological one. At the same time, the presence of Jews has been constitutive, by virtue of exclusion, of Polish national identity.[10] In the cultural imaginary, the Jewish 'stranger' was projected as a threat to the unity of the national community, a perception strengthened after Poland gained independence in 1918. Consequently, the Polish narrative of dignity, honor and pride was maintained at the cost of concealing the dark underside of the national myth, as it manifested in the widespread phenomenon of anti-Semitism. After the Shoah, the exclusionary nature of this Polish historical narrative, combined with the trauma of World War II and of the post-war imposition of Soviet rule, made it impossible for Poles to mourn the death of Poland's Jews, or to bear witness to their disappearance. The murder of Polish Jews during the Holocaust did not change the hostile view of the Jewish 'Other,' while the horrific facts of the extermination of Polish Jews during the Holocaust were largely forgotten.

Although Poles have always thought of themselves as privileged witnesses to the events of World War II, until 1989 – when the fall of communism in Poland ushered in renewed reflections on its dominant historical and cultural paradigm – they seem to have collectively reneged on their responsibility to also bear witness to what happened to Polish Jews. Gross' *Fear* asks whether what seems to be an instance of willed historical amnesia is not indicative of a deeper inability to engage in such testimony, especially when we consider the widespread, as Gross contends, Polish complicity in the destruction of Polish Jews. The possibility of bearing witness to the victims of the Holocaust in Poland is thus intricately related to the buried memory of what appears to be an unforgivable crime of having grossly violated the most fundamental tenets of neighborliness. Ethnic Poles' failure to come to terms with Poland's 'Jewish question,' to consider their double legacy of being both good neighbors and ruthless perpetrators, and, subsequently, their inability to mourn the disappearance of Poland's Jews continues to undermine the possibility of forgiveness and reconciliation (see Figure 10.1).

Relying on Emmanuel Levinas' ethical thought, I would like to explore what I see as the correlation between the necessity of bearing witness and the possibility of forgiveness and reconciliation, as it emerges in this morally and politically fraught context. I will focus on one particularly problematic dimension of this context, which I will call 'negative witnessing.' A constant motif in survivor testimonies is the image of cheering local onlookers, the victims' former neighbors. As Gross points out, in contrast to the secrecy and deception of the death camps, the murder of Jews during the Shoah in the rural areas of Eastern Poland took place in broad daylight and was witnessed by crowds of local inhabitants. Similarly, one of the most disturbing aspects of the

Figure 10.1 Tombstones in the Jewish cemetery in Kraków, Miodowa Street (Photograph by the author).

Kielce pogrom was the presence of gawking crowds, which included a number of children. The question I would like to explore is whether it is yet possible to find a passage between this negative witnessing and ethical testimony, and thus open up the possibility of forgiveness.

'Forgiveness must not annul the deed':[11] Levinas and the perplexities of forgiveness after the Shoah

In *Suffering Witness*, James Hatley engages Levinas' thought in order to examine literary testimonies that emerged from the Shoah: 'forgiveness [after the Shoah] is as impossible and yet as necessary as its witness.'[12] In suggesting that there exists an interdependence between bearing witness and the processes of atonement, forgiveness and reconciliation, Hatley raises perplexing questions about ethical responsibility in the wake of unprecedented murderous hatred on the one hand, and the aporias of forgiveness on the other.

Levinas' own conception of forgiveness was influenced by the crimes of the Shoah, which had claimed most of his family. His most sustained reflection on forgiveness is the essay 'Toward the Other,' from *Nine Talmudic Readings*, which consists of a detailed commentary on the passage quoted in the epigraph. Levinas insists that the injunction to grant forgiveness stems from the very teachings of Judaism:

> The Talmud teaches us that one cannot force men who demand retaliatory justice to grant forgiveness. It teaches us that I cannot deny this imprescriptible right to others. But it teaches us above all that if Israel recognizes this right, it does not ask it for itself and that to be Israel is to not claim it.[13]

Jews must consider the possibility of forgiving the crimes of the Shoah, no matter how difficult, or even impossible the task. How immensely challenging it is to implement these teachings in political praxis was revealed when Levinas himself refused to extend forgiveness to Klaus Barbie, the Butcher of Lyon, during his trial in France in 1987.[14]

Considering Levinas' insistence that self is hypostasized within the ethical relation of responsibility (i.e., my identity is derived from the Other), his reflection on forgiveness can be interpreted in the following way: because my responsibility is infinite and primordial, nothing I do or say can unburden me of my ethical obligation to be *for* the Other. Even though I may be innocent of any misdeeds toward others, I am guilty nevertheless: of having taken someone else's place under the sun or of not having done enough to come to another's aid. Since this 'guiltless guilt' can never be assuaged and only grows the more I try to help, I am always in need of forgiveness. Yet, at the same time, at every instant of my existence I am also being forgiven by the Other for the unwarranted usurpation implied by my very existence.

Levinas' understanding of forgiveness is profoundly informed by Judaism, where the meaning of the dialectic of atonement and forgiveness is revealed in the Hebrew word for repentance, *teshuvah*. It conveys the sense of 'returning to God,' with a resolve to repair the relationship with God and with those around us. According to Jewish law, the initiative in asking forgiveness must always come from the offender who is willing to repent, to offer restitution to the victim for his misdeed, as well as to prove that he or she would not repeat the act in similar circumstances. Levinas writes: 'No person can forgive if forgiveness has not been asked him by the offender, if the guilty party has not tried to appease the offended.'[15] As a number of theologians, both Jewish and Christian, have argued, it is on this point that the Jewish conception of forgiveness radically departs from the Christian, redemptive notion of unconditional forgiveness, extended to all wrongdoers – 'for they know not what they do.'[16] Jewish theologian Peter Haas argues that, as a result, despite the centrality of forgiveness in both Christianity and Judaism, 'notions of forgiveness and repentance as those being put forth by Christian communities have little meaning.'[17]

In the primordial ethical relation elucidated by Levinas, the self's obligation to the Other is asymmetrical: orienting myself toward the other, in the infinite movement of approach, I have already relinquished any expectation of the Other's gratitude or reciprocity. As he writes in 'The Trace of the Other,' 'a work conceived in its ultimate nature requires a radical generosity of the same who in the work goes unto the other. It then requires an *ingratitude* of the other. Gratitude would in fact be the *return* of the movement to its origin.'[18] So the movement of forgiveness in Levinas is asymmetrical: it does not involve the expectation that I will be forgiven in return. The symmetry of forgiveness, which calls for a calculation to be made between the assignation of blame and the distribution of responsibility, betrays forgiveness as that which is always primarily a gift to the Other.

Levinas' ethical reflection therefore draws critical attention to the normative symmetry of the Polish pleas for forgiveness (the symmetry prescribed in 'The Lord's Prayer': 'Forgive us our trespasses, *as* we forgive those who trespass against us'). The symmetry of 'I forgive and I ask forgiveness' implies an expectation of reciprocity, and the other's reluctance to grant pardon is accordingly read as ingratitude. In the morally and politically laden debates about Kielce, forgiveness becomes perverted into a barter (often overlaid with anti-Semitism): the Polish plea for forgiveness for the sins of anti-Semitism will be offered only if Polish Jews are prepared to beg forgiveness for the crimes of communism.

The essence of ethical forgiveness for Levinas, on the contrary, is always at work prior to the settling of political scores. Levinas refers to forgiveness as 'the very work of time;' that is, 'the infinite movement of pardon is constitutive of temporality.'[19] Pardon allows the subject to return to the past as if the deed had not happened and to embark on a new beginning. It is an ethical precondition of peaceful coexistence, especially in my relation to a former adversary. At the same time, pardon conserves the past, 'acts upon the past, somehow repeats the event, purifying it;'[20] it is thus the ground for working through the painful past. This implies that forgiveness does not amount to forgetting the past and thus need not efface the act or the offender's culpability. By suggesting that forgiveness is always a temporal process of *Durcharbeitung*, whereby I return to the past in which I encountered the Other, as well as anticipate the future in which I will welcome him or her, Levinas reveals that my relation to the past is indissociable from the way the Other appears in my memory of it. That is, my existence, my continuity in time, is first and foremost testimony that the Other has traversed my temporal horizon.

'The sincerity of testimony':[21] ethical witness

As Levinas elucidates, the subject is constituted in the world of others to whom it is beholden, and its self-revelation primordially bears witness to the life of another.[22] The infinity of the Other can only be revealed in the witness' speech, 'through what it is capable of doing in the witness.'[23] Such ethical testimony is not a form of knowledge or recognition, but a primordial obligation: 'This witness is true, but with the truth irreducible to the truth of disclosure, and it does not narrate anything that shows itself.'[24] As in his reflection on forgiveness, Levinas' articulation of subjectivity as the primordial structure of witnessing is informed by Judaism, where the obligation to bear witness is commanded by the law: 'You will always be my witness, says the Lord.'[25] Likewise, ethical witnessing is asymmetrical and excludes the expectation of reciprocity, in contradistinction to the Hegelian model of mutual recognition.[26] It is important to recognize, however, that although the self is always obliged to bear witness (since it is constitutive of its ontological structure), its *actual* response to the Other is often a negative one – of turning away from the Other. In its concrete relations with others, the self often relinquishes responsibility and becomes a negative witness.

What is the significance of Levinas' emphasis on witnessing in the constitution of the subject with respect to bearing witness after the Shoah? That is, if the Other was murdered, in what way is the annihilation of another's life inscribed in the *witnesses'* existence, especially in the existence of those who attest to events that took place a generation or two earlier? Does the logic of what Levinas calls, in *Otherwise Than Being*, 'substitution,' bear upon the past? In substitution, the self finds itself in the position of a hostage who answers for the Other's deeds as well as his misdeeds: 'I have not done anything and I have always been under accusation – persecuted.'[27] Within the ethical framework, insofar as the self is a witness after the Shoah, it expiates for the murder of the Other for which it is not guilty. At the same time, the self is thrust into the place of the victim and burdened with the suffering of the other, which, as Levinas writes in 'Useless Suffering,' exceeds its comprehension because it signifies the very 'refusal of meaning . . . the *way* in which, within consciousness, the unbearable is precisely not borne.'[28]

In the difficult and morally equivocal Polish Jewish contexts, however, can this imperative to bear witness be meaningfully articulated at all? After all, some of the Polish eyewitnesses to the events were guilty of the crimes in the most concrete and irrevocable sense. Emmanuel

Levinas often repeats that murder is always directed at the face of one's neighbor, *le prochain*. The face of the Other signifies exposure and vulnerability, almost 'inviting us to an act of violence.'[29] At the same time, the face in its very vulnerability proclaims 'Thou shalt not kill,' forbidding violence against it. In Polish Jewish contexts, however, during the Shoah and immediately in its aftermath, violence was perpetrated literally against neighbors, aimed at faces familiar from everyday encounters in the street, in the market place, even in each other's homes. As Levinas knew only too well, the ethical exigency of the face does not render murder impossible.

'Jews are human beings, but they are evil human beings':[30] the negative witness

Polish witnesses to the murder of Polish Jews can hardly be called compassionate, ethical witnesses. The reactions of the crowds present at the spectacle of Jewish suffering at the hands of ethnic Poles after the war were shocking. Gross writes: 'We read reports indicating that the spectacle of plundering, assaulting and killing Jews did not draw censure or criticism from casual spectators. On the contrary, accidental witnesses are found to have made derogatory comments, shared a laugh, or on occasion helped the assailants.'[31] Considering their tragic fate, one would expect compassion toward the few survivors who had suffered such unimaginable losses. 'But compassion was absent,' writes Gross, while the onlookers freely shared stories about the murders in a detached and matter-of-fact manner, occasionally with amusement.[32] Such absence of compassion seems not only morally outrageous, but incomprehensible in terms of existing explanatory frameworks.

Can there possibly be any relation between gleeful participation in the spectacle of murder and Levinas' ethical or, as he says in *Otherwise and Being*, prophetic witness? I would argue that the phenomenon of what I have called negative witnessing, shockingly ubiquitous during the Shoah and continuing after the war, necessitates that we consider even the guilty a witness, that we insist even more radically on the primordiality of witnessing as the trace of the Other and consider it in relation to the spectacle of murder.

In one of the chapters of *Suffering Witness*, Hatley interprets Polish writer Tadeusz Borowski's story 'This Way to the Gas, Ladies and Gentlemen.' Hatley argues that the rage directed at the victim by the perpetrator was a symptom of the perpetrator's attempt to turn away from the recognition of ethical obligation. Hatley adds that in order to commit murder, the perpetrator must strive to forget that the act being committed is indeed murder. Yet 'the forgetfulness of the perpetrator is self-defeating for it is built upon prior assignation to the other.'[33] Hatley concludes that Borowski's account 'gives witness to the persistence of the ethical order in spite of everything that one does to crush it.'[34] Thus, paradoxically, the ultimate effacement of the ethical relation may be signaled not by a frenzied act of murder but by absolute indifference and absence of emotion. The most disturbing and, according to one of the witnesses, most terrifying and 'incredible' episode recounted in Lozinski's documentary (which Gross also quotes at length) is an incident that took place several hours after the peak of the pogrom. The witness, a journalist, observed a group of Poles throwing stones at a young male Jew, standing in the middle of a stream, and they did so 'calmly, without excitement.' The crowd appeared leisurely, chatty, as if the occasion of stoning a man to death was 'a picnic.'

The paradox of ethical witnessing is that one bears witness even against oneself. In my speech, I am a witness to the existence of the Other, who 'glorifies itself in my saying, commanding me through my mouth,'[35] whether I will it or not. Thus even a murderer bears witness to the lives he has aided to extinguish, although he is a reluctant, forgetful and self-incriminating witness. It is imperative to recover the absolute and compassionate witness, the witness grounded in ethical involvement, from under the negative and murderous witness if the question of forgiveness and the path toward healing is to be opened up.

Gross provides one somewhat hopeful example of the transformation that might be undergone by a 'negative witness': one of the interviewees in Walery Lozinski's documentary about Kielce, who was then ten years old, saw an incident of violence against the Jews on the train on which he was traveling with his father. Although he was numb and indifferent during the events, the images of violence and the words of hate continued to disturb him, and later he felt compelled to give testimony. In the interview, the man says: 'If I am not an anti-Semite, having been brought up in this society, it is for two reasons: because my father was one and because of what I witnessed in Kielce.'[36] Such profound change requires, however, that the witness recognize the sanctity of the Other's death, that is, in Levinas' terms, the ethical fact that it takes precedence over the self's concern for itself, even for its own mortality. As Levinas argues in *God, Death and Time,* the significance of my own death cannot be disclosed without 'becoming responsible for another... It is for the death of the other that I am responsible to the point of including myself in his death.'[37] By extension, the sense of my own victimhood, and the belief in the martyrology of my own nation are only meaningful when they include the ethical significance the Other's death. I would argue that Poles' abrogation of responsibility for the death of the Other needs to be examined primarily in ethical terms, as a suppression of the paramount ethical affect of 'the culpability of the survivor' and a turning away from the primordial fact of the Other's death,[38] even if they were often present at the spectacle of that death. This failure to engage in ethical witnessing has in fact prevented Polish witnesses to the Shoah, even those who were not in the least involved in genocidal acts, from assuming the role of survivors in relation to the Polish Jews to whose extinguished lives they had been called upon to attest.

Levinas contends that ethical witnessing is the movement of substituting oneself for another. Yet what does it mean in the context of a lynching mob?[39] Such extreme circumstances require that the impossible be accomplished: that a negative witness turn away from the spectacle of murder in order to step over into the place of Jewish death, running the deadly gauntlet through the murderous crowd in Kielce. Based on Gross' findings, a change of heart from hatred or indifference to compassion, such as in the one example that he provides, was, sadly, an isolated case. Engaging Levinas' notion of substitution in order to reflect on what happened in Kielce has allowed me, however, to discern other such transformative moments in the voices of Lozinski's interviewees. One of the witnesses, a saleswoman, is indignant about the rumor of Jews using the blood of Christian children (unlike some other witnesses who seem to give the superstition some credence). Later in the documentary, she discloses that, at one point, she was stopped by a man in a uniform and 'taken for a Jewess. I looked like one.' Yet another witness describes the scene of the murder of an old Jewess at the train station. Speaking of himself as having been 'in shock' at such brutality, he also recalls that when he was younger, he was often told that he 'resembled a Jew'; like the saleswoman, he could have easily fallen victim to the violence himself. Another witness, who gives testimony about having seen wounded Jews being drowned in the river, also tells the story of having defended a Jew who worked for him. He explains that he knows what it is like to be victimized because he himself survived Oswiecim. It seems that all of the witnesses in the documentary who were sympathetic toward the Jews and outraged at what happened in Kielce that day, one way or another imagined themselves in the place of the persecuted Jews. Although Levinas' substitution is not a matter of imagination, such moments of empathy or 'putting oneself in another's shoes' allow the witness to return to – and subsequently act upon –

the ethical essence of substitution. As Levinas writes, 'Substitution is not a psychological event of compassion or intropathy in general, but it makes possible the paradoxical psychological possibilities of putting oneself in place of another.'[40]

On the other hand, neither Gross nor Lozinski (nor anyone else in the literature I have perused) ever quotes a perpetrator who has expressed contrition. The question then remains whether this movement can be accomplished by a vicarious witness. I would like to answer, although cautiously and with reservations, that it can. Again, such movement would entail recognizing the ethical necessity of turning toward the other, and in this case, of re-traversing the route from negative witnessing to ethical testimony to the existence of the Other and acknowledging the ethical fact of substitution.

It is not enough for Poles, as a nation, to admit their complicity as perpetrators and apologize for their crimes. They must also engage in ethical substitution. Levinas writes: 'It is through the condition of being hostage that there can be in the world pity, compassion, pardon and proximity – even the little there is.'[41] Recovering the shattered bonds of 'neighborliness' requires that Poles today hold themselves hostage to the past. Even if the new generations are not burdened with the guilt for the crimes, they must consider themselves accountable for passing on the memory of what happened. By taking ethical responsibility in this way, they can positively transform the Polish national myth of unsurpassable victimhood on the altar of history, a myth in which the Jewish Other has always been a scapegoat. My hope for the recovery of ethical witness has been fostered by some of the remarks offered in the context of the discussion about Kielce. Michal Bilewicz says, 'I wish every Polish politician realized that he is an heir to the Jewish citizens of Poland who became victims of their Christian neighbors and because of that to always put himself in the position of the victim.'[42]

It is undeniable that Poles were themselves the victims of history, both during World War II and under the Soviet occupation. As a result, they are resistant to being cast in the role of the perpetrator. Yet if we agree with Levinas that 'politics must be able in fact always to be checked and criticized starting from the ethical,'[43] a univalent assignation of the roles of victim and perpetrator is impossible. 'To be oneself [*pour soi*] is already to know the fault I have committed with regard to the other.'[44] Perhaps then the starting point for Poles in reflecting on crimes such as Kielce is that they begin to look at themselves otherwise and thus become capable of bearing witness after the fact.

Gross' thesis that Polish anti-Semitism after the war *resulted* from Poles' prior complicity in the Nazi crimes (however insufficient as the sole explanation of what happened), lends credence to Levinas' view. Polish perpetrators and bystanders had been already implicated in the acts of witnessing, and the murderous rage in Kielce arose not despite but *because* Poles and Jews were neighbors. Unlike the (non)relation of indifference between the Nazis and the Jewish victims, who in most cases were complete strangers and regarded each other as such, Polish Jewish contexts involved a prior relation of neighborliness and mutual speech, the framework that entirely collapsed during the Shoah. In several especially painful episodes recounted by Gross, the victims remonstrated with their murderers, calling them by their first names: 'Let me go, Olek [a diminutive form of Aleksander]'...or 'Franek [from Franciszek], where are you taking me?' to which the former neighbor replied, 'Go fuck yourself Jew' and proceeded to methodically clobber him to death.[45]

'In memory of the Jews murdered in Kielce': witnessing and forgiving

Once again, I would like to address the distressing paradoxes of post-Shoah witnessing by relating them to the question of forgiveness. As I have noted in my reading of Levinas, one becomes capable of granting or receiving forgiveness because, ethically, one is always in need of being forgiven for the 'guiltless guilt' of one's existence. Analogously, one can only become a witness, in the sense of giving testimony to the events, because as a subject, one is always already a witness to the Other. That is, only because to be a subject *means* to be a witness, is it possible to assume the concrete task of bearing witness and to become accountable for the ways in which this task is fulfilled. One is a witness, according to Levinas, whether one wills it or not. As James Hatley has remarked, 'The question is not whether one should bear witness to the victim but whether one is to embrace one's responsibility for that witness.'[46] It is in this sense that the progressive voices in the discussion about Kielce can be heard as bearing witness to the victims of the Shoah. It is significant, in the context of my argument, that the national debate over Polish attitudes *vis-à-vis* the fate of the Jews during the Holocaust was initiated in 1984 by Jan Blonski's essay 'Biedni Polacy patrzą na ghetto' [Poor Poles Look at the Ghetto], in which Blonski condemned Polish spectators' indifference to the plight of the Jews trapped within the burning ghetto at the close of the Warsaw Ghetto Uprising and called upon Poles to assume responsibility for the fate of Polish Jewry.

The Jewish memory of the Shoah has been scarred by the negative witness: as a result, to quote a recent visitor to Poland and a daughter of Holocaust survivors, 'For Jews, Poland is a cemetery and all Poles are evil.'[47] Hopefully, the ethical imperative of witnessing will also guide Polish historians' continuing efforts to establish the truth of the events that transpired in Kielce on July 4, 1946. Dr. Janusz Kurtyka, President of the Institute for National Memory, writes, 'We assume that even the most difficult truth serves the cause of reconciliation better than the wall of forgetting erected around the matters that are treated as a taboo.'[48]

Since, for Levinas, the duty to atone for one's misdeeds is commanded to the subject, whose existence acquires meaning because it is testimony to the life of another, the relation between forgiveness and witnessing is a necessary one. If forgiveness issues from the unforgivable, witnessing arises from the 'unwitnessable,' that is, from what cannot be truly testified to. First of all, in the ontic sense of complete knowledge about the events, the true or complete witnesses to the events of Kielce, as Primo Levi called 'the drowned' ones in the Nazi death camps,[49] were beaten or shot to death. Yet the events that befall the other are also unwitnessable in a primordial ethical sense since my life is testimony to the other whose 'glory' always exceeds my cognitive capacity and overflows my speech.[50] That to which the self bears witness is irreducible to the content of my consciousness and knowledge; it is 'a surplus of meaning of which consciousness all by itself would be incapable,'[51] and which signifies only as a sign of proximity with the other and responsibility without reserve.

Bearing witness is thus a continuous, unending process that bears upon the past and transforms the self's relation to that past into unceasing memory-work. Analogously, forgiveness, always in flux and oriented toward the unknown, must always recommence its work, must be continually rejuvenated. Levinas writes: 'For has anyone, in any case, ever finished asking for forgiveness?...The seeking for forgiveness never comes to an end.'[52] One does not discharge oneself of the debt by asking forgiveness. On the contrary, this is how one takes on the onus of the deed, regardless of whether one is actually guilty of the crime.

In relation to the memory of the Shoah as well, the plea for forgiveness has to be taken up again in each instance, as an expression of individual as well as generational responsibility, and it does not necessarily have to assume the form of loud expressions of contrition. As has been the case with Kielce and presumably with other, perhaps yet unacknowledged, dark moments of Polish history, the movement of repentance and asking for forgiveness is occurring whenever Poles experience genuine sorrow and thus begin to engage their responsibility as witnesses. The voices of a number of Polish intellectuals, who in the years 1945–1946 protested against the atrocities perpetrated on survivors, via publications in the press, exude a sense of moral duty and their despair at having failed to impart that sense to the majority of the Polish population. Wincenty Bednarczuk wrote, in September 1945, that '[i]t is a moral problem pure and simple. Today it is not a question of saving the Jews from misery and death, it is a problem of saving the Poles from moral misery and spiritual death.'[53] Jerzy Andrzejewski, in 1946, commented that '[w]ithout respect for a human being, without serious reflection about humanity ... no nation can be worthy of respect.'[54] Yet these writers' failure to engage the moral conscience of the nation immediately after the Shoah is now part of the legacy of the current generation of intellectuals, and it is becoming even more urgent in the current atmosphere of political and moral malaise in Poland.[55]

Like forgiveness, witnessing is not a task that can ever be accomplished. The Holocaust witness' very act of giving testimony, even if repeated numerous times, does not assuage the need to testify, and the witness can never disburden herself of the task; on the contrary, she suffers the *increasing* demand to bear witness. Paradoxically, the witness' responsibility is augmented the more she or he testifies because the debt is not dischargeable, and it grows with each act of testimony. The future (im)perfect tense of forgiveness thus corresponds to the unfinished work of witnessing as a demand for more witnessing, a continuous increase in debt. As is clear in the example of Kielce, this possibility, indeed, ethical necessity of turning toward the Other in responsibility is even more profound when we consider instances of negative witnessing. This leads me to conclude not only that forgiveness and witnessing are ethically intertwined but that repentance and working toward forgiveness are in themselves acts of bearing witness. Conversely, if we begin to think of negative witnessing in relation to the trace of ethical witnessing, then repentance, which is synonymous with turning toward the Other, and the possibility of forgiveness are always already inscribed in the act of witness, be it a negative one.

Despite his unequivocal insistence on the singularity of forgiveness, Levinas recognizes that the intimacy of deliverance must rely on the objective order of the community, even if its uniqueness is thus compromised. This is expressed in religious rituals, such as those involved in observing Yom Kippur, which are both intimate for each individual involved and yet possess a communal dimension. In the notion of the third, although he never develops it at length, Levinas acknowledges the need for justice within the space of human collectivity: 'I am responsible for the persecutor – but only me! For my people I demand justice.'[56] 'The drama of forgiveness involves not two players but three,'[57] writes Levinas, although the third interferes with the intimacy of ethical forgiveness. Yet Levinas invariably emphasizes the individual dimension of forgiveness in Judaism and the need to appease a particular person against whom the transgression has been perpetrated. God's forgiveness and, importantly for my argument, the forgiveness of history, 'cannot be given if the individual has not been honoured.'[58]

Just as 'pardon' – ethical forgiveness that obtains between two human beings – must become involved with 'the drama of forgiveness,' that is, with the social order of reconciliation, negotiation, reparations and adjudication of losses, the singularity of the ethical witness becomes translated into collective memory, into the Said, as it inevitably enters into the annals of history. Ethical witnessing must therefore also engage the social and political space. The hard and humiliating lesson imparted by Polish intellectuals' predecessors who, despite writing letters of protest against the pogroms in 1945–1946, failed to change the course of the tragic events, is that well-intentioned and sincere gestures will remain ineffective unless they become woven firmly into the social and political fabric of the national community. Undoubtedly, such interventions, which I argue are at least as important as the efforts to document the rescue of the Jews by Poles, always pose a risk of unravelling some of the most sanctioned national myths and of upsetting the very foundations of the tradition.

Polish intellectuals are beginning to accede to their responsibility for how the past is remembered and to accept their complicated, paradoxical legacy of both hospitality and hostility toward the Jews. I suggest, once again, that their own expressions of repentance and acts of asking forgiveness, both individual and collective, for the crimes of the past, are in fact instances of assuming their responsibility as witnesses, substituting for the negative witness and thus accounting for the past before the future. Substitution is the ethical condition of the possibility of neighborliness. As an example, journalist Jerzy Daniel's passionate account of the Kielce pogrom, entitled *Żyd w zielonym kapeluszu* [The Jew in a green hat], is largely based on his conversations with an adult Henryk Błaszczyk (the boy allegedly kidnapped by the Jews), with whom he 'has been talking for years now,' as well as on the perpetrators' testimonies before the court.[59]

Figure 10.2 White/Wash II – A Memorial for the Victims of the 1946 Pogrom (Photograph and design by Jack Sal).[60]

If both forgiveness and witnessing are open-ended, infinite and asymmetrical, if responsibilities are continually re-evaluated, never accomplished and always on the verge of collapse, it is only through the willingness to expose themselves to this risk that Poles can begin to reshape the contested memory and to forge a discursive space in which negative witnessing can be replaced by ethical witness. Such testimony both honors the dead and opens up a possibility of a conversation between neighbors, which recognizes its provenance in ethical speech. It is a conversation and an ethical transformation which the new monument in Kielce (see Figure 10.2) courageously inaugurates:

> 'In memory of the Jews murdered in Kielce on 4 July 1946. Before the war, 21 000 Jews lived in Kielce... On July 4, 1946, an incited crowd attacked and murdered Jews. In honor of the victims of the pogrom, let this monument be a warning and a call for tolerance and mutual understanding between neighbors.'

Notes

1. E. Levinas, 'Toward the Other,' *Nine Talmudic Readings*, trans. A. Aronowicz, (Bloomington: Indiana University Press, 1994) pp. 12–29.
2. The words of a witness to the pogrom in Kielce, a schoolteacher interviewed in Walery Lozinski's documentary film *Swiadkowie* [Witnesses], Polska Szkola Dokumentu 'Videonowa,' 1987.

3. Some of the estimates are as high as 3000 victims. See B. Szaynok, 'Polacy i Żydzi lipiec 1944–lipiec 1946' [Poles and Jews July 1944–July 1946], in, Ł. Kaminski and J. Żaryn (eds), *Wokół Pogromu Kieleckiego* [Around the Kielce Pogrom] (Warszawa: Instytut Pamięci Narodowej, 2006) pp. 9–24.
4. J. T. Gross, *Fear: Anti-Semitism in Poland After Auschwitz* (New York: Random House, 2006) p. 29.
5. Ibid., p. 29.
6. J. T. Gross, *Neighbors: The Destruction of the Jewish Community in Jedwabne, Poland* (Princeton: Princeton University Press, 2001).
7. I have relied on the English translation of the President's speech in Antony Polonsky and J. Michlic, *The Neighbors Respond* (Princeton and Oxford: Princeton University Press, 2004) p. 103.
8. In the letter from the President of the Republic of Poland, Lech Kaczyński, in *Gazeta Wyborcza*, July 5, 2005, p. 19 [translation mine].
9. From the voice-over in the 1946 *Polska Kronika Filmowa* [Polish Film Chronicle], accompanying the images from the funeral procession, in Walery Lozinski's *Swiadkowie.*
10. J. Michlic, *Poland's Threatening Other: The Image of the Jew from 1880 to the Present* (Lincoln: University of Nebraska Press, 2006).
11. Levinas, 'Toward the Other,' p. 27.
12. J. Hatley, *Suffering Witness: The Quandary of Responsibility After the Irreparable* (Albany: SUNY Press, 2000) p. 9.
13. Levinas, 'Toward the Other,' pp. 28–29.
14. See an interview with Emmanuel Levinas at the time of Klaus Barbie trial, entitled 'A quoi pensent les philosophes?' in *Autrement* 102 (1988) 53–60.
15. Levinas, 'Toward the Other,' p. 19.
16. *Luke 23:34.*
17. P. Haas, 'Forgiveness, Reconciliation and the Jewish Memory,' in D. Patterson and J. K. Roth (eds), *After-words: Post-Holocaust Struggles with Forgiveness, Reconciliation, Justice* (Seattle: University of Washington Press, 2004) p. 14.
18. E. Levinas, 'The Trace of the Other,' in M. C. Taylor (ed.), *Deconstruction in Context* (Chicago: Chicago University Press, 1996) p. 349.
19. E. Levinas, *Totality and Infinity: An Essay on Exteriority*, trans. A. Lingis (The Hague: M. Nijhoff Publishers, 1979) pp. 283–284 [hereinafter TI].
20. Ibid., p. 283.
21. E. Levinas, *Ethics and Infinity*, trans. R. E. Cohen (Pittsburgh: Duquesne University Press, 1985) p. 109.
22. E. Levinas, *Otherwise Than Being or Beyond Essence*, trans. A. Lingis (Pittsburgh, Pennsylvania: Duquesne University Press, 1998) p. 146 [hereinafter OBBE].
23. Levinas, OBBE, p. 145.
24. Levinas, *Ethics and Infinity*, p. 109.
25. *Isaiah 43:10.*
26. 'To the myth of Ulysess returning to Ithaca, we wish to oppose the story of Abraham who leaves his fatherland forever for a yet unknown land, and forbids his servant to even bring back his son to the point of departure:' Levinas, 'The Trace of the Other,' p. 348.
27. Levinas, OBBE, p. 114.

28. E. Levinas, 'Useless Suffering,' in *Entre Nous: Thinking-of-the-Other*, trans. M. B. Smith and B. Harshav (New York: Columbia University Press, 1998) pp. 91–92.
29. Levinas, *Ethics and Infinity*, p. 86.
30. Lozinski, *Świadkowie*.
31. Gross, *Fear*, p. 37.
32. Ibid., p. 43.
33. Hatley, *Suffering Witness: The Quandary of Responsibility After the Irreparable*, p. 86.
34. Ibid., p. 93.
35. Levinas, *Ethics and Infinity*, p. 110.
36. Gross, *Fear*, p. 116. This particular quote is not included in the final cut of Lozinski's documentary. It appears (from the footnote on page 283) that Gross derived this quote from an interview with Lozinski.
37. E. Levinas, *God, Death, and Time*, trans. B. Bergo (Stanford: Stanford University Press, 2000) p. 43. Levinas' argument about the primacy of the Other's death in the constitution of self is largely a polemic with Heidegger's existential analysis of death in *Being and Time*. Dasein's facing up to the existential truth of its mortality, its Being-toward-Death, opens up the possibility of authentic existence. Since no one can die in anyone else's place, Dasein faces death in solitude, and its relations with the world, including its involvements with others, disappear.
38. Ibid., p. 12.
39. The analogy between the participants of the anti-Semitic incidents and the racially motivated 'lynching mob' is Gross, *Fear*, pp. 163–164.
40. Levinas, OBBE, p. 146.
41. Ibid., p. 117.
42. In 'A jak bratem, a jak katem . . . ' ['A brother or an executioner?'] Discussion about Kielce, *Charaktery*, July 2006, p. 82, translation mine.
43. Levinas, *Ethics and Infinity*, p. 80.
44. E. Levinas, *Difficult Freedom: Essays on Judaism*, trans. S. Hand (Baltimore: Johns Hopkins University Press, 1990) p. 17.
45. Gross, *Fear*, p. 253.
46. Hatley, *Suffering Witness: The Quandary of Responsibility After the Irreparable*, p. 94.
47. I would like to thank Lilith Finkler for sharing with me her reflections on her trip to Poland. The stereotype recounted here by Lilith is an interesting counterpoint to the voice of the negative witness in Lozinski's documentary, quoted in the subheading of Section IV.
48. J. Kurtyka, 'Preface to *Wokól Pogromu Kieleckiego*' [Around the Kielce Pogrom], Ł. Kaminski and J. Żaryn (eds), (Warszawa: Instytut Pamieci Narodowej, 2006) p. 8.
49. P. Levi, *The Drowned and the Saved*, trans. R. Rosenthal (New York: Summit Books, 1988).
50. For instance, French philosopher, psychoanalyst and writer Sarah Kofman asks, 'Because he was a Jew, my father died in Auschwitz: How can it not be said? And how can it be said? How can one speak of that before which all possibility of speech ceases? Of this event, my absolute:' in *Smothered*

Words, trans. M. Dobie (Evanston, Illinois: Northwestern University Press, 1998) p. 9.
51. Levinas, OBBE, p. 152.
52. Levinas, 'Toward the Other,' p. 24.
53. Gross, *Fear*, p. 29.
54. Ibid., p. 132.
55. As I am writing these words in the summer of 2007, the antics of openly anti-Semitic Catholic priests, Father Jankowski and Father Rydzyk, continuously go unpunished, despite, in the case of the latter, the outrage of the international opinion and interventions from the Simon Wiesenthal Center.
56. Levinas, *Ethics and Infinity*, p. 99.
57. Levinas, 'Toward the Other,' p. 18.
58. Ibid., p. 20.
59. J. Daniel, *Żyd w zielonym kapeluszu* [The Jew in a green hat] (Kielce: Scriptum, 1996) p. 20. The trial, which both Daniel and Gross describe as a travesty of justice, was held in November 1946. Dozens of people were detained (including the Błaszczyks father and son). Nine people were sentenced to death and immediately executed, while several received prison sentences.
60. The photograph was accessed at http://www.jacksal.com/permanent_installations/kielce_memorial.htm. Permission to reproduce copyright material gratefully acknowledged.

Part V
Deuteronomy

11
Anarchic Law

Simon Critchley

Desmond Manderson's *Proximity, Levinas and the Soul of Law* is a deeply felt and powerful book which is marked by an utter and at times quite disarming moral sincerity.[1] Manderson displays a wonderful responsiveness to the compelling strangeness of Levinas's work, of both the way his language moves us and, more importantly in my view, the existential resonance of that language, or the way that language resonates within us, with our sense of self and world, of their connections and disconnections. Most importantly, in a year that was marked by largely turgid and conservative Centenary celebrations of Levinas's birth in 1906, Manderson's book does something new with Levinas. Indeed, what is most striking to the non-lawyer is the way Levinas's thinking is deepened and challenged by a thicket of cases, mainly drawn from common law, and most of those from the musings of the Australian High Court on the law of negligence. Broadly, the seven chapters of this book move from a presentation of Levinas's work in the early chapters through to the central chapters four and five, where Manderson moves from philosophy to law and where the central argument about the relation of ethics to law and more specifically to the law of torts is developed at length. In the final chapters, Manderson moves towards a critique of Levinas from the standpoint of law, showing the limitations of Levinas's work on the question of law and legal judgment and the potentially fatal confusions of law with justice and, more particularly, with politics, which led to Levinas's dreadful failure of political judgment in the case of the massacres in Sabra and Chatila in 1982.

To put it in Manderson's own oxymoronic terms, the aim of the book is to ask how Levinas might change how we understand law and how law might change the way we understand Levinas. As such, the argument of the book importantly cuts two ways: against law and against Levinas. What does that mean? Let's back up for a moment. As Manderson puts it, the soul is the name of that '... place we hold open, deep within ourselves, for others to enter' (p. 4). If law has a soul then it is to be found, Manderson claims, in the law of torts and the doctrines of negligence or the so-called 'duty of care'. The latter describes a personal responsibility that we owe to others and which has been placed on us without our consent. This responsibility is not a relation of equality, but asymmetry. As Manderson puts it in his Conclusion, 'In just the way that Levinas sees ethics as "first philosophy", so torts is "first law"' (p. 200). As such, common law is not based on individual rights, freedom, autonomy and contract, but on the individual's unchosen obligations where their autonomy and freedom are questioned.

At the centre of Manderson's book is an argument for a *prima facie* highly improbable link between the concept of proximity in Levinas, which figures powerfully in his work before and within *Otherwise Than Being*, and the legal opinions of the Australian High Court in the 1980s and 1990s. Refusing both Levinas's separation of proximity from the realm of law and indeed the hegemonic understanding of law in, say, contract and criminal law, Manderson argues that the common law tradition can show how proximity is not irrelevant to law, but is the best understanding of law and, indeed, the ethical component within law. This is what is at work in the law of torts with its distinctive blend of uncertainty, compassion and judgment that is not reducible to a rule; what we might think of as reflective rather than determinate judgment, although Manderson does not allude to this perhaps helpful Kantian distinction. Proximity is defined in relation to the infinitizing caress and not the totalizing grasp, as a sentient experience of the other's otherness that does not seize hold of the person or thing. Proximity is a non-conceptual, non-intentional contact with the other, expressed in the idea of *approach*, an approach irreducible to any account of intersubjectivity founded on recognition, as in Hegel or contemporary Hegelians like Axel Honneth.

Manderson's book might legitimately be approached as a meditation on the following four sentences from chapter 5 of *Otherwise Than Being*,

> Justice is impossible without the one that renders it finding himself in proximity. His function is not limited to the 'function of judgment', the subsuming of particular cases under a general rule. The judge is not outside the conflict, but the law is in the midst of proximity. Justice, society, the state and its institutions, exchanges and work are comprehensible out of proximity.[2]

As Manderson puts it in the final pages of the book, 'proximity is law deconstructed' (p. 199); by which he means that proximity is law's truth, the undeconstructible kernel at the heart of law's paper empire. In other words, proximity and not privity – as in contract and criminal law – is the truth of law, which takes place as a *pledge* to the other and not a contract with them. In torts, the 'I' is not the foundation of law as in contracts, neither is it the 'we' as in constitutional law, it is rather the third person singular 's/he'. This singular 's/he' appears in a unique set of circumstances and a legal decision with regard to them cannot be reduced to the application of a universal rule or the subsumption of the particular under the general. It is rather a question of the generation of the rule out of a response to particularity. Tort law, then, captures something that 'obliges beyond contracts'. This is clearest in the law of negligence, which seeks to attribute responsibility within discrete relationships. The law of negligence reflects our initial indebtedness to a neighbour, the human situation that has come to be known as 'the duty of care'. As such, the law of negligence recognizes, crucially, the *asymmetry* of the relation to the other. In the fifth and by far the longest chapter in the book, Manderson presents a fascinating, intricate and tightly-argued thicket of legal cases which culminate in showing that the common law 'is a discourse and not a machine' (p. 142): a fluid, responsive, open-ended and ongoing process of law-making in response to the experience of proximity.

So, Manderson wants to oppose the separation of ethics from law that one finds in Levinas with the claim that the law of torts as first law and ethics as first philosophy are in a relation of proximity, although not identity. This is an important point, particularly for those of us reared on and afeared by the Hegelian criticisms of Gillian Rose, who argued that Levinas offers a pure and puerile ethics without any connection to *sittlich* morality and legality. Legality is not morality, and law is not ethics. Ethics is rather the scruple within law, where scruple is understood as the irritating pebble in our shoe that both constantly discomforts law and impels it to move. On Manderson's interpretation, Levinas offers the possibility of a 'jurisprudence for adults' that, as he nicely expresses it, 'requires us to give up forever a concept of rule-fetishism and absolute obedience that tends to obsess six-year olds' (p. 200). In short, proximity is that place where the law is a student of the other and not its master and the experience of proximity in common law keeps the wounds of law open and makes sure that the scrupulous ethical pebble rubs the tender soft skin on the sole of the judge's foot.

However, despite this book's many merits, I want to register a slight disagreement or difference of emphasis on the reading of Levinas. Manderson asks whether the move from ethics to justice in *Otherwise Than Being*, as a move from the other to all the others, from ethical asymmetry to judicial symmetry, simply abandons us to totality (p. 186). Firstly, what is wrong in Levinas – and I completely agree with Manderson and it can be seen in the final sentence of the quote from *Otherwise Than Being* that I just cited – is the identification of justice with the state, society, politics and legality, as if these things were in any imaginable sense identical features of totality, however that might be understood. What is particularly awry in Levinas is the seemingly strict separation of ethics from law that is implied in the move from the other to the third party. As such, I think Levinas's understanding of law is flat and simplistic and thus, to quote Manderson, 'we need to rescue Levinas from himself' (p. 193). Another subsidiary claim that Manderson makes, with which I would also concur, is that Derrida's picture of legal judgment as marked by the aporia of regulation and a lack of regulation – that is, both a conservation of the law and its destruction where both conservation and destruction are part of the experience of deconstruction – is much closer to the truth or to the experience or even the procedure of legal decision-making. So, Manderson's entire argument is that if we begin thinking about law from the perspective of the law of torts and the law of negligence, then ethics and law – whilst not identical – are in a greater relation of proximity than Levinas allows. But does this argument do justice to Levinas's position, particularly the way that position is developed in *Otherwise Than Being*? I have my doubts, so let me sketch an alternative way of approaching this issue and turn to the question of anarchy.

The logic of the law in Levinas's work may be understood according to a threefold schema. Arguably, such an approach demonstrates that the separation between ethics and law is not as radical as Manderson imagines and the relation between ethics and law is arguably of a different character:

1. In *Otherwise Than Being*, chapter 5, Levinas writes of 'the inscription of law in consciousness' (p. 148), by which he means the break up of the unity of transcendental apperception through a moment of trauma, where alterity, as he says, slips into me 'like a thief'. Importantly, this is the moment of anarchy, of what we might call an anarchic law, which means the moment of proximity and responsibility for the neighbour.

So, the bringing together of law and proximity which Manderson attempts is also an identification of law with anarchy. Levinas's theme of anarchism is of great interest, particularly the way this theme is handled by Miguel Abensour when he speaks of an anarchic disturbance of politics.[3] Levinas introduces the notion of anarchy in 'Substitution', the pivotal chapter of *Otherwise Than Being or Beyond Essence,* where it is employed as a name for that which precedes any principle or *archè*. Levinas understands *archè* in philosophical terms where the first 'scientific' principle is the positing of the subject, as for example in Fichte's *Wissenschaftslehre*. On this account, philosophy begins with the idea of intellectual intuition as the self-intuiting or self-positing of the subject in terms of activity. Gently chiding talk of 'subject-positions', we might say that the principled subject *is* position. The subject is self-positing, it puts itself in place through an act of will. This self-positing might be linked to the notion of the spontaneity of the subject in Kant's first critique or the concept of autonomy in the second critique, what Rawls in a rare rhapsodic moment describes as Kant's 'aristocracy of all', where each moral subject would be sovereign over itself insofar as it was freely determined by the moral law. On Levinas's view, it is the sovereign self-positing subject that has dominated modern philosophy. This is what I elsewhere call the 'autonomy orthodoxy', where the *archè* is understood as *autarchy*, as self-origination or self-legislation – we might want to add self-satisfaction to this list. For Levinas, on the contrary, ethical subjectivity is the experience of being affected by an other in a way that precedes consciousness and which places in question our spontaneity and sovereignty. Our autonomous majesty is deposed and decapitated, our autonomous self-binding is unbound and we are undone. Our posturing subject-position is deposed. It is in this sense that Levinas claims that the heteronomous ethical experience of the relation to the neighbour is anarchical, the other posits me under their demand despite myself and before any act of the will. In Manderson's terms, this anarchic experience of proximity is first law, which means that *first law is no law*. In a fascinating footnote to *Otherwise Than Being,* Levinas comes close to defining what he means by anarchy in relation to its customary political signification,

> The notion of anarchy we are introducing here has a meaning prior to the political (or anti-political) meaning popularly ascribed to it. It cannot, under pain of contradiction, be set up as a principle (in the sense that anarchists understand it). Anarchy, unlike *archè,* cannot

> be sovereign. It can only disturb, albeit in a radical way, the State, prompting isolated moments of negation *without any* affirmation. The State, then, cannot set itself up as a Whole. (p. 194, translation modified)

Anarchy should not seek to mirror the archic sovereignty that it undermines. That is, it should not seek to set itself up as the new hegemonic principle of political organization, but remain the negation of totality and not the affirmation of a new totality. Anarchy is a radical disturbance of the state, a disruption of the state's attempt to set itself up or erect itself into a whole (*s'ériger en Tout*). In my jargon, anarchy is the creation of *interstitial distance* within the state, the continual questioning from below of any attempt to establish order from above. We might say that ethical anarchy is the experience of the multiple singularities of encounter with others that defines the experience of sociality. Each of these singularities overwhelms and undoes us and we can never do enough in response. Any attempt to order these singularities into a shoulder-to-shoulder 'fighting collectivity', as Carl Schmitt might say, is doomed to fail. Despite the political problems inherent to Levinas's work, and which I have tried to catalogue elsewhere – fraternity, monotheism, androcentrism, filiality and the family schema and Israel – this is the anti-authoritarian kernal to Levinas's work.[4]

2. The second moment in the logic of law in Levinas is the entry of the third party, *le tiers*, which is famously described as 'the comparison of incomparables' (OB 158), where the inequality and asymmetry of the ethical relation becomes a symmetrical relation of equals. This is the moment when myself and the other appear on an equal footing 'as before a court of justice' (OB 157), as Levinas very interestingly adds. With the entry of the third, 'the contemporaneity of the multiple is tied around the diachrony of the two', which is to say that the temporal order of synchrony is added to and interrupted by the diachronic non-coincidence of the anarchic relation of proximity. Anarchy becomes *archè*. Importantly, this is also the moment of *philosophy* understood as the domain of archic judgment, of a judicial decision. Philosophy is here the moment of the legal decision, which has to be based on a principle, say the principle of autonomy, equal treatment or whatever. Levinas's point, however, is that this principled judgment has to flow from and be informed by the anarchy of the relation of proximity to the neighbour. There is a thus a disjunction between ethics and law, the disjunction that Manderson criticizes.

3. Yet, what is the relation between the first and second moments in the logic of law in Levinas? It is here that we approach a crucial third moment in the logic of law, which is something upon which Levinas insists, although I don't really think Manderson does justice to the idea. The relation between ethics and law, and this is a word that appears countless times in these pages of *Otherwise Than Bring*, is the experience of *ambivalence* or *ambiguity*, which Levinas links here and elsewhere to the experience of an *enigma*. He writes, 'it is through its ambivalence which always remains an enigma that infinity or the transcendent does not let itself be assembled' (p. 161). And again, 'there is an ambiguity of the order that orders to me the neighbour who obsesses me...' (162) It is here that a different meaning is given to the idea and practice of philosophy. That is, philosophy is not just the moment of archic judgment or sovereign legal decision. Rather, philosophy is the name of that practice – what he calls 'the wisdom of love at the service of love', rather than the more sovereign love of wisdom, the Socratic gadfly rather than the Platonic philosopher king – that has to attend to the movement of ambivalence or ambiguity. This ambivalence is precisely the movement between the first and second moments in the logic of law, between anarchy and arche, or between the saying and the said. To understand this ambivalence, it is essential in my view to have a clear sense of the concept of *reduction* in Levinas's work (see, e.g., pp. 43–45, p. 152 & p. 181), a concept which has been far too little understood, with certain noble exceptions, say the important work of William Large, and which I think provides the key to understanding the movement of Levinas's later work.[5]

Let me try to explain. Levinas claims that the philosopher's effort consists in the reduction of the Said to the Saying, to show how my anarchic ethical proximity to the other underlies any ontological exposition, where ontology is identified with the category of totality and the refusal of ethics. But how is this reduction to be *shown*? Levinas insists that everything that shows itself takes place at the level of the Said. We should recall that, for the Heidegger of *Sein und Zeit*, phenomenology is defined as the letting be seen *(logos)* of that which shows itself *(phainomenon)*. But if this is the case, then how does the Saying show itself, particularly when Levinas persistently identifies it in his work with enigma as the counter-concept to phenomenon, that is as that which does not show itself? In other words, how can there be a phenomenology of the enigmatic? For Levinas, the Saying can only be conveyed or *traduit* to the extent that it is *trahit* or betrayed within the Said. This means that a more complex discursive procedure is involved in the Levinasian idea of reduction. That is to say, the Saying is not the Husserlian *epoche* or bracketing out of the Said, nor is it the Heideggerian letting be seen of the Saying as a phenomenon. Rather, the reduction is the exposure of the Saying by way of a continual contestation of the Said. The Saying shows itself within the Said by interrupting it. This logic of interruption is analogous to the logic of scepticism as it is developed in the vitally important closing pages of chapter 5 of *Otherwise Than Being*, the pages that close the argument of the book. Levinas asserts, classically enough, that the sceptic can only expose the thesis of scepticism – for example, 'all truth is subjective' – in a language that refutes that thesis – namely, in a propositional language that presupposes the very shared understanding which the sceptical thesis denies. But, and this is Levinas's point, this is not an end to scepticism, for the sceptic will return to interrupt the language of philosophical refutation by both conveying and betraying his thesis. Levinas writes, 'language is already skepticism'. That is, the Said is always subverted by a Saying that speaks at the price of betrayal. The Saying is the performative disruption of the Said that is immediately refuted by the language in which it shows itself. The method of reduction – a method that is *enacted* by the writing of the later Levinas – performs a kind of spiralling movement or what he calls '*un mouvement en vrille*', between the unavoidable language of the Said and the attempt to unsay that Said in order to locate the Saying within it. For Levinas, the philosopher's effort is dedicated towards the production of this spiralling movement in language and experience, a movement that attempts to unsay the Said and find the Saying within it. Yet – and for my understanding of Levinas this has always been crucial – *the reduced Said retains a residue of the unsaid Said within the Saying*. That is, the reduction is never pure or complete. This leaves philosophy in a spiralling movement of ambivalence between two orders of discourse, the Saying and Said, where ethics only signifies through the oscillation or ambiguity of these orders. The enigma of philosophy consists in nothing else but the enactment of this ambiguity.

My closing thought is highly speculative but hopefully simple: what if the practice of law, the very activity of law-making or the writing of legal opinions and the taking of legal decisions were conceivable in relation to this method of reduction? What if we thought of law in terms of this movement of ambivalence and oscillation between the Saying and Said, between the experience of proximity and the taking of legal decisions? What if the very movement of law were both informed and deformed by the experience of anarchic proximity, an experience that can only be conveyed at the price of its betrayal in the Said? What if we took seriously the idea of the enigma of philosophy in the later Levinas, as the spiralling movement between the Saying and the Said, an endless ambivalence or oscillation, and extended it to law? What if the Saying that law attempts to convey, the experience of proximity with the neighbour, could only be achieved at the price of its betrayal in the codification of a black letter Said? Might this not be an anarchic law, a law that has no law at its base and as its basis, where anarchy is understood as the relation of proximity to the neighbour? Might this not also be a *sceptical* law, which is another way of thinking about an adult jurisprudence rather than law as a rule-obsessed six-year-old's policing function? If, as Levinas suggests, language is already scepticism, then might not law also already be scepticism? If the relation between scepticism and its refutation suggests a movement of ambivalence between the Saying and the Said, an unsaying of the Said and the retention of the unsaid Said within the saying, then might not this movement be approached as the enigma of the relation between ethics and law? Might we not be able to rewrite *Law's Empire* as *Law's Enigma*, where the activity of the judge and the reflective activity of judgment itself might be approached in terms of the spiralling movement between the Saying and the Said? Might we begin to think of law not as determination but as reflection generated out of the ambiguity the Said of law, legal opinion and legal precedent and the Saying of a responsibility that might anarchically and sceptically both inform and deform that Said? Might such a thing be possible? I do not know. It depends upon the outcome of a fight for the soul of law.

Notes

1. D. Manderson, *Proximity, Levinas and the Soul of Law* (Montreal, Kingston: McGill-Queen's University Press, 2006). All subsequent page references given in the text.
2. E. Levinas, *Otherwise Than Being or Beyond Essence,* trans. A. Lingis (Kluwer, Dordrecht & Boston, 1981) p. 162. All subsequent pages references given in the text.
3. M. Abensour, 'An-archy Between Meta-politics and Politics', *Parallax* 24 (July–September 2002) 5–18.
4. See S. Critchley, 'Five Problems in Levinas's View of Politics and the Sketch of a Solution to Them', *Political Theory* 32 (April 2004) 172–185. See also Howard Caygill, *Levinas and the Political* (London, New York: Routledge, 2002).
5. W. Large, *Emmanuel Levinas and Maurice Blanchot. Ethics and Ambiguity of Writing* (Manchester: Clinamen Press, 2005).

Response

Desmond Manderson

Like Professor Critchley, I approached with some enthusiasm *Proximity, Levinas and the Soul of Law*, a taste of whose curious mixture of doctrinal law and Levinasian ethics can be found elsewhere in this volume.[1] But I find on reflection that the author's tiger, when shaken vigorously, turns out to be a kitten, after all. Although we are promised a new way of thinking about tort theory, and a new development of Levinas's own understanding of the relationship between ethics and law, the book is always teetering on the precipice of its various stools. Ultimately it raises questions as to the genuine effectiveness of interdisciplinary dialogue between two such specialized terrains. Manderson's effort to show how the so-called 'trace' of ethics, 'of infinite responsibility', can nevertheless continue to contaminate the work of law will seem far too airy-fairy for the lawyers and far too down-'n'-dirty to the philosophers. No doubt to be attacked from both sides in this way is the peril that awaits all interdisciplinary research but it seems in this case unusually acute. In attempting to establish a dialogue between legal and philosophical perspectives, not by 'applying' the agent Levinas to the object law, but rather by allowing each to modify our appreciation of the other, I fear he has created Frankenstein's monster, neither one thing nor the other.

In the end, the novelty of Manderson's vision of law lies in his insistence on the necessity and indeed value of indeterminacy, the 'trace' or 'fresh judgment' that each new case must confront and must contribute to an ongoing dialogue. This, for the author, is the moment in which we can detect the 'trace' of the Saying within the law's pedantic Said. Critchley rightly pushes the argument to its logical conclusion and exposes within Levinas the workings of an 'anarchic law.' 'The first law', he concludes, 'is no law at all'. But who amongst us, not just lawyers but citizens too, will be comforted by that? Critchley, the philosopher, wonders whether such a moment might be preserved within the law. 'Might such a thing be possible?' he wonders, and has no answer. Manderson, the lawyer, wonders whether such a moment might be controlled and corralled by the law; and he too has no answer.

This brings us to the other side of the book. Manderson's vision of ethics insists with 'disarming moral sincerity' – a back-handed compliment if ever there was one – on its pragmatic relevance to concrete legal problems. But in the process, the wildness of Levinas's ethical position and the *difficulty* of living by its lights become domesticated.[2] Perhaps, as Critchley – and others – sometimes imply, it is the very impossibility of applying Levinas to law that is its value. *Traduttore, traditore*, they say. Indeed, Manderson goes so far as to defend betrayal as a genre, arguing that without the inevitable failures of translation new knowledge and new understanding would never emerge. That is what traitors always say and in this case I suspect the author is a traitor not to one discipline but two. Whether that balances the injustice or merely doubles it will depend on your view of the loyalty owed to the genres he has mixed and matched here.

As an instance of the way in which law domesticates everything with which it comes into contact, perhaps inevitably but in which case most instructively, Manderson hastily shies away from the 'infinite' aspect of Levinasian responsibility, arguing that this infinity is 'infinitely deep, not infinitely wide'; that it does not mean that we are all responsible to everybody, but rather that to those with whom we are 'proximate', our responsibility can never be defined or limited in advance. There are those who are rightly sceptical of this interpretation which it seems to me is a bit of a sleight of hand;[3] and it must be said that it is not always easy to see where Levinas ends and Manderson's development and correction of him begins.

Even within the carefully constrained understanding of infinite responsibility he sets himself, I remain unsure whether Manderson has not finessed the problem. Chapter 5 is, as Critchley observes, key to the argument. To paraphrase Dr Johnson, while not every reader has wanted it shorter, no reader has ever wanted it longer. Here and in the chapters that follow, Manderson reconstructs the legal history of negligence in the High Court of Australia in the process defending, rather quixotically, its flirtation with proximity during the 1980s and 1990s. Yet in the end the exercise of establishing the duty of care is only a preliminary step. Once a responsibility has been established, the court must still determine if that responsibility has been breached by the defendant. On this point, the author is largely silent. I cannot help wondering if, for all its symbolic value, by which the author appears to be immensely taken, the 'duty of care', broad or narrow, is really only of minor importance as we go about the daily grind of acting responsibly. Manderson might even be accused – and this is for others to examine and explore – of reinstating the same dichotomy between responsible 'ethics' and the calculus of law, that he wished to tear down. The duty issue is the realm of responsibility, our infinite relationship with the suffering other. But the breach issue seems here to remain the province of law, rule-bound and finite as ever.

The author is less interested in the results that legal tribunals deliver to parties before them than in the discourse in which they are couched. For him, the legal discourse which has developed around the idea of responsibility to others has a force and a cultural significance quite apart from the actual decisions and consequences of individual cases. The attraction of Levinas, then, is that his work offers the analysis of tort law a register that captures something of its distinct blend of uncertainty, judgment and compassion. Above all, the common law offers us an ethical ideal of teaching in which law's instability, its constant reassessment and transformation of its own principles, allows us all, judges and citizens alike, to keep learning from a process that is never entirely settled or rigid.[4] I have some sympathy for this position which seems to me to bring together the very heart of both the common law and ethics. Both are exegetical practices and therefore dialogic and responsive, rather than monologic and declaratory.[5] And I say this despite law's increasingly anxious and, particularly in the case of the jurisprudence of negligence, hopelessly untenable self-image to the contrary.[6]

Nonetheless, I wonder whether the focus on discourse at the expense of results is, at best, only half the story. Do people really *care* very much what the High Court of Australia says about their duty to their fellow man? And what price do we pay for this sentimental commitment to law as a narrative of history and culture? Many scholars, of course, find the whole structure of negligence law, which almost arbitrarily chooses to compensate the victims of some accidents while ignoring others, illogical and unjust.[7] The more we understand the law of negligence as a means of providing necessary compensation to those who have been injured, and the more we think of insurance as a necessary means of financing that compensation, the less appropriate or even honest seems a tort system which focuses, in rhetoric though not in reality, on fault and individual responsibility. So we find the trend, de facto and de jure, towards no-fault liability. *Proximity, Levinas and the Soul of Law* tells the story of negligence as if these realities hardly existed.

Its approach is to focus on the duty of care as a social vision, without unduly heeding its actual operation. Yet surely we should not ignore a focus on law's outcomes merely to preserve a certain 'conversation' in which few participate. Despite Manderson's attachment to the particularity and suffering of individual lives, the discourse about discourse that he privileges operates at quite a high level of abstraction.

I suppose that is the value of this odd research. It is not entirely a work of philosophy, and it is hardly a piece of law reform. It is instead, I think, an interdisciplinary history of a moment – within ethics and within law. The book is at its most convincing when it envisages a connection between disparate histories and disparate discourse, and labours to bring them together. In the particular case of the duty of care, I do not think that the parallels in language and approach between Levinas and the developing ideas about the duty of care, both in Australian jurisprudence and to some extent around the world (the House of Lords, for example, was very influenced by the Australian trends), were coincidental. From the early 1980s, the Anglo-American common law was searching for resources to reconfigure an ethical coherence in law at a unique moment in their jurisprudential history. It was the heyday of 'critical legal studies',[8] a brash outpouring by principally US academics which insisted on the absolute impossibility of the coherence of rules or meaning within the law. Law: was power. In philosophy, aspects of the emerging field of post-structural theory (on which CLS drew clumsily) were also casting doubt on the legitimacy and interpretative stability of institutions of authority.[9] Power: was law. In society as a whole, the myth that judges do not 'make' law, the bread-and-butter of judicial mythology since the time of Coke and Blackstone, had been comprehensively debunked. This had gradually exposed courts around the world to an increasingly virulent criticism, in the light of which judges were undoubtedly facing growing pressure from social critics to find new ways to justify and explain their craft. In Australia, the appointment of left-leaning politician Lionel Murphy to the High Court was like a red rag to a bull. He, more than any judge before him, espoused a critical approach to law. Yet he had personal reason to come to regret the demystification of the judiciary. In 1984 the 'Murphy affair' broke, and there followed the shameless excoriation of a High Court judge, in the media, parliament and the courts.[10] Where now was the line between law and politics?

So comprehensively under siege from these various social forces, the Australian High Court, for one, seems to have set out on a quest to revive law's goodness – trying to explain to an increasingly sceptical world why law as an institution was worth caring about despite the fact that it could no longer be defended as simply the 'application' of objective 'rules'. It was perhaps more than a little naïve that the court took as its target for this renewal an area of law as chaotic, hopelessly subjective – indeed, 'anarchic' – as the duty of care. But faced with the cynicism and hostility that encircled it, the effort was courageous and even inspiring. With the help of Levinas, one can begin to detect a trace not of what the High Court actually said about our responsibility to others, but what lay behind it and why it was saying.

Notes

1. See D. Manderson, ' "Current Legal Maxims in which the word neighbour occurs": Levinas and the Law of Torts' in this volume.
2. J. de Ville, 'Levinas on Law: A Derridean Reading of Manderson's *Proximity*, Levinas, and the Soul of Law', *Griffith Law Review* 16 (2007) 225–47 is particularly critical of Manderson's *taming* of the radicalism of Levinasian ethics.
3. See J. Crowe in Book Symposium: D. Manderson, *Proximity, Levinas, and the Soul of Law, Aust. J. Legal Philosophy* 33 (2008).
4. R. Gibbs, 'The Other Comes to Teach Me: A Review of Recent Levinas Publications', *Man and World* 24 (1991) 219–233, 219–220.
5. R. Cohen, *Ethics, Exegesis and Philosophy: Interpretation After Levinas* (Cambridge: Cambridge University Press, 2001) pp. 225–245.
6. P. Goodrich, *Reading the Law: A Critical Introduction to Legal Method and Techniques* (Oxford and Cambridge, MA: Basil Blackwell, 1986).
7. P. Atiyah, *Accidents, Compensation and the Law*, 4th ed. (London: Weidenfeld and Nicholson, 1987); 7th ed., P. Cane (ed.) (Cambridge: Cambridge University Press, 2006) is rightly the classic in the field.
8. R. Gordon, 'Critical Legal Histories', *Stanford Law Review* 36 (1984) 57–125; M. Kelman, *A Guide to Critical Legal Studies* (Cambridge, Mass: Harvard University Press, 1987); A. Hutchinson, *Critical Legal Studies* (Lanham: Rowman and Littlefield, 1989); D. Kennedy and K. E. Klare, 'A Bibliography of Critical Legal Studies', *Yale Law Journal* 94 (1984) 461–490; M. Tushnet, 'An Essay on Rights', *Texas Law Review* 62 (1984) 1363–1403; D. Kennedy, 'The Structure of Blackstone's Commentaries', *Buffalo Law Review* 28 (1978) 205–382.
9. J. Derrida, 'Before the Law' and 'The Law of Genre', in D. Attridge (ed.), *Acts of Literature* (New York: Routledge, 1992) pp. 181–220 and 221–252; M. Foucault, *Power/Knowledge: Selected Interviews and Other Writings, 1972–1997*, C. Gordon (ed.) (New York: Pantheon, 1980); *Discipline and Punish: The Birth of the Prison,* trans. A. Sheridan (New York: Vintage Books, 1979).
10. See T. Blackshield, M. Coper and G. Williams, *The Oxford Companion to the High Court* (Melbourne: Oxford University Press, 2001) pp. 486–489; G. Sturgess, 'Murphy and the Media' and T. Blackshield, 'The "Murphy Affair" ', both in J. A. Scutt (ed.), *Lionel Murphy: A Radical Judge* (Melbourne: Macmillan Australia, 1987) chapters 11 and 12.

12
Exceptional Justice, Violent Proximity

Jesse Sims

Grounding violence: From application to force of law

Discussions of the relationship between Levinas's philosophy and politics or law typically envision an engagement of Levinasian ethics with a conception of justice drawn from the Kantian, liberal tradition. However, there has been increasing recognition of a strange proximity of Levinas's thought to quite another perspective on the juridical-political, that of Carl Schmitt. For instance, in *Levinas and the Political*, Howard Caygill observes that

> War and the political assume a proximity in Levinas's thought that were it recognized would prove extremely uncomfortable for liberal readers accustomed to keeping war – as the alleged pathology of civility – separate from peace. The proximity of war and politics is a thought that brings Levinas closer to the thought of Clausewitz and Carl Schmitt than to the liberal ethical theory issued from Kant.[1]

With respect to the question of justice, the temptation to treat Levinasian ethics in terms of a dialogue with the dominant juridical and political tradition – Kantian, liberal and universalist – arises in part from Levinas's well-known introduction of the third party into the ethical relation, notably in chapter V of *Otherwise Than Being*.[2] However, the possibility of treating the relationship between ethics and justice within a Kantian framework is equally precluded by a proper reading of that text.

Two facets of Levinas's discussion of the third party seem to lend themselves to a Kantian interpretation. In the first place, the third party refocuses our attention from the absoluteness and intimacy of the ethical relation between self and other to the possibility, indeed the necessity, of a justice that mediates between multiple and conflicting demands – a justice based on universal categories, such as equality, reciprocity and autonomy. More than a supplement to the proximity of the ethical relation, the third party upsets this proximity, placing 'distance between me and the other and the third party' and forcing the question: 'What do I have to do with justice?'[3] With this question, the asymmetry of ethical responsibility gives way to the familiar juridical-political expectations of the liberal tradition: universality, equal treatment, rights, citizenship. Justice permits the weighing and judging of terms as though on a common scale, requiring the submission of self and other to a 'calculus' in which responsibility, ethically incalculable, can be measured.[4] Justice thus establishes between me and the other and the third 'a copresence on an equal footing as before a court of justice.'[5] This reference to the judicial institution is meant literally, as the work of justice requires the protection of 'the State and its institutions,' that the 'saying' of ethics congeal into a fixed 'said,' becoming 'book, law and science,' and that the subject be understood as 'a citizen with all the duties and rights measured and measurable which the equilibriated ego involves.'[6]

Levinas's introduction of the question of justice through the arrival of the third party thus appears to move him in the direction of the Kantian tradition, in its insistence on the law's universality and institutional realization. Of course, the unique ethical demands of the other, which resist universality, do not disappear with the entry of the third. But this emphasis on ethical resistance itself provides a second route to the Kantian perspective. The other's allergy to the universality of law is essential to the structure of justice insofar as it opens a dimension of *problems* to be taken up by the law; that is to say, the very conflict between singular ethical imperatives and universal legal norms can be taken to fall within the universal sphere of practical reason, discourse and compromise. For Levinas, justice is necessary because of this problematic dimension: it is the way 'from responsibility to problems,' problems that do not exist in the ethical dyad, but that remain problematic on its account. The order of justice does not supplant ethics, but is rather 'superimposed' upon 'the extravagance of substitution,' in which I am an irreplaceable 'hostage' for the other.[7] The relationship with the third is thus 'an *incessant correction* of the asymmetry of proximity in which the face is looked at,' and as such, justice assumes the impossible task of a 'comparison of the incomparable.'[8] Without reducing the difference of the terms, the comparison itself remains necessary: 'There must be a justice among incomparable ones.' Justice occurs when responsibility for the other 'is also a responsibility for the third party,' when there is a 'synchrony of being and peace,' that is, of the contradictory demands of equity and proximity.[9]

Given both of these features that the third party introduces into Levinas's account of justice – the necessity of universal justice itself and the tension with the demands of the other that is thereby produced – it is unsurprising that this account is sometimes misinterpreted as a sort of regulative dilemma. There is, I think, a Kantian misreading of Derrida's frequent characterization of Levinas's problematic as an aporia. The classic statement of this aporia, and the most fecund for relating the legal and ethical dimensions of Levinasian justice, occurs in Derrida's essay 'Force of Law.' On one level, it consists in the tension between justice as the asymmetrical ethical relation (its meaning in *Totality and Infinity*) and the regulated, symmetrical nature of law.[10] But the same aporia is also internal to the exercise of justice – and here Derrida is clearly influenced by *Otherwise Than Being* – in that a relation to the other is at once 'the condition of all possible justice' and 'excluded by justice as law, inasmuch as justice as right seems to imply an element of universality, the appeal to the third party.' The question prompted by justice is how to reconcile the act of justice that respects the singularity of the other or the unique situation with the act of justice that imposes universal rules and norms.[11]

This is where one might be tempted, in a Kantian vein, to consider justice as an arena of negotiation between the irreducible poles of singularity and universality, necessitating perhaps ethical checks on institutional normalization and flexibility in judicial applications. But it would be a misreading of Levinas to treat ethics and law at the same level, as competing normative claims in a regulative context. Such a negotiation would already be internal to the juridical-political, leaving the central question of Levinasian justice – the relation of this sphere to that of ethics – untouched.[12] The attempt to reduce justice to the application of competing criteria to particular cases is already narrowly juridical. For Levinas, the tension between ethical responsibility and legal normalization does not signify first of all competing standards that arise in concrete cases, but rather an inescapable ambiguity in my relation to the other, who is at once 'comparable and incomparable, a unique face and in relationship with faces.'[13] The law itself is already 'in the midst of proximity,' unable to take an objectifying position by which the demands of other and third could be considered as discrete criteria for juridical application. Justice is not a question of accommodating the requirements of ethical responsibility in the face of competing expectations of universality (or vice versa). Levinas is explicit that justice is not simply a matter of 'the subsuming of particular cases under a general rule'[14] – even if that rule or its application is specifically designed to respect the alterity of the other or the singularity of a case.

This position is echoed by Derrida, for whom the aporia of justice consists in the fact that justice, while requiring its own application, resists application as such. The difficulty consists in reconciling a 'justice that must always concern singularity' with a justice that, as law, always has 'a general form, *even if this generality prescribes a singular application in each case*.'[15] Even if we 'apply a good rule to a particular case, to a correctly subsumed example,' says Derrida, we have not accounted for the justice he calls 'incalculable.'[16] Derrida's interest in 'Force of Law' to get behind the sphere of the law's application, while indebted to Levinas's account of law's ethical justification, is perhaps better understood from his account of Benjamin's analysis of the originary violence at the foundation of law. Derrida argues that the concept of applicability in law implies the force with which the law is applied, 'a force that justifies itself or is justified in applying itself.'[17] In 'Critique of Violence,' Benjamin insists that violence must be analyzed at a level more fundamental than the 'sphere of its application'; to consider the justness of the ends violence is used for (say, in legal enforcement) is not to consider 'violence itself as a principle, but, rather, the criterion for cases of its use.'[18] He traces the various functions of violence in law to the immediate violence present at the moment of lawmaking, a violence he calls 'mythical.'[19] For Derrida, this means that behind the justifiable violence of the law's application there is a foundational and alegal 'violence without ground,' instituting authority in a wholly performative manner, itself neither just nor unjust.[20]

This characterization of Benjamin's analysis is intended to recall the thought of Schmitt, and Derrida mentions several times the mutual admiration and troubling affinity of the two thinkers.[21] If the liberal lens through which Levinas's account of justice is sometimes viewed misses its deeper and more troubling dimensions, then perhaps the alternative juridical tradition represented by Schmitt can provide a more penetrating understanding of the nature and implications of Levinas's ethical grounding of law. Despite the distance separating ethical proximity in Levinas from the mythic violence postulated by Benjamin – the former is identified with passivity, the latter with power – both conceptions follow an analogous logic, resisting the reduction of law to generalization and application, and finding behind its regulative function a singular event that remains beyond the law. The problem of the relationship of the thought of Levinas and Schmitt with respect to justice is thus suggested prior to any dialogue with the Kantian tradition. I will argue that there is an implicit Schmittianism in Levinas's attempt to ground law and politics in a conception of the ethical inseparable from violence – though this violence can only be found, paradoxically, at the level of peace and proximity. In order to identify this strain in Levinas's thought, we will pass through two stages of argument, establishing firstly the irreducibility of violence in Levinas's account of the relation of ethics and politics, and secondly the manner in which this violence subtly underpins Levinas's introduction of the third and justice into the ethical relation.

Exceptional violence: Enmity in the ethical

As suggested by Caygill's observation of 'the proximity of war and politics' in Levinas, *Totality and Infinity* seems the most promising place to seek the Schmittian moment in his work. However, that work concerns the political more directly than the juridical. The claim is already made that fraternity and equality require the presence of the third party,[22] but a sustained account of the essential relationship between reciprocal justice and the ethical is not developed until *Otherwise Than Being*. Unlike the latter work, which we have seen envisions justice as an essential (if interminable) corrective to ethical responsibility, *Totality and Infinity* identifies justice with the ethical relation itself,[23] as 'the uprightness of the face to face,'[24] in contrast to the 'equilibrium' of 'universal and objective law.'[25] Nevertheless, in the earlier work's understanding of the relationship between ethics and politics, there is an underlying Schmittian logic that can also be found in Levinas's later account of justice.

The theme of war dominates *Totality and Infinity*, and according to Levinas constitutes the essential characteristic of both ontology and politics. In the preface, Levinas envisions politics as 'the art of foreseeing war and of winning it by every possible means.' On this view, war is truth itself, 'the pure experience of pure being,' and a politics based on this realism poses a fundamental challenge to morality, making it appear a fool's game.[26] Bettina Bergo has noted the disturbing correspondence of this conception of the political to Schmitt's reduction of politics, in *The Concept of the Political*, to the 'friend-enemy' distinction.[27] This distinction, to which all 'political actions and motives can be reduced'[28] according to Schmitt, amounts to a principal of polemics or enmity as such.[29] War has 'no normative meaning' on Schmitt's account,[30] and conversely morality can be reduced to the political insofar as its antitheses approach the friend–enemy distinction.[31]

Of course, this challenge to ethics is what Levinas confronts in *Totality and Infinity*, and is introduced so that he can demonstrate how, despite the seemingly unsurpassable political logic of antagonism, ethical peace can yet dominate. 'The moral consciousness can sustain the mocking gaze of the political man only if the certitude of peace dominates the evidence of war.'[32] Later in the book Levinas argues that ultimately, war signifies not the irreducibility of hostility, but the fact of a relationship to the other even in violence, 'since in war the adversaries seek each other out.' This 'refusal of totality' and embrace of relation in war means that 'only beings capable of war can rise to peace.'[33]

However, this meditation on the priority of peace may bring Levinas close to Schmitt in the same movement that appears to separate them. In *Adieu to Emmanuel Levinas*, Derrida declares Schmitt, the thinker of hostility and the irreducibly political, the 'absolute adversary' of Levinas, the thinker of hospitality and the irreducibly ethical. Each system of thought seems to demand confrontation with the other, 'with all the paradoxes and reversals that such an absolute opposition might harbor,'[34] and, according to a maxim shared by both thinkers, their antagonism attests to an essential relationship. For Levinas, the condition of the victory of morality is that 'the eschatology of messianic peace will have come to superpose itself on the ontology of war.' This eschatological conception of peace is not the opposite of war, but is presupposed both by war and the politically instituted peace that opposes it.[35] In this respect, Levinas's eschatology of peace has a structure analogous to Schmitt's conception of the political, which Schmitt says tends neither to war nor pacifism in its content, but concerns the very possibility of hostility presupposed by this opposition.[36] Both thinkers are skeptical of an institutional, generalizable peace in the tradition of Kant's 'Perpetual Peace'; indeed, it is in the course of distinguishing Kantian from Levinasian peace that Derrida remarks on the connection to Schmitt. Regarding eschatological peace, Derrida also worries: if war bears witness to peace as Levinas claims, then in terms of political content, might not war be interpreted as the 'continuation of peace by other means'?[37] Ethical peace may constitute the formal condition of politics and law, but the fact that their content remains indeterminate means that such a peace 'still allows any State ... to feel justified in raising an army, in making war or keeping law and order, in controlling its borders – in killing.'[38]

What would a peace based on singularity rather than universality, outside institutional realization, look like, and what value would this apparent reversal of Schmittianism have if it still allowed the same killing?

The question here is whether, at the pre-political level where Levinas situates peace, there remains an inescapable violence inherent in the logic of ethical singularity. The question is more interesting from a juridical perspective because it brings Levinas into relation with the Schmitt of *Political Theology*, that is, with his account of the exception. In establishing ethics and peace as the condition of war and violence, Levinas applies the logic of the exception, in a way that problematizes the meanings of both Schmitt's political and Levinas's ethical.

Let us isolate certain features of Schmitt's logic before considering its place in *Totality and Infinity*. Schmitt likens the operation of the exception to that of the miracle in Christian theology,[39] in that it constitutes a 'suspension of the entire existing order.'[40] This possibility is the alegal requirement of any coherent legal system. The rule cannot of itself account for the exception, whereas the exception justifies both itself and the rule, a principle Schmitt intends concretely as well as abstractly, since a legal or political system can function only against the backdrop of the exception.[41]

Secondly, the exception bears a necessary, yet ambiguous, relationship to the decision. The sovereign has the power to decide whether the exceptional or normal situation obtains; by virtue of this exercise of will he is at once inside and outside the law. But ultimately the exception has priority over the decision, for as the 'circumstance that requires the decision,' the exception 'remains an independently determining moment.'[42] The exceptional situation requires a decision because the normal situation 'in which legal prescriptions can be valid must first be brought about.'[43]

Thirdly, there is an irreducible violence in the sovereign's power to announce and enforce a state of exception. In *Political Theology*, this is evident in the exception's appearance as the 'extreme case' or emergency, but the meaning of this violence is not concretely described until *The Concept of the Political*. Schmitt writes that the meaning of the exception consists in the 'extreme possibility' of 'real war' or 'real combat,' and thus also the political distinction of friend and enemy.[44] The essence of war consists in the bare possibility 'of physically killing human beings.'[45] The conceptual symmetry of the friend–enemy distinction and the exception is such that the enemy is defined at once by the priority of exceptionality and this possibility of killing. The primal relationship to the other in war cannot be defined by any 'general norm' or 'a disinterested and therefore neutral third party,' but only by the fact that 'in the extreme case conflicts with him are possible.'[46]

In Levinas's *Totality and Infinity* an analogous logic of exceptionality underpins an apparently opposite project, the attempt to ground violence on the ethical relation or peace. Ultimately this logic works against that attempt, as it reveals an inherent violence in the exceptionality of the ethical foundation.

The attestation of violence to an antecedent ethical relation depends on Levinas's analysis of the exceptional *way of being* of the other at whom violence aims. Violence can only aim at 'a being both graspable and escaping every hold' – there is a 'living contradiction in the being that undergoes violence,' without which violence would signify only labor, a normalized economy of force-relations.[47] This contradiction is found in the face of the other, where 'the sensible, still graspable, turns into total resistance to the grasp.' The other resists in such a way that the power to which it is exposed is fundamentally transformed, from possession to murderous violence; murder demonstrates that the other's 'being cannot be suspended by an appropriation.' The possibility of murder fascinates Levinas precisely because of its exceptional status within the economy of the same: 'This most banal incident of human history *corresponds to an exceptional possibility* – since it claims the total negation of a being.'[48]

As with Schmitt's 'real possibility of physical killing,' the possibility of murder here is inseparable from the exception. But Levinas's analysis of the exceptional status of killing exceeds Schmitt's, for this exception depends on the 'ethical resistance' offered by the face. Ethics is found already in the possibility of murder, because the resistance that would make murder possible announces beforehand the commandment against murder.[49] The possibility of killing reveals itself simultaneously as 'the purely ethical impossibility of this temptation and attempt.' The ethical interdiction, by which the other expresses an absolute resistance to all attempts at control, is the frustration of murder in the very act of carrying it out. The other eludes the murderer's attempts at appropriation even in the moment of death. Through the paradoxical logic of this relationship, Levinas finally establishes the priority of peace over violence: 'War presupposes peace, the antecedent and non-allergic presence of the other; it does not represent the first event of the encounter.'[50]

If this were Levinas's final word, it might pose a fundamental challenge to Schmitt's political logic, a demonstration that the foundation of the juridical-political is exceptional only in its being ethical, that is, in its prohibition of the same possibility it announces. But Levinas does not take the exceptionality of this prohibition for granted. He admits that while the other announces the '*moral* impossibility of annihilating,' at the level of action 'this interdiction is to be sure not equivalent to *pure and simple* impossibility, and even presupposes the possibility which precisely it forbids.'[51] To establish the primacy of peace, what has to be shown is that, in the very structure of the will and not just the face at which it aims, the resistance of the other 'dwells in this very possibility rather than presupposing it.'[52]

At this point in the argument there is a crucial shift of the locus of hostility from self to other. According to Levinas, the work of my will, including its willing against the other, presupposes an exposure to the will of the other. 'I am a passivity threatened... by a will in my will. In my action, in the for itself of my will, I am exposed to a foreign will.'[53] The other is resistant to murder as the sole being who does not simply oppose the weakness of my power, but paralyzes my very 'power for power.'[54]

The other's challenge to sovereignty is essential to Levinasian ethics, but is portrayed in terms of violence, suffering and death – not the other's, but coming *from* the other. The 'will in my will' is a 'hostile will,' from which proceeds 'the violence of death.'[55] 'The Other,' writes Levinas, 'is situated in the region from which death, possibly murder, comes.' This 'consciousness of hostility' alone 'renders possible an appeal to the other.'[56] The exceptional moment of ethics depends as much on the threat of my death as the other's, because the exception requires my passivity before the other: the menace of death 'is a relation with an instant whose exceptional character is due... to the fact that, in life, it is the impossibility of every possibility, the stroke of a total passivity....'[57] The violence of death is met 'in the suffering called physical,' through which the will 'turns despairingly into total submission to the will of the Other. In suffering the will is defeated by sickness.'[58]

Thus the exceptionality of the 'impossibility' of killing the other is complicated by the fact that enmity and violence belong to the structure of this exception at a level deeper than the prohibition. I am affected by the commandment against murder only insofar as in my very will I am subject to the violence of the other as a hostile force. It remains to be seen how the exception and its essential violence continue to operate within Levinas's later account of justice.

Enigmatic violence: From suffering to justice

Totality and Infinity describes how the ethical exception operates in relation to the political. But to see how this exceptionality functions with respect to the juridical, we need to turn to the discussion of justice in *Otherwise Than Being*.

As noted, the aporia of justice cannot be reduced to the conflict between the demands of the other and the third. Levinas is unequivocal that as far as justice is concerned, the relationship with the other is prior to, and the justification for, relationships with third parties. The concerns of the third party are already immersed in the fact of proximity, which 'gives meaning to my relations with all the others.' Consequently, nothing that concerns justice, including all political and juridical institutions, 'is outside the control of the responsibility of the one for the other.'[59] This priority of the other is what resists the reduction of justice to the procedural application of rules, however comprehensive, nuanced and flexible. We might already say that the basis of law here, as of politics, is in exceptionality rather than universality. The relation with other is not only exceptional in its being outside the system of rules, but in its logical and methodological priority over that system – justifying both itself and the rules to which it is an exception.

Caygill worries about the political consequences of the priority of proximity, which 'potentially leaves intact the worst forms of state in the name of the other. It seems as permissible on Levinas's account to wage war by forgetting the self in the proximity of the other as it is to pursue the work of justice.'[60] He suspects in *Otherwise Than Being* an ineffaceable persistence of the dominance of war in *Totality and Infinity*.[61] This may be true, insofar as the logic of the exception, by which Levinas's account of peace cannot break with violence, carries over into the later work. But in *Otherwise Than Being*, the foremost concern is not political violence, the discourse of the other as an enemy, but rather the ethical violence at the heart of subjectivity, a violence essential to the passivity of the subject in the ethical relation.

This violence should be distinguished from that inherent in the fact that justice considers competing claims and incommensurable responsibilities – the 'comparison of incomparables' and all the dilemmas this entails. In the midst of opposing obligations to alterity and equity, justice must try to mitigate violence: neither imposing equality upon the other, nor ignoring the demand for equal treatment by all the others. To some degree, this violence is unavoidable, in the limit justice places upon my infinite responsibility to the other, and in my obsession with such responsibility at the expense of duties toward my fellows. But these difficulties only arise from the prior fact of a command, issuing from the other, to *reduce* violence. Reason, made possible by the third party, has for Levinas 'the virtue of arresting violence,' but only insofar as it arises from 'the order of peace,' the 'disinterestedness, passivity or patience' of responsibility for the other.[62]

Although the modalities of violence arising from the clash between ethics and law could be endlessly discussed, the relation of justice and violence must be pursued further, at the very level of proximity, if we are to find its place at the foundation and not merely the application of justice. Concerning the priority of proximity in justice, Levinas says:

> The equality of all is borne by my inequality.... The forgetting of self moves justice. It is then not without importance to know if the egalitarian and just State in which man is fulfilled... proceeds from a war of all against all, or from the irreducible responsibility of one for all....[63]

Levinas assumes that 'the egalitarian and just State' is not justified on its own merits, but must proceed from the foundation of war or asymmetrical responsibility. By putting the question in this form, he essentially asks, *from which of two violences does justice proceed?* The meaning of justice's grounding in responsibility is revealed in the claim that 'the equality of all is borne by my inequality,' and a good deal of *Otherwise Than Being* is devoted to exploring the sense of that inequality in a violently disturbed subjectivity. If there is a violence at the heart of Levinasian justice, it is that suffered by the subject for the other. Only through an account of the *exceptional* status of this suffering can Levinas portray it as more than violence – indeed, as the Good that justifies the appearance of justice.

To understand the role this violence plays relative to justice, we must consider the context of Levinas's discussion of justice. 'From Saying to the Said,' the section in which it appears, does not mention justice or the third as such until quite late, but begins with a description of ethical subjectivity, rehearsing formulations from the book's pivotal chapter, 'Substitution.' The singular identity of the subject is due to its extreme exposure to the other that accuses and persecutes it. The patience required by responsibility is that of a passivity which 'must be always at the limit, exceeded by a demented suffering, "for nothing," a suffering of pure misery.'[64] In 'Substitution,' Levinas is clear that this suffering is meant literally and corporeally. The body is the site of 'the other in the same,'[65] of my exposure to the other, 'that by which the self is susceptibility itself. Incarnation is an extreme passivity.'[66] But this violence, even as a corporeal suffering, has a deeply ethical sense. The 'persecuting hatred' of the neighbor's face prompts me to 'answer for the persecutor,' to responsibility, and thus to pass 'from suffering to expiation for the other.'[67] In the suffering of my exposure 'the Good reabsorbs, or redeems, the violence of non-freedom.' There is a redemption of violence by virtue of the trace of *illeity*, or God, in responsibility, giving the violence suffered by the subject the sense of an 'inspiration,' rather than a force, issuing from the other.[68]

In 'From Saying to the Said,' however, the goodness of this violence is not assumed, but from the outset treated as problematic, and it is only from this problematic that the problems of justice arise. After describing the extreme suffering of responsibility, Levinas says that we are confronted with 'a new dilemma': does the infinite responsibility at the heart of subjectivity 'confer upon me a new identity, that of being the unique chosen one,' elected and able to support the other? Or in this election by the Infinite is the self not rather reduced to 'an articulation in its divine economy,' 'equivalent to the entry of the subject into the play or designs of the Infinite'?[69]

The section is thus from its initial question concerned with the question of an originary violence. Does the ethical relation that will underpin justice designate a subject with obligations issuing from the Good, or simply a violence (even if this is a 'divine violence')? Rather than opting for either horn of this dilemma, Levinas challenges its very status. To see a 'dilemma or an alternative' here, he says, is already to restrict oneself to the domain of the said, of knowledge, where phenomena are treated as exclusive choices. But the meaning of ethical subjectivity is in the signification of the other's *saying* in me. At this level, there is no dilemma, but only an 'ambivalence' or an 'enigma.' The 'enigma of the Infinite' in me signifies both the uniqueness of my responsibility and a tension with the Infinite whereby I contest my subjection to it. The enigma is 'the hesitation between knowing and responsibility' in the relation of proximity by which the Infinite 'comes to pass.'[70]

The 'enigma' is thus the device by which Levinas is able to maintain an originary violence in the subject, without this violence proving fatal to Levinas's attempt to ground justice on an experience that remains ethical. For Levinas, this enigmatic quality of original ethical violence circumvents a worry like Caygill's, above, that the priority of proximity might serve to justify violence from or on behalf of the other. Such a concern arises only from the point of view of the said, whereas in saying, the priority of proximity signifies an ambivalence of violence and the good. The violence of the said is that of the dilemma, entailing sacrifice and exclusivity, but prior to this there is the violence of the enigma, which denotes a traumatic rupturing as the very condition of ethical subjectivity.

Despite establishing this fundamental difference between the 'good' violence of ethics – a violence that is always only enigmatically so – and the unambiguous violence that forms the subject matter of legal and political problems, the whole point of Levinas's discussion in 'From Saying to the Said' is to show how the violence of the enigma *becomes* a problem precisely in justice. The title of the section tips us off to the fact that the necessity of justice is not simply political or juridical, but metaphysical. The third party opens the possibilities of comparison and thematization *as such*, not only pragmatically; the 'entry of the third party is the very fact of consciousness.'[71] 'The foundation of consciousness is justice,' for justice allows for the synchronization and measuring of the said.[72] Levinas introduces justice in answer to the question of why proximity, as enigmatic, should also show itself in the said.

> If proximity ordered me to only the other alone, there would have not been any problem .... The responsibility for the other is an immediacy antecedent to questions, it is proximity. It is troubled and becomes a problem when a third party enters.[73]

The third party answers the question of how the enigma of ethical proximity – the violence of which is, on its own terms, unproblematic – *becomes* a dilemma, that is, presents a problem. The enigma as such demands justice, because proximity shows itself in the said, while still signifying 'as an enigma.'[74] Levinas must thus preserve the 'enigmatic' nature of the original ethical trauma *within* the problems of justice if it is to exceed its own violence and signify also the good. The special status of the enigma in relation to justice resembles the exception in Schmitt, which lies simultaneously inside and outside the law that it grounds. In fact, Levinas expresses the same thought by reference to the exception: what shows itself in the said is an '*ex-ception* to being, as though being's other were an event of being.' Saying 'forms an exception' with respect to cognition, 'but it is in the said that both this exception and the birth of cognition show themselves.'[75] The enigmatic nature of the ethical relation hinges on this characterization of the exception, as that which enables both itself and being to be expressed together in the said – a co-expression of the demands of the other and the third, and thus of justice.

The exception takes its essential place, then, in the passage from the discussion of ethical subjectivity to that of justice and law. If the enigma describes the ethical violence operating beneath the workings of justice, it is the enigma's 'exceptional' status that allows it to be not only prior to, but also expressed within, the language of the third to which it is an exception. By virtue of this dual function, the ethical nature of the violence underpinning law is attested to even in its interruption of the law.

As we have seen in the case of *Totality and Infinity*, the qualification of this exceptionality as 'ethical' is not enough to annul its Schmittian resonance. There, we saw the ultimate reference of the ethical relation to the exception evinced the basic hostility with which the other threatened the self. In *Otherwise Than Being*, what is most troubling is the extent to which the exception operates through what Levinas calls *illeity*. *Illeity* is Levinas's word for the remote alterity of God – at once the beyond being through which ethical responsibility takes place, but also the distant 'thirdness' of the divine, manifest only as a 'trace' rather than the immediate exposedness of the other's face. While we cannot begin to unpack this concept, one of Levinas's densest, in these pages, we can, with an understanding of this basic structure and the essential reference to divinity, see how the idea underpins the operation of justice in *Otherwise Than Being*.

The figure of the 'enigma' already invokes that of illeity – first of all because the enigma is for Levinas that of 'a God speaking in man' or of an 'extraordinary illeity,'[76] but more importantly because the persistence of the enigma in justice reveals the exceptionality of the relation with illeity: it comprises 'a betrayal of my anarchic relation with illeity, but also a new relationship with it,' in a reciprocity traced with the other's transcendence.[77] The concept of illeity is invoked because it provides the conceptual unity needed to ground justice in this exceptional fashion – signifying at once the ethical violence of subjectivity, the priority of responsibility and the necessity of the third – but only in its identification with divinity or the 'name of God.' Without this reference, the exception underlying justice risks collapsing into an unredeemed violence.

Illeity performs the work of the exception because it signifies both the irreducibility of ethical violence and the discourse of the third in which that violence reappears. Levinas describes these multiple functions of illeity in 'The Glory of the Infinite,' the section that immediately precedes 'From Saying to the Said.' Like the latter, this section begins by repeating the book's central theses on substitution, a structure that is explained by reference to the exception: the state of being hostage for another is 'in its "essence" an ex-ception to essence, or a substitution.' This exceptional nature of substitution is presented as the paradoxical character of responsibility, where the subject, in responsibility for the other, is exposed to 'the command exercised by the other in me over me,' 'prior to every decision' that could arise from my will.[78] The interdependence of the decision and the exception again recalls Schmitt, as well as Levinas's earlier attempt to locate in self's will an exceptional encounter that undoes and threatens it. *Otherwise Than Being* deepens this account by insisting on the essential heteronomy of the decision, by virtue of which the other's command over me is beyond the 'insurmountable adversity' of same and other.[79]

It is in the attempt to portray this heteronomy in terms other than violence that Levinas appeals to the concept of illeity. The 'exception to essence' by which the other 'circumscribes me and orders me by my own voice' even as I obey, is simply the manner in which the Infinite, as illeity, 'passes.'[80] In this usage, illeity is 'the coming of the order to which I am subjected before hearing it, or which I hear in my own saying.'[81] Illeity thus accounts for the enigma that constitutes 'the exception and subjectivity of the subject,' and its passing, as the 'reverting of heteronomy into autonomy,' is the condition of possibility for a subject capable of justice, the matrix of 'the inscription of the law in consciousness.'[82]

However, illeity does not simply denote the condition of justice in the exceptional status of the ethical subject, but also the very happening of justice as the advent of the third. Although one might expect that Levinas would identify illeity, as the device of the subject's ethical suffering, with the alterity of the other, in fact illeity is meant to convey the remoteness of God as opposed to the immediacy of the face. From this remoteness, Levinas extends the definition of illeity to the third party and the institution of justice:

> [the Infinite] signifies as *illeity*, in the third person. This 'thirdness' is different from that of the third man, it is the third party that interrupts the face to face of a welcome of the other man, interrupts the proximity or approach of the neighbor, it is the third man with which justice begins.[83]

Illeity makes justice possible not only by virtue of this thirdness, but because in the same movement it 'ordains me to the other' and imposes 'the presence of the third party alongside of the neighbor approached.'[84] While making possible both the subject and the symmetrical relationships required by justice, illeity carries with it the persecutory asymmetry at the heart of these. Illeity is thus identical with both the exceptional moment of the subject's traumatization prior to the law and the persistence of this exception within the law.

The most crucial role of illeity, however, consists in qualifying the violence of this exception as something beyond violence, as enigmatic. In all of the functions of illeity, the 'enigma' underlying justice is preserved only by reference to the divinity of illeity. It is through the trace of illeity that 'the reciprocal relationship binds me to the other man,' and it is only 'thanks to God' that as a unique subject I can be 'an other like the others.' The transformation of the subject into an equal among equals, a member of society capable of political and juridical relations, takes place 'in reference to God,' through an 'Infinite which enigmatically commands me.'[85] In the end, this divine reference is powerful enough in Levinas's discourse that it proves prior not only to justice, but to the enigma itself: 'Illeity,' writes Levinas, 'overflows both cognition [that is, justice] and the enigma through which the Infinite leaves a trace on cognition,' and in this overflowing 'makes the word God be pronounced.'[86] If Schmitt likens the place of the exception in law to that of the miracle in theology, Levinas does not hesitate to ascribe this exception to its divine source.

Divine violence: Infinite justification

Let us review how Levinas's discussion of justice arrives at this intractable point before considering, in conclusion, some of its implications. The impetus for seeking a Schmittian moment in Levinas's account of justice is due to the fact that, even with the arrival on the scene of the third party, the question of the law's applicability to the conflicting demands of other and third gives way to the grounding of the juridical-political sphere as such in the ethical relation. With respect to the political, the intrinsic violence of that relation is described in *Totality and Infinity*, in a way that brings Levinas close to Schmitt's descriptions of the friend–enemy distinction and the exception. Despite challenging the dominance of war as a model for politics with an account of its grounding in an eschatological and ethical peace, Levinas does so on the basis of the *exceptional* status of the other's ethical resistance. This account resembles Schmitt's not only formally – in the priority of the exception to systematic political or legal relations – but substantively, since the exceptionality of the ethical relation ultimately refers to the irreducible hostility of the other to my designs.

In *Otherwise Than Being*, there is also a priority assigned to the violence issuing from the other, not as the political figure of the enemy but as the source of the ethical subject's traumatization. The question is how this ethical violence suffered by the subject (the book's central thesis) leads to the question of justice for Levinas, and the sections 'The Glory of the Infinite' and 'From Saying to the Said,' read together, provide an answer. The concept of *illeity* is meant to signify both the exception of the subject persecuted by the other and the advent of a third party external to the ethical relation; the ensuing discussion of justice is thus not primarily concerned with the conflict between other and third, but the inseparability of the whole of justice and law from an exceptional and violent heteronomy. But the role of illeity here is also meant to allay this fundamental violence: the reference to the infinite and the divine renders the suffering of the subject enigmatic rather than problematic. Consequently, for Levinas, the violence exercised by the other can only be considered a 'problem' within the sphere of law and the said, but not at the level of the law's foundation.

Though the ultimate reference of Levinasian justice to the exception and to the divine might appear to be purely formal, there are grounds for substantive concern here. It is helpful to consider again Derrida's reading of Benjamin, which emphasizes his proximity to Schmitt, particularly in their critique of liberalism and parliamentarism as a degeneration from the law's pure and violent foundation – a perspective Derrida calls 'archeo-eschatological.'[87] If Schmitt's understanding of the basis of law in the exception seems the epitome of what Benjamin critically names 'mythical violence,' the alternative proposed by Benjamin does not escape its essential logic. Benjamin asks whether there is a 'pure immediate violence that might be able to call a halt to mythical violence,' and finds this in 'divine violence' – a violence that remains immediate, but which issues from God rather than temporal power. Divine violence is expiating, 'lethal without spilling blood,' and ultimately revolutionary.[88] For Derrida, this eschatological perspective remains too close to 'the very thing against which one must act and think, do and speak, that with which one must break.'[89]

Of course, there are crucial differences between Benjaminian 'divine violence' and the justification of ethical violence in illeity, or between an eschatology of revolution and an eschatology of peace. But with respect to the question of justice, Derrida sees Benjamin's reference to God as 'nothing other than a reference to the irreducible singularity of each situation,' to the contradiction between God and the universality of law – that is, it corresponds to the Levinas-inspired aporia with which Derrida begins his essay.[90] And the same is surely true of Levinas. If the ethical priority of singularity over universality translates into the grounding of law in the exception, we are left with the insoluble problem that the exception can, in practice, justify anything, and the characterization of the exception as divine adds to the justification without improving the practice.

The place of killing in the discourse of thinkers like Schmitt, Benjamin and Levinas is instructive here. Like Schmitt, Benjamin sees in the possibility of putting to death 'law itself in its origin.' However, he claims that 'in this very violence something rotten in the law is revealed,'[91] a phrase that for Derrida is the deconstructive heart of Benjamin's text.[92] But is the violence of the exception overcome when killing is condemned by a new exception, be it ethical or divine? Benjamin identifies divine power, opposed to mythical violence, with the commandment 'Thou shalt not kill,' and even analyzes this prohibition in the same terms used by Levinas: the 'commandment precedes the deed,' murder presupposes the divine injunction. However, Benjamin is clearer than Levinas that no universal condemnation of killing can be derived from this formal commandment, and that practically there is no stopping the exception from carrying over to the level of content:

> It exists not as a criterion of judgment, but as a guideline for the actions of persons or communities who have to wrestle with it in solitude and, in exceptional cases, to take on themselves the responsibility of ignoring it.[93]

In the case of Schmitt's personal politics and his relationship with Nazism, one knows too well what excesses the exception justified.[94] Even with Benjamin, Derrida fears that 'divine violence,' in its desire for an 'expiatory and bloodless' justice, would leave open the temptation of justifying a 'final solution.'[95] In Levinas's case, it doubtless serves to justify his notorious unwillingness to criticize the 'prophetic' political actions of Israel, not excluding concrete events like the Sabra and Shatila massacre, in reference to which he makes the claim that 'in alterity we can find an enemy.'[96] The danger here is that with respect to Levinas's theory of justice, the injustice of this strain of his personal politics does not amount to an aberration, but rather demonstrates what conclusions might be drawn from that theory's ethical grounding, for which an inner hostility and divinely legitimated violence remain basic.

Notes

1. H. Caygill, *Levinas and the Political* (London: Routledge, 2002) p. 3. Bettina Bergo made similar comments in her paper, 'A Critique of Political Utopianism,' given at the conference that spawned this volume (*Centennial Conference on Levinas and Law*, McGill University, Montreal, September 17, 2006). To my knowledge, Jacques Derrida is the first to have made the connection, which bears a highly adversarial sense for him – implicitly in *Politics of Friendship*, where he insists that the decisionism of Schmitt's theory of sovereignty cannot evade, and opens onto, a heteronomous responsibility [*Politics of Friendship*, trans. G. Collins (New York: Verso, 1997) pp. 68–69], and explicitly in *Adieu to Emmanuel Levinas*, in a passage I discuss below, where Derrida declares Schmitt and Levinas 'absolute adversaries' [*Adieu to Emmanuel Levinas*, trans. M. Naas and P. Brault (Stanford University Press, 1999) p. 147, n. 95]. I discussed some of the dynamics of a Schmitt–Levinas encounter in 'Absolute Adversity: Schmitt, Levinas, and the Exceptionality of Killing' [*Philosophy and Social Criticism* 31 (2005) 223–252], an article that was largely sympathetic to Derrida's use of Levinasian ideas to undermine the Schmittian theory of sovereignty (which for Derrida is also implicit in mainstream juridical discourse). As will be evident from the present chapter, I now understand the Schmitt–Levinas relationship to be more complicated than this, problematizing the meaning of ethics, peace and justice in Levinas no less than sovereignty and the political in Schmitt.
2. Specifically, in Section 3, entitled 'From Saying to the Said, or the Wisdom of Desire.' Some of the formulations below are also drawn from Levinas's introductory summary of the book's argument as a whole, in Chapter I.
3. E. Levinas, *Otherwise Than Being or Beyond Essence*, trans. A. Lingis, (Dordrecht: Kluwer Academic Publishers, 1991) p. 157 [hereinafter OBBE].
4. Ibid., pp. 159, 161.
5. Ibid., p. 157.
6. Ibid., p. 160.
7. Ibid., p. 161.
8. Ibid., p. 158 (my emphasis).
9. Ibid., p. 16.
10. J. Derrida, 'Force of Law: The "Mystical Foundation of Authority",' trans. M. Quaintance, in D. Cornell, M. Rosenfeld and D. G. Carlson (eds), *Deconstruction and the Possibility of Justice* (New York: Routledge, 1992) p. 22.
11. Ibid., p. 17.
12. A prime example of this tendency would be Axel Honneth's attempt to formulate Derrida's aporetic reworking of Levinas (in an early version of *Politics of Friendship*) in terms of a point-counterpoint structure of two normative principles – 'care' and 'equal treatment' – in a state of necessary and productive tension. See A. Honneth, 'The Other of Justice: Habermas and the Ethical Challenge of Postmodernism,' trans. J. Farrell, in S. K. White (ed.), *The Cambridge Companion to Habermas* (New York: Cambridge University Press, 1995) pp. 309–315. By calling these two principles 'patterns of recognition' (Ibid., p. 309), Honneth implicitly suggests that the conflicts they engender could be accommodated within his own normative social theory, firmly grounded in a Kantian understanding of ethical universality [see *The Struggle*

for Recognition: The Moral Grammar of Social Conflicts, trans. J. Anderson (Cambridge: MIT Press, 1996].
13. Ibid., p. 158.
14. Ibid., p. 159.
15. Derrida, 'Force of Law,' p. 17 (my emphasis).
16. Ibid., p. 16.
17. Ibid., p. 5.
18. W. Benjamin, 'Critique of Violence,' in *Reflections: Essays, Aphorisms, Autobiographical Writings*, trans. E. Jephcott (New York: Schocken Books, 1986) pp. 277–279.
19. Ibid., pp. 294–295.
20. Derrida, 'Force of Law,' pp. 6, 14.
21. See ibid., pp. 29–30, 46, 48, 66 note 6.
22. E. Levinas, *Totality and Infinity: An Essay on Exteriority*, trans. A. Lingis, (Pittsburgh: Duquesne University Press, 1969) pp. 213–214 [hereinafter TI].
23. Ibid., p. 89.
24. Ibid., p. 78.
25. Ibid., p. 245.
26. Ibid., p. 21.
27. Bergo, 'A Critique of Political Utopianism,' September 17, 2006.
28. C. Schmitt, *The Concept of the Political*, trans. G. Schwab (University of Chicago Press, 1996) p. 26.
29. Ibid., pp. 30–32.
30. Ibid., p. 49.
31. Ibid., p. 37.
32. Levinas, TI, p. 22.
33. Ibid., pp. 222–223.
34. Derrida, *Adieu to Emmanuel Levinas*, p. 147, n. 95.
35. Levinas, TI, p. 22.
36. Schmitt, *The Concept of the Political*, pp. 33–34.
37. Derrida, *Adieu to Emmanuel Levinas*, p. 95.
38. Ibid., pp. 115–116.
39. C. Schmitt, *Political Theology: Four Chapters on the Concept of Sovereignty*, trans. G. Schwab (Cambridge: MIT Press, 1985) p. 36.
40. Ibid., p. 12.
41. Ibid., p. 15.
42. Ibid., p. 30.
43. Ibid., p. 13.
44. Schmitt, *The Concept of the Political*, p. 35.
45. Ibid., p. 33.
46. Ibid., pp. 26–27.
47. Levinas, TI, p. 233.
48. Ibid., pp. 198–199 (my emphasis).
49. Ibid., p. 199.
50. Ibid.
51. Ibid., p. 232.
52. Ibid., p. 233.
53. Ibid., p. 236.
54. Ibid., p. 198.

55. Ibid., p. 236.
56. Ibid., pp. 233–234.
57. Ibid., p. 235.
58. Ibid., p. 238.
59. Levinas, OBBE, p. 159.
60. Caygill, pp. 142–143.
61. Ibid., p. 143.
62. Levinas, OBBE, p. 16.
63. Ibid., p. 159.
64. Ibid., p. 153.
65. Ibid., p. 109.
66. Ibid., p. 195 note 12.
67. Ibid., p. 111.
68. Ibid., p. 123.
69. Ibid., p. 153.
70. Ibid., pp. 155–156.
71. Ibid., p. 158.
72. Ibid., p. 160.
73. Ibid., p. 157.
74. Ibid.
75. Ibid., p. 6.
76. Ibid., p. 154.
77. Ibid., p. 158.
78. Ibid., p. 141.
79. Ibid.
80. Ibid., p. 147.
81. Ibid., p. 150.
82. Ibid., p. 148.
83. Ibid., p. 150.
84. Ibid., p. 16.
85. Ibid., pp. 158, 161.
86. Ibid., p. 162.
87. Derrida, 'Force of Law,' pp. 46, 62.
88. Benjamin, 'Critique of Violence,' pp. 297, 300.
89. Derrida, 'Force of Law,' p. 62.
90. Ibid., p. 51.
91. Benjamin, 'Critique of Violence,' p. 286.
92. Derrida, 'Force of Law,' p. 39.
93. Benjamin, 'Critique of Violence,' p. 298.
94. If we consider the entire trajectory of his philosophy dispassionately, we must at least consider the possibility, however hazardous, that Levinas does not entirely escape this association either. The structural precedence of corporeal suffering and death to ethics has a long prehistory in Levinas's thought to which the Levinas–Schmitt proximity inevitably leads us. But if this proximity lies beyond, or rather before, the horizon of Levinas's ethical thought (Levinas does not mention ethics until 1951), it likewise exceeds the attempted formalism of Schmitt's project. I have in mind Giorgio Agamben's view that Schmitt's theory of sovereignty provides a key to understanding not only the specific politics of National Socialism, but

the foundation of Western politics as such in 'biopower.' What Agamben (following Benjamin) calls 'bare life,' the body of the citizen politicized by the sovereign, is 'included in politics in the form of the exception' [*Homo Sacer: Sovereign Power and Bare Life*, trans. D. Heller-Roazen (Stanford University Press, 1998) p. 11]; 'human life is included in the juridical order solely in the form of its exclusion (i.e., of its capacity to be killed):' ibid., p. 8. Agamben approvingly cites Levinas's 1934 article, 'Reflections on the Philosophy of Hitlerism,' as a way of understanding the relation to 'bare life' in both Nazism and, implicitly, Heidegger's philosophy. In this article, Levinas describes the philosophy of Hitlerism as a sort of bio-ontology. Its basic premise is that the subject experiences itself as an enchainment to the body at 'the very base of its being.' With this new understanding of human being, says Levinas, comes a 'new ideal of truth,' that of violence: the universality presupposed by liberalism 'must give way to the idea' of 'the expansion of force,' which 'brings with it its own form of universalization: war and conquest' [see 'Some Thoughts on the Philosophy of Hitlerism' in *Unforeseen History*, trans. N. Poller (Urbana: University of Illinois Press, 2004) pp. 17–21]. For Agamben, this 'facticity of the body' can be read as 'a radicalization without precedent of the state of exception.... It is as if... bare life..., whose exclusion founded sovereign power, now became – in assuming itself as a task – explicitly and immediately political': Agamben, p. 153.

If Levinas's early description of corporeal facticity in Hitlerism can be seen as a radicalization of the state of exception, this raises for me the pressing question: what is the connection in Levinas's philosophy between this early ontology of the body and the figure of the other as enemy and death in *Totality and Infinity*, or as the corporeal suffering of subjectivity obsessed with the other in *Otherwise Than Being*, in both cases crucial descriptions of the exceptional nature of the Levinasian ethical?

'Reflections on the Philosophy of Hitlerism' is, to be sure, a warning of the threats entailed by the corporeal ontology it describes, but what is most striking in the essay is that it does not explicitly challenge this ontology, which has more in common with Levinas's own enthusiasms in the period 1929–1933 than with anything imagined by Nazi ideologues. Levinas's philosophical position at this moment in far from unambiguous. Despite a clear antipathy toward the ontology he describes, evident in its association with racism, the valorization of the 'community of blood,' the spread of 'war and conquest,' Levinas also gives this worldview a certain dignity, and he will later regret it, by calling it a 'philosophy.' This philosophy of corporeal enchainment exceeds 'racist particularism' and amounts to a new conception of the 'humanity of man,' challenging at the deepest level the freedom presupposed by Western liberalism, which degenerates into 'deceit' and a 'lack of conviction' (Levinas, *Unforeseen History*, pp. 19–21). There is in this essay, as in Levinas's earliest work on Heidegger, a sense of the inevitability of this philosophy in the face of the relatively weak position of liberalism.

It would be easy enough to discount 'Reflections on the Philosophy of Hitlerism' as a curiosity of Levinas's pre-ethical period, but its implications for our understanding of the genesis of his later thought are profound. The connections between the philosophy described in 1934 and the ontology Levinas develops beginning with *On Escape* in 1935 are well documented, and provide the key to understanding how his early conception of being and corporeality (and arguably, politics) carry forward into his mature ethical thought. To sketch this trajectory briefly: *On Escape*, with its thesis of 'being riveted' to being (again experienced through bodily suffering in the form of nausea) and need to escape it, sets the itinerary Levinas pursues in his immediate post-war works, *From Existence to the Existent* and *Time and the Other*. These works, particularly *Time and the Other*, can be read as a culmination of Levinas's early ontology, while also introducing the other – but by reference to suffering and death and not yet ethics. Corporeal suffering is experienced as the 'irremissibility of being' that holds the subject fast, but also the 'proximity of death' through which I encounter alterity as a threat to my power. Thus, Levinas writes, 'only a being whose solitude has reached a crispation through suffering, and in relation with death takes its place on a ground where the relationship with the other becomes possible' [see *Time and the Other*, trans. R. A. Cohen (Pittsburgh: Duquesne University Press, 1990) pp. 69–76]. This thesis of a subjectivity threatened by hostility and physical pain as the basis for a relation of transcendence is repeated in *Totality and Infinity*, where we have seen it take its place in establishing the exceptional character of the ethical relation.

95. Derrida, 'Force of Law,' pp. 62, 63–65 note 6.
96. E. Levinas, 'Ethics and Politics,' interview with S. Malka and A. Finkielkraut, trans. J. Romney, in S. Hand (ed.), *The Levinas Reader* (Oxford: Blackwell, 1989) p. 294.

13
Rethinking Justice with Levinas

Sarah E. Roberts-Cady

Introduction

Emmanuel Levinas argues that justice is meaningful only to the extent that other persons are encountered in their individuality, as neighbors, and not merely abstract citizens of a political community. Further, he claims that equality before the law only emerges from this unequal, asymmetrical moral responsibility for others. Levinas writes, 'The equality of all is borne by my inequality, the surplus of my duties over my rights. The forgetting of self moves justice.'[1] Thus Levinas writes that the call to justice is a call to think the abstraction of law together with the uniqueness of every face, the call to think the equality of every citizen together with their inequality. The following is an exploration of Levinas's views on justice. I will contend that, despite his revolutionary ideas about the origins of justice, Levinas ultimately appeals to a very traditional view of justice in which persons are considered equal and comparable, and responsibilities and rights are distributed evenly among them. In response to Levinas, I will argue that insofar as justice is constructed by and for the ethical relationship, it must also be deconstructed by that relationship. If one takes seriously Levinas's claim that asymmetrical ethical responsibility is the origin of justice, then one must also reject Levinas's suggestion that justice requires viewing persons and responsibilities as comparable and symmetrical.

The self as asymmetrical responsibility

Levinas argues that my subjectivity can never be understood as an ontological package which is sufficient in itself because who I am is always affected by that which is outside me. I am affected despite myself (without having asked for it, having earned it, or having the ability to decline it).[2] Respiration, or breathing, is an apt metaphor which Levinas uses to explain this. My very first breath of life is an exposure to the outside. The very air I breathe is other than me, an otherness on which I sustain myself.[3] Of course it is not just the air on which I depend. I develop in response to my parent's genes, my mother's womb, and every person I encounter from the moment of birth. Subjectivity is a kind of response to otherness; I find myself involved with others in the very moment of finding myself.

For this reason, Levinas claims that the answer to the question, 'Who am I?' is not ontological, but ethical. What makes me the unique person I am? It is not an unchanging essence or any other ontological or epistemological trait. He argues that the self is best understood as a kind of responsibility to and for the other – a radically unique task. In that sense, the self is not a noun in the nominative form, but rather the accusative. It is not the case that I am first a self, who *afterwards* takes on responsibilities; instead my unique selfhood enters the picture in the first place when I am accused, called, blamed, and held responsible by the other. Levinas writes, 'An identity individuates itself as unique, without recourse to any system of references in the impossibility of evading the assignation of others without blame.'[4]

Not only does my uniqueness arise through my responsibility, but also I am called to responsibility as a unique individual. While philosophers theorize about the responsibilities we have as abstract citizens and members of the human species, any one of them will admit that no abstract citizen ever took responsibility for anything. It is only as the real, unique person that I am that I have ethical responsibilities or take responsibility for others. Nevertheless, there is a tradition in Western philosophy to explain or justify my responsibilities as a unique individual in terms of qualities that I have in common with others – my reason or my humanity are popular candidates. Levinas is arguing that my responsibilities to others arise and are justified before and without this kind of theorizing about our common attributes. I have a responsibility to drive my neighbor to her chemotherapy appointment because she asked me to do it and she needs me to do it, not because I theorize that we have some essential traits in common. The face of the other issues the ethical commands to me directly, as a unique individual. Any theorizing comes afterward.

In this respect, Levinas argues that he is challenging Soren Kierkegaard's distinction between the ethical and the religious.[5]

Kierkegaard had argued that the ethical sphere is the sphere of the universal. The moral action is the rational action – the one that can be understood and approved by all other rational beings. But the religious sphere is different. In faith, Kierkegaard argues, one is totally alone – one cannot be understood by others or aided by others, because one acts beyond and against reason. The call of God is addressed to the unique individual and the individual alone can respond. Levinas argues that Kierkegaard was mistaken to confine this singular subjectivity to the realm of the religious. He argues that ethical responsibility also addresses me as singular and irreplaceable. Levinas writes,

> The ethical means the general, for Kierkegaard. The singularity of the I would be lost, in his view, under a rule valid for all. Generality can neither contain nor express the secret of the self. However, it is not at all certain that the ethical is to be found where he looks for it. *Ethics as the consciousness of a responsibility towards the other... does not lose one in the generality, far from it, it singularizes, it posits one as a unique individual, as a Self*... In evoking Abraham he describes the meeting with God as occurring where subjectivity is raised to the level of the religious that is to say above ethics. But one can posit the contrary: the attention Abraham pays to the voice that brings him back to the ethical order by forbidding him to carry out the sacrifice is the most intense moment of the drama... It is there, in the ethical, that there is an appeal to the uniqueness of the subject and sense is given to life in defiance to death.[6]

In responsibility, I am unique and incomparable. Levinas writes, 'The self in a being is exactly the not-being-able-to-slip-away-from an assignation that does not aim at any generality. There is no ipseity in common to me and the others; "me" is the exclusion from this possibility of comparison, as soon as comparison is set up.'[7]

Further, Levinas argues that the one who calls me to respond is also a radically unique other. Responding to the other is not responding to an instance of humanity, but to the other who eludes categorization.[8] The other is never fully encompassed by the familiar and limited terms of human discourse. The other surpasses me, in that she is always more than I can understand. On the one hand, Levinas is merely pointing out the widely accepted fact that individuals are unique and immensely complex, and thus never completely comprehensible. On the other hand, Levinas is making a point that moral philosophers (with the exception of some recent feminist thinkers) have not discussed enough: responding appropriately to the other requires acknowledging her uniqueness and complexity. If I assume that I already understand who she is and what she needs, I am likely to represent her and her needs in terms of my own biases. As a result, I will fail to respond to her adequately.

Again, this is a challenge to Kierkegaard's distinctions. Kierkegaard writes that the relationship with God is different from our relationship with people because it is a relationship with that which is completely other. He claims God is radically transcendent. God is not just other than me, but completely outside the metaphysical categories through which I make sense of the world – paradox, transcendence. Levinas argues that the otherness attributed to God is paradigmatic of the otherness of all others. *Tout autre est tout autre.* Every other is every bit other.

Levinas holds that my unique responsibility to this unique other is asymmetrical in at least two different ways. First, Levinas claims that moral responsibility is asymmetrical in the sense that I am held responsible before I earn that responsibility. It is a 'debt prior to any loan.'[9] It is a responsibility which does not arise from any tacit or literal commitment I made, any action I took, or any rational, autonomous, or emotional quality that I have. Indeed, for Levinas, responsibility could not possibly arise from something in me; he argues that the self first arises in that responsibility. Thus, rather than having its source in me, this responsibility draws its authority solely from the face of the other before me, experienced as a demand or a call for help. I am responsible, not because of who I am or what I owe, but simply because the other needs something, forbids something, or calls me to respond. Levinas argues that I need neither an ontological nor a deontological theory to tell me that I should not kill – that demand is issued directly from the face of the other before me.

Second, Levinas argues that responsibility is asymmetrical in the sense that my responsibility is not dependent on and cannot be compared to, other people's reciprocal responsibilities. This claim follows directly from his argument that responsibility is not derived from universal principles, but rather from the concrete demands of the unique person who faces me. If there were one set of universal ethical principles which applied to everyone equally, then there would be comparable and reciprocal responsibilities. But when ethical requirements come from the face-to-face encounter with the other, responsibilities must be conceived differently. The face of the other issues the demand to me, not as an instance of some general category of rational beings, but simply as a radically unique, irreplaceable person. Because of this, I can only talk about what is ethically demanded of me. Thus, for Levinas, ethics is not about what you owe me, but only about what I owe. It is an 'order that one cannot preach.'[10]

This asymmetry is even more radical than it first appears insofar as that which is demanded of me is infinitely large. Levinas contends that the asymmetry of my responsibility for the other is so extreme that I, as a unique individual, bear the responsibility for every other. 'The word *I* means *here I am*, answering for everything and everyone.'[11] In my exposure to the other, I have no choice but to be concerned with, to be involved in, to take on as my affairs the affairs of the others. It is impossible for me to be concerned only with myself.[12] Every face I encounter is making demands on me. All their faces have ethical authority over me. Further, I am responsible for the whole world in the sense that I must respond to and before and for them all. Thus, the asymmetry is unfathomably large. I am 'under the weight of the universe, responsible for everything.'[13]

Justice and the third person

At this point, the reader may begin to get uncomfortable, or likely even skeptical. Isn't this view of our ethical responsibilities excessive? How could I respond to the demands of so many others? If I cannot respond to everyone, how do I choose between this other and that one? What is more, certainly not everything that other people demand of me is ethically acceptable. How do I distinguish the morally acceptable from the unacceptable demands? Further, it seems likely that people will make ethical demands of me which conflict with each other. How can I respond to them all? In addition, if ethics only concerns my responsibilities and I am responsible for the whole world, then am I not leaving myself open to exploitation and oppression? How does Levinas account for my right to protect myself and meet my own needs? Finally, isn't there an ethical requirement that I think about the responsibilities of other people to each other? Do I have no recourse for arguing that the others should not rape, harm, oppress, or kill each other? How can anyone's (mine or other's) rights be protected on this view? How can fairness be achieved? What about justice?

Levinas agrees that there is a vulnerability involved in the asymmetries of the ethical situation. Indeed, he argues that it is because of these vulnerabilities that the asymmetrical relationship with the other must be 'interrupted' by justice, in the form of law, equality, and reciprocity, the balancing of demands and symmetrical responsibility. He argues that justice arises when a 'third person' comes into the ethical scene. The third person, who was actually always already there, disrupts the relationship between myself and the other, and demands that responsibilities be thought in a new way.

How does my radically unique and asymmetrical ethical responsibility relate to this universal, symmetrical concept of justice through the entrance of a third party? I see at least four possible interpretations of what Levinas means when he writes that justice arrives with the entrance of a third party. One possible interpretation is that the need for justice arises when I find that I must divide my attention and responsibilities between multiple others. In my lifetime I am faced, not just with one other person, but with countless people whose needs are so vast and diverse that it seems that I could not possibly take responsibility for them all. Levinas might be arguing that the third party is 'one too many' and justice would involve the calculating, dividing, and rationing of my responsibilities between all the faces making demands on me. John Caputo seems to accept this interpretation when he argues, 'Justice for Levinas intervenes in order to limit, to calculate – by dividing and multiplying – my obligation among the entire community. Justice for Levinas is a way of stopping me from spending everything on one account.'[14]

This interpretation is not entirely satisfactory. First, it suggests that justice involves placing a limit on my responsibilities to the unique person before me, so that I can have something left to give to the others. Yet Levinas makes it clear that my responsibility to the singular other is not diminished by considerations of justice. He writes, 'In no way is justice a degradation of obsession, a degeneration of the for-the-other, a diminution, a limitation of anarchic responsibility...'[15]. As such, it seems unlikely that Levinas was arguing that justice involves placing a limit on my responsibilities to the others or rationing my efforts.

Second, this interpretation isn't satisfactory because, although it gets us to part of what Levinas sees as justice – the need for calculation, measure, and so on – it demonstrates no need for anything like reciprocity. In order for there to be justice, Levinas writes that there must be some reciprocal responsibilities of the other for me. I must also be an 'other.' He writes:

> Justice can be established only if I, always evaded from the concept of the ego, always desituated and divested of being, always in a non-reciprocal relationship with the other, always for the other, can become an other like the others.[16]

The first interpretation of the role of the 'third person' does not adequately explain the need for justice as reciprocity. My having to divide up my attention between many different people does not require that anyone else have any reciprocal responsibilities for me.

A second, more plausible interpretation is that justice is the tool through which I take full responsibility for all the others. In this case, the third are all the innumerable others whom, though I cannot help them face to face, I can protect by means of laws, institutions, and social organizations. I may not be able to personally put food in every mouth, but I can fight for a social system which will create a set of duties, rights, and opportunities that will best provide for others' needs. Perhaps this is what Levinas meant when he wrote that in taking responsibility for the others, I must take responsibility for all the others' responsibilities. In order to protect the others, I must fight for policies and laws that establish and enforce their responsibilities to each other. This interpretation is more satisfactory because it both accounts for my total responsibility for every other, and introduces laws and systems through which other people are given reciprocal responsibilities.

A third possible interpretation (which is compatible with the second) is that the entry of the third party brings recognition that my neighbor also has a neighbor. That is, I note that the others who hold me responsible also stand in relation to each other, and likewise hold each other responsible. This seems to be what Levinas means when he writes,

> The third party is other than neighbor, but also another neighbor, and also a neighbor of the other, and not simply his fellow. What then are the other and the third party for one another? The other stands in a relationship with the third party, for whom I cannot entirely answer, even if I alone answer, before any question, for my neighbor.[17]

In my concern for the other, I realize I need to be concerned about how the others treat each other. My taking responsibility for one other person requires my thinking about the responsibilities of all the others who surround her: How can I protect the person before me from the others? How do the others help me care for her? What sorts of laws or institutions would best protect this other from those others, and enforce their responsibilities to each other? In taking responsibility, I become conscious that it is not just me who has a responsibility for others. I see that the others are also called to respond and to confront each other.

The radical uniqueness of my responsibility is generalized and compared to the responsibilities of others. Indeed, I compare the incomparable. In doing so, I begin to see how others' responsibilities include a responsibility to me. As a consequence, I gain a notion of something like reciprocal and universal responsibilities.

A fourth plausible interpretation (which is compatible with the second and third) is that the third person functions as a witness to my responsibility. By witnessing my relationship to the other, the third party transforms my radically unique relationship to the other into something repeatable. That is, my unique situation can be articulated in a shared language, repeated to others, and then generalized to include others. One can begin to talk about 'human rights' and 'universal moral duties.' In Levinas's own terms, it transforms the 'saying' into a 'said.' This seems to be what Levinas means when he writes,

> It will turn out to be possible to understand the manifestation of being on the basis of justice, to which is led a saying which is not only addressed to the other, but is addressed to the other in the presence of a third party. Justice is this very presence of the third party and this manifestation, for which every secret, every intimacy is a dissimulation.[18]

All of these interpretations provide an interesting picture of how my unique responsibility to my neighbor can lead me to a conception of universal and reciprocal responsibilities. But this discussion also raises an apparent problem for Levinas. A careful look at Levinas's description of justice reveals that he includes in justice almost everything he rejected in his description of asymmetrical responsibility. Levinas describes justice in a very conventional way. First, in contrast to the radical asymmetry of ethical responsibility, Levinas argues that justice involves symmetry. Persons must be considered equal, and responsibilities should be distributed evenly among them. I become an other like the others. My responsibilities and rights become symmetrical with yours. 'In justice the dissymmetry that holds me at odds with regard to the other will find again law, autonomy, equality.'[19]

Second, Levinas argues that in order to achieve this symmetry, one thinks about persons as ontological packages, and responsibilities as a function of universal laws. We become equal because we are presented and represented as equal before the law. Justice arrives, at least in part, in the form of systems – philosophical theories, political machinery, courts, and laws. Responsibilities are defined and dictated by those systems.

Thus, he writes, 'in comparison of the incomparable there would be the latent birth of representation, logos, consciousness, work, the neutral notion of *being*.'[20]

How can Levinas reconcile these claims about justice with his claims about asymmetrical responsibility? How can one treat persons as equal and symmetrically situated before the law, without neglecting (or even suppressing) the absolute uniqueness and alterity of the face before me? What is the relationship between the symmetry of legality and the asymmetry of ethics?

In part, answering these questions involves sorting out what Levinas means by 'comparing the incomparable.' It either involves doing that which is completely impossible (and thus it is paradoxical), or it involves a comparison which fails to fully capture that which it compares. Levinas seems to intend the latter. Talking about people and responsibilities in terms of universal categories will always fail to accurately represent who one is and what one's responsibilities are. Indeed, Levinas argues that any way of representing selfhood and responsibilities cannot capture them, insofar as they are always more than what can be presented. But he argues that one can and will adopt systems by which one, however inadequately, represents, compares, and classifies. In Levinasian terms, the saying always solidifies into a said, while at the same time overflowing the content of the said. What's more, he argues that this movement from the saying to the said, from the incomparable to the comparable, from the radically singular to the universal, is something which *ought* to occur. Levinas seems to think that it is necessary to adopt this 'inadequate' vocabulary for real, ethical, and political reasons – in order to accomplish justice in the world. That is, in order to achieve justice, one must conceive of people as comparable 'members' of a human race, who all have a similar set of human rights and moral duties.

But there is a second part to this story, which is perhaps even more important. Although Levinas seems to believe that justice necessarily involves some universal principles or laws which provide symmetry and reciprocity, he argues that the authority of justice is not derived from those universal principles. Instead, the authority of justice is derived from the face of the other before me. The face of the suffering other does not reach me as an instance of a general or universal category. The face of the other only reaches me as an alterity which can never be sameness. It is this unique alterity, rather than some universal principles, which demands justice. My relationship with the other in proximity gives meaning to my relationship to all others as citizens or abstract members of a moral community. The homeless child I pass on the street, the woman down the hall who has no health insurance, the photographs of the prisoners at Abu Ghraib; each call us to create systems and laws by which we can attempt to address the responsibilities of the 'third party,' of each member of the community, in order to achieve something like fairness and the protection of basic rights. Thus, justice doesn't eliminate my personal asymmetrical responsibility, but is motivated by it and draws its authority from it.

Because the call of the other is the source of the authority of justice, it is also the standpoint from which any theory of justice must be critiqued. As noted earlier, Levinas argues that the otherness of the human other is never fully encompassed in that which is present, and its radical alterity can never be encompassed fully by the familiar and limited terms of human discourse. Insofar as the other does not fit into human logos, he or she exposes the limitations of the logos. Every face I encounter is a face which disrupts my theory, which forces me to rethink my assumptions, which renews my passion for finding a better way of conceiving and accomplishing justice. For this reason, Levinas would be skeptical of any theory of justice that made claims to completeness. Any theory or system of justice would always be subject to critique and revision from the perspective of the face-to-face encounter. Perhaps it is with this in mind that Levinas once said, 'justice is always a justice which desires for a better justice.'[21]

In sum, Levinas argues that there is a sense in which one must fight for the equality, reciprocity, and symmetry of justice, while at the same time critiquing it from the standpoint of the call of the other. He writes that justice requires 'political simultaneousness.'[22] It requires thinking the universal together with the unique and unsubsumable particular, creating systems while critiquing systems, fighting for symmetry only because of the asymmetry of my responsibilities.

Rethinking justice

In this spirit, I want to use Levinas's ideas to critique Levinas's ideas. Levinas rightly pointed out that the fight for justice is inspired and challenged by the face of each unique person who stands before me. But I will argue for a stronger claim. If one takes seriously the assertion that the call of the unique other is the beginning of justice, then it may be that justice itself should no longer be thought, even critically, in terms of symmetry and comparability. Perhaps justice is best accomplished by maintaining a recognition of the uniqueness of individuals and the asymmetry of responsibilities. One way to approach this is to argue, with thinkers such as Iris Marion Young, Drucilla Cornell, Patricia J. Huntington, and Martin J. Beck Matustik, that justice requires a kind of 'asymmetrical reciprocity.' While it is important that justice include some notion of reciprocity and mutual respect, they argue that it is essential that this reciprocity be accompanied by recognition of difference. Every other must maintain her status as 'wholly other.' I will explore this viewpoint through Iris Marion Young's critique of Seyla Benhabib's book *Situating the Self*.

Benhabib argues that equal respect for others can arise from imaginatively putting oneself in the place of others. One is better able to understand and address the needs and interests of everyone equally through imaginatively considering how a situation looks from another person's point of view.[23] Young argues, to the contrary, that adopting the standpoint of others is impossible, and that attempting to do so is politically dangerous. Instead she suggests that the moral ideal ought to be asymmetrical reciprocity – a mutual respect between people which takes into account unbridgeable differences between them.[24]

Young argues that it is impossible to adopt the viewpoint of others for two reasons. First, it is impossible because each person has her own history, which transcends what could be communicated. In that sense, reciprocal respect will always inevitably be accompanied by certain asymmetries in our historical perspective. Second, Young claims that one could not adopt another person's perspective because one's perspective is partly constituted by other people's perspective on oneself.[25] She argues that who I am is in part a product of who others are, and how others see me as other. Suspending this viewpoint, which is constituted by one's position in relation to multiple others, in order to take on the viewpoint of others, which is constituted by their position in relation to multiple others, is impossible. I can attain reciprocity in the sense that I know that I am other for you in the same way that you are other for me, but there will always be certain asymmetries in our positions in that relation.[26]

Attempting to understand the perspective of other persons by imagining oneself 'in their shoes' fosters a tendency to overlook the differences between one's own perspective and that of others. Young argues that this can become politically suspect when the differences in perspective which are overlooked include differences of privilege and power. Young writes, 'When privileged people put themselves in the position of those who are less privileged, the assumptions derived from their privilege often allow them unknowingly to misrepresent the other's situation.'[27] The other's 'viewpoint' is represented in terms of one's own stereotypes, biases, and ideologies. As a result, existing privileges, prejudices, and forms of oppression are reinforced beneath a veneer of complacent assumptions.

Young argues that moral judgments are better made on the basis of *asymmetrical reciprocity*. She argues that moral respect requires *reciprocity* in the sense of a mutual recognition of communicating parties. However, she argues that mutual recognition must be *asymmetrical* in the sense that it involves recognition of the irreducible character of the other's perspective. There must be acknowledgement that the other's perspective will always transcend one's own – that the other will always remain other.

Young offers a helpful example to illustrate the way in which justice requires recognition of asymmetry:

> When Anita Hill claimed she had been sexually harassed by Clarence Thomas, many men, including several senators questioning her, did not believe her. How could she have experienced the violations and indignities she claims, and not have filed any complaint at the time, continued to work with the perpetrator and even to go with him to another position? Men who put themselves in Hill's alleged position knew that they would never have remained silent and compliant. But many women told these men that they just did not 'get it,' that their sexual privilege prevents them from understanding the reasoning and motives of an ambitious career woman being sexually harassed by her boss.
>
> Many white feminists claimed that they did 'get it,' and claimed Anita Hill as a martyr for feminism. They were baffled when some African-American women denied the ability of white feminists to take Hill's standpoint; at least on issues of sexual harassment, many white feminists thought, women's interests and experiences are symmetrical. But even many African-American women who believed Hill were nevertheless sympathetic to Thomas's claim that he was being subject to a 'high-tech lynching.' For them, unlike for many white feminists, the case did not concern sexual harassment 'pure and simple,' but a complex racial drama in which once again white society was acting out its fears and power struggles through the body of a black man.

> There are certainly dynamics of sexual privilege between African-American men and women, but when these come before a white public, they are so intertwined with the dynamics of racism that other women simply cannot take the perspective of African-American women.[28]

The Anita Hill case illustrates that even (and perhaps especially) at the level of social and political policy, assuming that persons are symmetrically situated can result in injustice. Anita Hill may not react to sexual harassment the same way as certain men, professional white women, working class African-American women, or even other professional African-American women. Likewise, different members of the public may react differently to allegations of sexual harassment by a black man than they would react to similar allegations directed at a white man, a white woman, or a black woman. Overlooking these difference, especially when they include differences of privilege and power, may result in a failure to protect people's rights, or in a reinforcement of oppression. In this particular case, one risks failing to prosecute a man guilty of sexual harassment, or condoning racially biased hearings.

Although she did not intend it as such, Young's discussion of asymmetrical reciprocity can be read as an important critique of Levinas's views on justice. He argues that achieving social justice sometimes requires thinking about persons in terms of general categories by which we can compare and classify them. At first glance, this comparison seems constructive. It involves looking for commonalities by which we can understand each other, communicate, and create laws which apply to each member of a community. But Levinas himself admits that any such comparison is bound to fail; radically unique individuals cannot be boxed into tidy categories of comparison. What Young points out is that attempting to understand other persons in terms of these 'universal' categories of comparison will translate into understanding you on my terms, or on the terms accepted by some dominant social group. In other words, any 'comparing of incomparables' will involve understanding others based on biases created by one's own limited perspective, experiences, and culture. While there certainly are identifiable similarities between persons, viewing those similarities as symmetries is a mistake. It fosters the tendency to overlook the fact that any similarity will be accompanied by difference. The failure to recognize these differences at the political level can result in injustice. For that reason, it is dangerous to use the vocabulary of symmetry or comparability in conjunction with justice. Any 'comparing incomparables' will more likely lead to injustice than justice.

Of course, this isn't an argument for abandoning the concept of justice. We can and should enact laws and policies that are driven by a respect for every person. This is an argument for rethinking justice. Justice requires recognition of the asymmetry of persons; it requires recognition of the unique position and viewpoint of any person in a community. Fighting for justice in the case of Clarence Thomas and Anita Hill means seeing them as unique individuals, and hearing their case as such.

Recognition of the asymmetry of persons also entails asymmetry of responsibility. While I am inclined to grant that we all have an *equal* obligation *not* to sexually harass people, I do not think that obligation is symmetrical in a meaningful way. First, people encounter different situations and are in different positions of power within those situations. For some people, the opportunity and temptation to use sexual harassment to exert power will not arise. Further, fulfilling the obligation *not* to sexually harass persons requires sensitivity to differences between people and situations. One of the key elements of most proposed definitions of sexual harassment is that it involves 'unwelcome' sexual attention. Defining sexual harassment in terms of the victim's mental state makes it clear that avoiding sexual harassment requires being attentive to the response of the unique person with whom one is interacting. Thus, even this apparently symmetrical negative responsibility will be different with different people in different situations. In fact, it will be a perfect example of Levinas's conception of responsibility as a response to the face of the other.

Further, achieving justice requires more than negative responsibilities. Social justice has only ever been achieved by individuals who fight for positive change, taking on more than their fair share of responsibility. Achieving justice for women in part requires fighting for a world in which women won't have to face sexual harassment. But the causes of sexual harassment can be traced back (at least in part) to a complicated history of gender socialization. No single person is responsible for creating this sex/gender system. Yet individuals have to take responsibility for it in order to change it and achieve justice for women. Turning back to Levinas again, this is a perfect example of the asymmetry of a responsibility that is not earned. I am not responsible for overcoming the injustice of sexism because of who I am or what I have done; I am responsible because victims of sexism are calling for change, and because of my singular capacity to do something about it.

Parting words

Following Young, I have argued that viewing people as symmetrical and comparable obscures important differences, and may even create injustices. I have argued that justice is best achieved by recognizing people as unique and responsibilities as asymmetrical. But can one create laws and policies that avoid categorizing or comparing people and responsibilities? Wouldn't it be more reasonable to conclude that people tend to overemphasize the usefulness of categorization and comparison and be insufficiently attentive to their dangers? Wouldn't it be more reasonable to conclude, with Levinas, that justice requires thinking the universal categories together with the unique and incomparable? It is probably true that laws cannot avoid generality. But I don't think this generality must involve assuming people are symmetrically situated. Let me close with one more example, suggesting how one may achieve generality without symmetry, and therefore how one may understand justice in the spirit and novelty of Levinasian ethics. Among advocates for persons with disabilities, there is much discussion of 'universal design' in teaching. This conception of universality is interesting because it is not about similarities; it's about respecting everyone by responding to differences. It entails adopting teaching techniques which will work for students with a wide variety of learning styles and disabilities. In other words, it is all about respecting everyone by recognizing and responding to the uniqueness of every student. How might that serve as a model for our conception of justice? How might we reconceive the generality of law and policy in a way that is truly – and ethically – responsive to difference? This chapter only provides hints at the answer, but perhaps those hints can serve as a challenge to pursue the question further.

Notes

1. E. Levinas, *Otherwise Than Being or Beyond Essence* (Boston: Kluwer Academic Publishers, 1997) p. 159 [hereinafter OBBE].
2. Ibid., p. 55.
3. Ibid., pp. 115, 107.
4. Ibid., p. 112.
5. Levinas may have been too hasty in his criticism of Kierkegaard. Kierkegaard himself suggested that the religious sphere would transform the ethical sphere. Indeed, Levinas's project may just be an extension of Kierkegaard's project in this way. In *Fear and Trembling*, Kierkegaard's pseudonym, Johannes de Silentio writes, 'The paradox [of faith] may also be expressed in this way: that there is an absolute duty to God, for in this relationship of duty the individual relates himself as the single individual absolutely to

the absolute. In this connection, to say that it is a duty to love God means something different from the above, for if this duty is absolute, then the ethics is reduced to the relative. From this it does not follow that the ethical should be invalidated; rather, the ethical receives a completely different expression, a paradoxical expression, such as, for example, that love to God may bring the knight of faith to give his love to the neighbor – an expression opposite to that which, ethically speaking, is duty: *Fear and Trembling (with Repetition)*, trans. H. V. Hong and E. V. Hong (Princeton: Princeton University Press, 1985) p. 70.

6. E. Levinas, *Proper Names*, trans. M. B. Smith (Stanford: Stanford University Press, 1996) pp. 76–77, my italics.
7. Levinas, OBBE, p. 127.
8. As such, people have argued, there is no reason to assume that it is a human face. Perhaps animals or plants also have faces, calling us to respond and to responsibility.
9. Ibid., p. 111.
10. E. Levinas, 'The Paradox of Morality: An Interview with Emmanuel Levinas Conducted by T. Wright, P. Hughes, and A. Ainley' in R. Bernasconi and D. Wood (eds), *The Provocation of Levinas: Rethinking the Other* (New York, London: Routledge and Kegan Paul, 1988) p. 175.
11. Levinas, OBBE, p. 114.
12. Ibid., p. 114.
13. Ibid., p. 116.
14. J. D. Caputo, *The Prayers and Tears of Derrida: Religion without Religion* (Bloomington: Indiana University Press, 1997).
15. Levinas, OBBE, p. 159.
16. Ibid., pp. 160–161.
17. Ibid., p. 157.
18. Ibid., p. 191 n2.
19. Ibid., p. 127.
20. Ibid., p. 158.
21. Levinas, 'The Paradox of Morality: An Interview with Emmanuel Levinas Conducted by T. Wright, P. Hughes, and A. Ainley,' p. 177.
22. Levinas, OBBE, p. 161.
23. S. Benhabib, *Situating the Self* (New York: Routledge, 1991).
24. I. M. Young, 'Asymmetrical Reciprocity: On Moral Respect, Wonder, and Enlarged Thought,' *Constellations: An International Journal of Critical and Democratic Theory* 3/3 (1997) 340–363.
25. Levinas would, of course, state this differently than Young. For him, my selfhood is wholly constituted in the response to the other.
26. Levinas might challenge the claim that I can know that I am other for you in the same way that you are other for me.
27. Young, 'Asymmetrical Reciprocity: On Moral Respect, Wonder, and Enlarged Thought,' p. 349.
28. Ibid., p. 345.

Bibliography

Writings of Emmanuel Levinas

Autrement qu'être ou au-delà de l'essence (Paris: Kluwer, 1974).

R. Bernasconi, S. Critchley, and A. Peperzak (eds), *Basic Philosophical Writings* (Bloomington: Indiana University Press, 1996).

Collected Philosophical Papers, trans. A. Lingis (Pittsburgh: Duquesne University Press, 1987).

Difficult Freedom: Essays on Judaism, trans. S. Hand (Baltimore: Johns Hopkins University Press, 1997).

'Dialogue with Emmanuel Levinas,' in R. Cohen (ed.), *Face to Face with Levinas* (Albany: SUNY, 1986) (with R. Kearney).

En découvrant l'existence avec Husserl et Heidegger (Paris: Vrin, 1949, 1967).

Entre Nous Thinking-of-the-Other, trans. M. Smith and B. Harshav (London: Continuum, 2006, New York: Columbia University Press, 1998, New York: Columbia University Press, 1991).

Ethics and Infinity: Conversations with Phillip Nemo, trans. R. E. Cohen (Pittsburgh: Duquesne University Press, 1985).

Éthique et Infini: Dialogues avec Philippe Nemo (Paris: Fayard Radio-France, 1982).

God, Death, and Time, trans. B. Bergo (Stanford: Stanford University Press, 2000).

The Levinas Reader, trans. S. Hand (Oxford: Blackwell, 1989).

Nine Talmudic Readings, trans. A. Aronowicz (Bloomington: Indiana University Press, 1994).

Of God Who Comes to Mind, trans. B. Bergo (Palo Alto: Stanford University Press, 1998)

On Escape, trans. B. Bergo (Stanford: Stanford University Press, 2003).

Otherwise Than Being or Beyond Essence, trans. A. Lingis (Dordrecht & Boston: Kluwer, 1981).

Outside the Subject (London: The Athlone Press, 1993).

'The Paradox of Morality: An Interview with Emmanuel Levinas Conducted by Tamra Wright, Peter Hughes, and Alison Ainley' in R. Bernasconi and D. Wood (ed.), *The Provocation of Levinas: Rethinking the Other* (New York: Routledge and Kegan Paul, 1988).

Proper Names, trans. M. B. Smith (Stanford: Stanford University Press, 1996).

'Reflections on the Philosophy of Hitlerism,' *Critical Inquiry* 17 (Autumn 1990) 62–71; reproduced in G. Horowitz and A. Horowitz (eds), *Difficult Justice – Commentaries on Levinas and Politics* (Toronto: Toronto University Press, 2006).

Théorie de l'intuition dans la phénoménologie de Husserl (Paris: Vrin, 1930, 1963).

Time and the Other, trans. R. A. Cohen (Pittsburgh: Duquesne University Press, 1990).

Totalité et infini: essai sur l'extériorité (Paris: Kluwer, 1961).

Totality and Infinity: An Essay on Exteriority, trans. A. Lingis (Pittsburgh: Duquesne University Press, 1968, 1969).
'The Trace of the Other' in M. C. Taylor (ed.), *Deconstruction in Context* (Chicago: Chicago University Press, 1996).

Cases and legislation

Airedale NHS Trust v. Bland (1993) 2 WLR 316 (House of Lords, hereinafter HL).
Anns v. London Borough of Merton (1978) AC 728 (HL).
Caltex Oil (Australia) Pty Ltd v. The Dredge 'Willemstad' (1976) 136 CLR (High Court of Australia, hereinafter HCA).
Chae Chan Ping v. United States (1889) 130 U.S. 581, 606 (United States Supreme Court, hereinafter US).
Cook v. Cook (1986) 162 CLR 376 (HCA).
Cruzan v. Director, Missouri Dept of Health (1990) 110 S Ct 2841 (US).
Dorset Yacht Co. Ltd v. Home Office (1970) AC 1004 (HL).
Eskimo Amber Pty Ltd v. Pyrenees Shire Council (1998) 192 C.L.R. 330 (HCA).
Gala v. Preston (1991) 172 CLR 243 (HCA).
Geyer v. Downs (1977) 138 CLR 91 (HCA).
Hall v. Hebert (1993) 101 DLR (4th) 129; 2 SCR 159 (Supreme Court of Canada).
Hargrave v. Goldman (1963) 110 CLR 40 (HCA).
Hedley, Byrne & Co. Ltd v. Heller & Partners Ltd (1964) AC 465 (HL).
Henwood v. Municipal Tramways Trust (1938) 60 CLR 438 (HCA).
Hill v. Van Erp (1997) 188 CLR 159 (HCA).
Illegal Immigrant Reform and Immigrant Responsibility Act of 1996 (1996) 8 U.S.C.A. 1252.
Illinois v. Allen (1970) 397 U.S. 337 (US).
Jackson v. Harrison (1978) 138 CLR 438 (HCA).
Jaensch v. Coffey (1984) 155 CLR 549 (HCA).
Lowns v. Wood (1996) *Australian Torts Reporter* 81–376 (NSW Court of Appeal).
Medical Practitioners Act 1938 (NSW).
Mental Capacity Act 2005 (UK).
Moy Wing Sun v. Prentis (7th Cir. 1916) 234 F.2d 24, 25–26.
Nelson v. Nelson (1995) 184 CLR 538 (HCA).
NHS Trust A v M (2001) 1 All E.R. 801 (HL).
Nishimura Ekiu v. U.S. (1892) 142 U.S. 651, 661 (US).
Perre v. Apand Pty Ltd (1999) 198 CLR 180 (HCA).
Progress and Properties v. Craft (1976) 135 CLR 651 (HCA).
Protocol Additional to the Geneva Convention of 12 August 1949 and Relating to the Protection of Victims of Non-International Armed Conflict, June 8, 1977, 1125 U.N.T.S. 609.
Protocol Additional to the Geneva Convention of 12 August 1949 and Relating to the Protection of Victims of Internal Armed Conflict, June 8, 1977, 1125 U.N.T.S. 3.
Pyrenees Shire Council v. Day (1998) 192 CLR 330 (HCA).
Re D (Adult: Medical Treatment) (1998) 1 F.L.R. 411.
Re G (Adult Incompetent: Withdrawal of Treatment) (2002) 65 B.M.L.R. 6.
Re H (a patient) (1998) 2 F.L.R. 36.
Re J (a minor) (1990) 3 All ER 930 (HL).

Riggs v. Palmer (1889) 22 NE 188 (New York Court of Appeals).
Smith v. Jenkins (1970) 119 CLR 397 (HCA).
Stevens v. Brodribb Sawmilling Co Pty Ltd (1986)160 CLR *16*.
Superintendent of Belchertown State School et al v. Joseph Saikewicz, Mass (1977) 370 N.E.2d 417.
Sutherland Shire Council v. Heyman (1985) 157 CLR 424 (HCA).
Yee Won v. White (1921) 256 U.S. 399 (US).

Secondary materials

Abensour, M., 'An-archy Between Meta-politics and Politics,' *Parallax*, 24 (July-September 2002) 5–18.
Adorno, T. W., 'Extorted Reconciliation: On Georg Lukacs' Realism in Our Time,' in *Notes to Literature I*, trans. S. W. Nicholsen (New York: Columbia University Press, 1991).
Adorno, T. W., *Minima Moralia*, trans. E. F. N. Jephcott (New York: Verso, 1974).
Agamben, G., *The Coming Community*, trans. M. Hardt (Minneapolis: University of Minnesota Press, 1993).
Agamben, G., *Homo Sacer: Sovereign Power and Bare Life*, trans. D. Heller-Roazen, (Stanford: Stanford University Press, 1998).
Alford, C., *Levinas, the Frankfurt School, and Psychoanalysis* (Middletown: Wesleyan University Press, 2003).
Angel Island Immigration Station Foundation, http://www.aiisf.org/history.
Anghie, A., *Imperialism, Sovereignty and the Making of International Law* (Cambridge: Cambridge University Press, 2005).
Annan, K., *Report of the Secretary General, 54 GAOR, 4th Plenary Meeting*, 20 September 1999, A/54/PV.4.
Arendt, H., *On Violence* (San Diego, New York, London: Harvest, 1970).
Atiyah, P., *Accidents, Compensation and the Law* 4th ed. (London: Weidenfeld and Nicholson, 1987) 63–72; P. Cane (ed.), 7th ed. (Cambridge: Cambridge University Press, 2006).
Atterton, P., 'Face to Face with the Other Animal?' in P. Atterton, M. Calarco, and M. Friedman (eds), *Levinas and Buber: Dialogue and Difference* (Pittsburgh: Duquesne University Press, 2004).
Bauman, Z., *Postmodern Ethics* (Oxford: Blackwell, 1993).
Beaulac, S., 'The Westphalian Legal Orthodoxy – Myth or Reality?' *Journal of the History of International Law*, 2 (2000) 148–177.
Benhabib, S., *Situating the Self* (New York: Routledge, 1991).
Benjamin, W., 'Critique of Violence,' in *Reflections: Essays, Aphorisms, Autobiographical Writings*, trans. E. Jephcott (New York: Schocken Books, 1986).
Bergo, B., Levinas between Ethics and Politics: For the Beauty that Adorns the Earth (Pittsburgh: Duquesne University Press, 2003).
Bergson, H., *The Creative Mind*, trans. M. L. Andison (New York: Philosophical Library, 1946).
Berman, R., 'Adorno's Politics,' in N. Gibson and A. Rubin (eds), *Adorno: A Critical Reader* (New York: Blackwell, 2003).
Bernasconi, R., 'Deconstruction and the Possibility of Ethics,' in J. Sallis (ed.), *Deconstruction and Philosophy: The Texts of Jacques Derrida* (Chicago, University of Chicago Press, 1987).

Bernasconi, R., 'The Third Party: Levinas on the Intersection of the Ethical and the Political,' *Journal of the British Society for Phenomenology*, 30 (1999) 76–87.

Bernasconi, R., 'What is the Question to Which "Substitution" is the Answer?' in S. Critchley and R. Bernasconi (eds), *The Cambridge Companion to Levinas* (Cambridge: Cambridge University Press, 2002).

Bezdek, B., 'Religious Outlaws: Narratives of Legality and the Politics of Citizen Interpretation,' *Tennessee Law Review* 62 (1995) 899–996.

Biersteker, T. and C. Weber (eds), *State Sovereignty as Social Construct* (Cambridge: Cambridge University Press, 1996).

Bilewicz, M., Kapralski, S., Kofta, M., Weigl, B. and Żbikowski, A. ' "A jak bratem, a jak katem..." [A brother or an executioner?]. Discussion about Kielce,' *Charaktery*, July 2006: 74–82.

Binder, G. and R. Weisberg, *Literary Criticisms of Law* (Princeton: Princeton University Press, 2000).

Blackshield, T., M. Coper, and G. Williams, *Oxford Companion to the High Court* (Melbourne: Oxford University Press, 2001) pp. 486–489.

Bowden, B., 'In the Name of Progress and Peace: The "Standard of Civilization" and the Universalizing Project,' *Alternatives* 29 (2004) 43–68.

Bullock, M. and M. Jennings (eds), *Walter Benjamin: Selected Writings,* vol. 1 (Cambridge: Harvard University Press, 1996).

Burggraeve, R., 'Violence and the Vulnerable Face of the Other: The Vision of Emmanuel Levinas on Moral Evil and Our Responsibility,' *Journal of Social Philosophy* 30 (1999) 29–45.

Byers M. and S. Chesterman, 'Changing the Rule about Rules: Unilateral Humanitarian Intervention and the Future of International Law,' in J. L. Holzgrefe and R. O. Koehane (eds), *Humanitarian Intervention: Ethical, Legal, and Political Dilemmas* (Cambridge: Cambridge University Press, 2003).

Calarco, M., 'Deconstruction is not Vegetarianism: Humanism, Subjectivity, and Animal Ethics,' *Continental Philosophy Review*, 36 (2004) 175–201.

Caputo, J. D., *The Prayers and Tears of Derrida: Religion without Religion* (Bloomington: Indiana University Press, 1997).

Caygill, H., *Levinas and the Political* (London, New York: Routledge, 2002).

Charlesworth, H. and C. Chinkin, *The Boundaries of International Law: A Feminist Analysis* (Manchester: Manchester University Press, 2000).

Ciaramelli, F., 'Levinas's Ethical Discourse between Individuation and Universality,' in R. Bernasconi and S. Critchley (eds), *Re-Rading Levinas* (Bloomington: Indiana University Press, 1991).

Clark, D., 'On Being "The Last Kantian in Nazi Germany": Dealing with Animals after Levinas,' in J. Ham and M. Senior (eds), *Animal Acts: Configuring the Human in Western History* (New York: Routledge, 1997).

Cohen, J., *Interrupting Auschwitz: Art, Religion, Philosophy* (New York: Continuum Press, 2003).

Cohen, R., *Ethics, Exegesis and Philosophy: Interpretation After Levinas* (Cambridge: Cambridge University Press, 2001).

Cole, R. and G. Chin, 'Emerging from the Margins of Historical Consciousness: Chinese Immigrants and the History of American Law,' *Law & History Review* 17 (1999) 325–364.

Cornell, D., *The Philosophy of the Limit* (New York: Routledge, 1992).

Cornell, D., Rosenfeld, M., and Carlson, D. G. (eds), *Deconstruction and the Possibility of Justice* (New York: Routledge, 1992).

Cover, R., 'Nomos and Narrative,' *Harvard Law Review* 97 (1983) 4–68.

Critchley, S., 'Five Problems in Levinas's View of Politics and the Sketch of a Solution to Them,' *Political Theory*, 32 (2004) 172–185.

Critchley, S., 'Introduction' in S. Critchley and R. Bernasconi (eds), *The Cambridge Companion to Levinas* (Cambridge: Cambridge University Press, 2002).

Critchley, S., *The Ethics of Deconstruction: Derrida and Levinas* (New York, Oxford: Blackwell 1992).

Crowe, J., 'Dworkin on the Value of Integrity,' *Deakin Law Review*, 12 (2007) 167–180.

Crowe, J., 'Existentialism and Natural Law,' *Adelaide Law Review*, 26 (2005) 55–72.

Crowe, J., 'Natural Law in Jurisprudence and Politics,' *Oxford Journal of Legal Studies*, 27 (2007) 775–794.

Crowley, M., 'Border War,' *New Republic Online*, 24 March 2005, http://www.tnr.com/doc.mhtml?i=20050328&s=crowley032805.

Daniel, J., *Żyd w zielonym kapeluszu* [The Jew in a green hat] (Kielce: Scriptum, 1996).

de Ville, J., 'Levinas on Law: A Derridean Reading of Manderson's Proximity, Levinas, and the Soul of Law,' *Griffith Law Review* 16 (2007) 225–247.

de Vries, H., *Minimal Theologies: Critiques of Secular Reason in Adorno and Levinas*, trans. G. Hale (Baltimore: Johns Hopkins University Press, 2005).

Deleuze, G., *Difference and Repetition*, trans. P. Patton (New York: Columbia University Press, 1994).

Derrida, J. *Acts of Literature*, D. Attridge (ed.) (New York: Routledge, 1992).

Derrida, J., 'Force of Law: The "Mystical Foundation of Authority,"' trans. M. Quaintance, in Cardozo Law Review 11 (1990) 920–1045; and in D. Cornell, M. Rosenfeld and D. G. Carlson (eds), *Deconstruction and the Possibility of Justice* (New York: Routledge, 1992).

Derrida, J., 'Bois,' in S. Critchley, *The Ethics of Deconstruction* (Oxford: Blackwell, 1999).

Derrida, J., *Adieu to Emmanuel Levinas*, trans. M. Naas and P. Brault (Stanford University Press, 1999).

Derrida, J., *Politics of Friendship*, trans. G. Collins (New York: Verso, 1997).

Derrida, J., *The Gift of Death*, trans. D. Wills (Chicago: University of Chicago Press, 1995).

Diamantides, M., 'Ethics in Law: Death Marks on a Still Life,' *Law and Critique* 6 (1995) 209–228.

Diamantides, M., *The Ethics of Suffering* (Aldershot: Ashgate, 2000).

Duncan, D. M., *The Pre-Text of Ethics: On Derrida and Levinas* (New York: Peter Lang, 2001).

Dworkin, R., *Taking Rights Seriously* (London: Duckworth, 1978).

Dworkin, R., *Law's Empire* (London: Fontana, 1986).

Elias, T. O., *Africa and the Development of International Law*, 2nd ed., rev. R. Akinjide (Boston: Martinus Nijhoff, 1988).

Elshtain, J., 'Sovereign God, Sovereign State, Sovereign Self,' *Notre Dame Law Review* 66 (1991) 1355–1378.

Fauchille, P., *Traité de droit international public* (Paris: Rousseau, 1922).

Finnis, J., *Natural Law and Natural Rights* (Oxford: Clarendon Press, 1980).

Finnis, J. M. 'Bland: Crossing the Rubicon,' *Law Quarterly Review*, 109 (1993) 329–337.
Fitzpatrick, P., 'Death as the Horizon of Law' in D. Manderson (ed.), *Courting Death* (London: Pluto Press, 1999).
Foucault, M., *Discipline and Punish: The Birth of the Prison*, trans. A. Sheridan (New York: Vintage Books, 1979).
Foucault, M., *Power/Knowledge: Selected Interviews and Other Writings, 1972–1997*, C. Gordon (ed.) (New York: Pantheon, 1980).
Foucault, M., *Society Must Be Defended* (New York: Picador, 2003).
Fraser, N., *Justice Interruptus: Critical Reflections on the Post-Socialist Condition* (New York: Routledge, 1996).
Fuller, L. L., 'Positivism and Fidelity to Law: A Reply to Professor Hart,' *Harvard Law Review* 71 (1958) 630–672.
Gallop, J., *Reading Lacan* (Ithaca, NY: Cornell University Press, 1985).
Gibbs, R., 'The Other Comes to Teach Me: A Review of Recent Levinas Publications,' *Man and World* 24 (1991) 219–233.
Goodrich, P., *Reading the Law: A Critical Introduction to Legal Method and Techniques* (Oxford and Cambridge, MA: Basil Blackwell, 1986).
Gordon, R., 'Critical Legal Histories,' *Stanford Law Review* 36 (1984) 57–125.
Gross, J. T., *Neighbors: The Destruction of the Jewish Community in Jedwabne, Poland* (Princeton: Princeton University Press, 2001).
Gross, J. T., *Fear: Anti-Semitism in Poland After Auschwitz* (New York: Random House, 2006).
Gunning, I., 'Expanding the International Definition of Refugee: A Multicultural View,' *Fordham International Law Journal* 13 (1989–1990) 35–85.
Gunning, I., 'Modernizing Customary International Law: The Challenge of Human Rights,' *Vanderbilt Journal of International Law* 31 (1991) 211.
Haberfield, L., 'Lowns *v.* Woods and the Duty to Rescue,' *Tort Law Review* 6 (1998) 56–80.
Habermas, J., 'The New Obscurities: The Crisis of the Welfare State and the Exhaustion of Utopian Energies,' *Philosophy and Social Criticism*, 11 (1986) 1–18.
Hall, W., A *Treatise on International Law* (Oxford: Clarendon, 1909).
Hammer, E., *Adorno and the Political* (New York: Routledge, 2005).
Hammer, E., 'God Squaddy,' *Radical Philosophy*, 134 (2005).
Hand, S. (ed.), *The Levinas Reader* (London: Basil Blackwell, 1989).
Hart, H. L. A., *Essays on Bentham: Studies in Jurisprudence and Political Theory* (Oxford: Clarendon Press, 1982).
Hart, H. L. A., 'Kelsen Visited,' *UCLA Law Review* 10 (1963) 709–728.
Hart, H. L. A., 'Positivism and the Separation of Law and Morals,' *Harvard Law Review* 71 (1957–1958) 593–629.
Hart, H. L. A., *The Concept of Law*, 2nd ed. (Oxford: Oxford University Press, 1994).
Hass, P., 'Forgiveness, Reconciliation and the Jewish Memory,' in D. Patterson and J. K. Roth (eds), *After-words: Post-Holocaust Struggles with Forgiveness, Reconciliation, Justice* (Seattle: University of Washington Press, 2004).
Hatley, J. , *Suffering Witness: The Quandary of Responsibility After the Irreparable* (Albany: SUNY Press, 2000).
Herzog A., 'Is Liberalism "All We Need"?: Levinas' Politics of the Surplus,' in *Political Theory* 30 (2002) 204–227.

Higgins, R., *Problems & Process: International Law and How We Use It* (Oxford: Clarendon, 1994).

Honneth, A., *The Struggle for Recognition: The Moral Grammar of Social Conflicts,* trans. J. Anderson (Cambridge: MIT Press, 1996).

Honneth, J., 'The Other of Justice: Habermas and the Ethical Challenge of Postmodernism,' trans. J. Farrell, in S. K. White (ed.), *The Cambridge Companion to Habermas* (New York: Cambridge University Press, 1995).

Honoré, T., 'Are Omissions Less Culpable?' in T. Honoré (ed.) *Responsibility and Fault* (Oxford: Portland, 1999).

Horkheimer, M. and T. W. Adorno, *Dialectic of Enlightenment,* trans. J. Cumming (New York: Continuum, 1972).

Horowitz, A., '"By a Hair's Breadth": Critique, Transcendence, and the Ethical in Adorno and Levinas,' *Philosophy and Social Criticism* 28 (2002) 213–248.

Horowitz, A. and G. Horowitz (eds), *Difficult Justice – Commentaries on Levinas and Politics* (Toronto: Toronto University Press, 2006).

Husserl, E., *Analyses Concerning Passive and Active Synthesis,* trans. A. J. Steinbock (Dordrecht: Kluwer, 2001).

Husserl, E., *Cartesian Meditations,* trans. D. Cairns (The Hague: Martinus Nijhoff, 1960).

Hutchinson, A. *Critical Legal Studies* (Lanham: Rowman and Littlefield, 1989).

Jackson, F., 'Epiphenomenal Qualia,' *American Philosophical Quarterly* 32 (1982) 127–136.

Jager, L., *Adorno: A Political Biography,* trans. S. Spencer (New Haven: Yale University Press, 2004).

James, A., 'The Practice of Sovereign Statehood in Contemporary International Society,' *Political Studies* XL:VII (1999) 457–473.

Jennings, R. and A. Watts, *Oppenheim's International Law* 9th ed. (London: Longmans, 1993).

Jochnick, C. af and R. Normand, 'The Legitimation of Violence,' *Harvard International Law Journal* 35 (1994) 49–95.

Jodoin, S., 'Terrorism as a War Crime,' *International Criminal Law Review* 7 (2007) 77–115.

Kamiński, Ł. and J. Żaryn (eds), *Wokół pogromu kieleckiego* [Around the Kielce Pogrom] (Warszawa: Instytut Pamięci Narodowej, 2006).

Kelman, M., *A Guide to Critical Legal Studies* (Cambridge, Mass: Harvard University Press, 1987).

Kelsen, H., *General Theory of Law and State,* trans. A. Wedberg (New York: Russell and Russell, 1961).

Kelsen, H., *General Theory of Norms,* trans. M. Hartney (Oxford: Clarendon Press, 1991).

Kennedy, D., 'The Structure of Blackstone's Commentaries,' *Buffalo Law Review* 28 (1978) 205–382.

Kennedy, D. and K. E. Klare, 'A Bibliography of Critical Legal Studies' *Yale Law Journal* 94 (1984) 461–490.

Kierkegaard, S., *Fear and Trembling,* trans. H. V. Hong and E. V. Hong (Princeton: Princeton University Press, 1985).

Kofman, S., *Smothered Words,* trans. M. Dobie (Evanston, Illinois: Northwestern University Press, 1998).

Korsgaard, C., *The Sources of Normativity* (Cambridge: Cambridge University Press, 1996).

Koskenniemi, M., *From Apology to Utopia* (Cambridge: Cambridge University Press, 2006).

Kostal, R., 'Currents in the Counter-Reformation,' *Tort Law Review* 3 (1995) 100.

Krahl, H., 'The Political Contradictions in Adorno's Critical Theory,' in J. M. Bernstein (ed.), *The Frankfurt School: Critical Assessments*, vol. 4 (New York: Routledge, 1994).

Kramer, A., 'Proximity as Principles: Directness, Community Norms and the Tort of Negligence,' *Tort Law Review* 11 (2003) 70–103.

Large, W., *Emmanuel Levinas and Maurice Blanchot. Ethics and Ambiguity of Writing* (Manchester: Clinamen Press, 2005).

Lingis, A., 'Translator's Introduction' in E. Levinas, *Otherwise Than Being, or Beyond Essence*, trans. A Lingis (Pittsburgh: Duquesne University Press, 1981).

Llewellyn, K., *Jurisprudence: Realism in Theory and Practice* (Chicago: University of Chicago Press, 1962).

Llewelyn, J., 'Am I Obsessed by Bobby? (Humanism of the Other Animal),' in R. Bernasconi and S. Critchley (eds), *Re-Reading Levinas* (Bloomington: Indiana University Press, 1989).

Lochhead, C., 'Immigration Deal Already Appears to be Unraveling: Immigration Bill Has Something for All to Oppose,' *San Francisco Chronicle* (May 22, 2007).

Lo Monaco, C., 'Child, Hundreds of Photos Lead Pair to Dead Daughter,' *Tucson Citizen* (Friday, 29 July 2005).

Łoziński, W., *Świadkowie* [Witnesses], documentary film, *Polska Szkoła Dokumentu* 'Videonowa,' 26 min., 1987.

Lukács, G., *The Theory of the Novel*, trans. A. Bostock (Cambridge, MA: MIT Press, 1974).

Mackie, J. L., *Ethics: Inventing Right and Wrong* (Middlesex: Penguin, 1977).

Malanczuk, P., *Akehurst's Modern Introduction to International Law* (London: Routledge, 1997).

Manderson, D., *Proximity, Levinas and the Soul of Law* (Montreal, Kingston: McGill Queen's University Press, 2006).

McHugh, M., 'Neighbourhood, Proximity and Reliance,' in P. Finn (ed.), *Essays on Torts* (Sydney: Law Book, 1989).

Mertus, J., 'Considering Non-state Actors in the New Millennium: Toward Expanded Participation in Norm Generation and Norm Application,' *NYU Journal of International Law & Politics* 32 (2000) 537–566.

Michlic, J. B., *Poland's Threatening Other: The Image of the Jew from 1880 to the Present* (Lincoln: University of Nebraska Press, 2006).

Moore, J., 'From Nation State to Failed State: International Protection from Human Rights Abuses by Non-state Actors,' *Columbia Human Rights Law Review* 31 (1999) 81–121.

Natale, *v.* 'Angel Island: "Guardian of the Western Gate,"' *Modern American Poetry*, http://www.english.uiuc.edu/maps/poets/a_f/angel.natale.htm.

No More Deaths 2005 Year End Report, http://www.nomoredeaths.org/Endof SummerReport 2005.html.

Noortmann, M., 'Non-State Actors in International Law' in B. Arts, M. Noortmann and B. Reinalda (eds), *Non-State Actors in International Relations* (Aldershot: Ashgate, 2001).

Oladosu, A., 'H. L. A. Hart on Legal Obligation,' *Ratio Juris* 4 (1991) 152–176.
Oppenheim, L., *International Law* (London: Longmans, 1905).
Otto, D., 'Subalternity and International Law: The Problems of Global Community and the Incommensurability of Difference,' *Social & Legal Studies* 5 (1996) 337–364.
Peperzak, A., 'Illeity According to Levinas,' *Philosophy Today* 42 (suppl) (1998) 41–46.
'Photographer Recounts Crossing U.S. Border with Mexican Illegal Immigrants,' *National Geographic Adventure*, 23 January 2003.
Poirié, F., *Emmanuel Levinas: Qui êtes-vous?* (Lyon, France: La Manufacture, 1987).
Price, P., 'Alien Land Restrictions in the American Common Law: Exploring the Relative Autonomy Paradigm,' *American Journal of Legal History* 43 (1999) 152–208.
Rajagopal, B., *International Law from Below: Development, Social Movements and Third World Resistance* (Cambridge: Cambridge University Press, 2003).
Raz, J., 'Hart on Moral Rights and Legal Duties,' *Oxford Journal of Legal Studies* 4 (1984) 123–131.
Raz, J., 'Incorporation by Law,' *Legal Theory* 10 (2004) 1–17.
Raz, J., *Practical Reason and Norms* (Oxford: Oxford University Press, 1999).
Raz, J., *The Authority of Law* (Oxford: Clarendon Press, 1979).
Robbins, J. (ed.), *Is It Righteous to Be? Interviews with Emmanuel Levinas* (Palo Alto: Stanford University Press, 2001).
Robbins, J., 'Aesthetic Totality and Ethical Infinity', *Créateur* 35, 3 (1995) pp. 66–79.
Roberts, S., 'Rethinking Justice: Levinas and Assymetrical Responsibility,' *Philosophy & the Contemporary World* 7 (2000) 5–12.
Röling, B. V. A., *International Law in an Expanded World* (Amsterdam: Djambatan, 1960).
Roth, B., 'The Enduring Significance of State Sovereignty,' *Florida Law Review* 56 (2004) 1017–1050, 1019.
Rubinton, D., 'Towards a Recognition of the Rights of Non-States in International Environmental Law,' *Pace Environmental Law Review* 9 (1992) 475–494.
Ruggie, J., 'Territoriality and Beyond: Problematizing Modernity in International Relations,' *International Organization* 47:1 (1993) 139–174.
Saturno, L. Borderland Photos, http://www.jmc.kent.edu/kpa/stories3/ls_borderland/content/borderland_14_large.htm.
Schmitt, C., *The Concept of the Political*, trans. G. Schwab (Chicago: University of Chicago Press, [1927] 1996).
Schmitt, C., *Political Theology: Four Chapters on the Concept of Sovereignty*, trans. G. Schwab (Cambridge: MIT Press, [1922] 1985).
Shapo, M., *The Duty to Act* (Dallas: University of Texas Press, 1978).
Simmons, W. P., 'The Third: Levinas' Theoretical Move from An-archical Ethics to the Realm of Justice and Politics,' *Philosophy and Social Criticism* 25 (1999) 83–104.
Simpson, G., *Great Powers and Outlaw States* (Cambridge: Cambridge University Press, 2004).
Simpson, G., 'The Guises of Sovereignty,' paper presented at SAID workshop, London: January 2006.

Simpson, G., 'Piracy and the Origins of Enmity' in M. Craven, M. Fitzmaurice, and M. Vogiatzi (eds), *Time, History and International Law* (Leiden: Martinus Nijhoff Publishers, 2006).

Sims, J., 'Absolute Adversity: Schmitt, Levinas, and the Exceptionality of Killing' *Philosophy and Social Criticism* 31 (2005) 223–252.

Singer, P., *Causing Death and Saving Lives* (London: Penguin, 1990).

Singer, P., *Rethinking Life and Death – The Collapse of Our Traditional Ethics* (Oxford: Oxford University Press, 1995).

Smith, N., 'Adorno vs. Levinas: Evaluating Points of Contention,' *Continental Philosophy Review* 40 (2007) 3.

Smith, N., 'Incommensurability and Alterity in Contemporary Jurisprudence,' *Buffalo Law Review* 45 (1997) 503–553.

Smith, N., 'Making Adorno's Ethics and Politics Explicit,' *Social Theory and Practice* 29 (2003) 487–498.

Snyder, F., 'Sharing Sovereignty: Non State Associations and the Limits of State Power,' *American University Law Review* 54 (2004) 365–399.

Spruyt, H., *The Sovereign State and its Competitors* (Princeton: Princeton University Press, 1994).

Stauffer, J., 'The Rule of Law and its Shadow: Ambivalence, Procedure, and the Justice Beyond Legality,' *Journal of Law, Culture and the Humanities* 3 (2007) 225–243.

Sturgess, G., 'Murphy and the Media' and T. Blackshield, 'The "Murphy Affair" ' in J. A. Scutt (ed.), *Lionel Murphy: A Radical Judge* (Melbourne: Macmillan Australia, 1987).

Taylor, C., 'A Modest Proposal: Statehood and Sovereignty in a Global Age,' *University of Pennsylvania Journal of International Economic Law* 18 (1997) 745–809.

Tushnet, M., 'An Essay on Rights,' *Texas Law Review* 62 (1984) 1363–1403.

Vines, P., 'Fault, Responsibility and Negligence in the High Court of Australia,' *Tort Law Review* 8 (2000) 130–145.

Vines, P., 'The Needle in the Haystack: Principle in the Duty of Care in Negligence,' *University of New South Wales Law Journal* 23 (2000) 35–57.

Viorst, M., 'The Colonel in His Labyrinth,' *Foreign Affairs* 78 (1999) 60–75.

Visker, R., 'Is Ethics Fundamental? Questioning Levinas on Irresponsibility,' *Continental Philosophy Review* 36 (2003) 263–302.

Walker, T., A *History of the Law of Nations* (Cambridge: Cambridge University Press, 1899).

Walker, T., A *Manual of Public International Law* (Cambridge: Cambridge Universtiy Press, 1895).

Weinrib, E., 'The Case for a Duty to Rescue,' *Yale Law Journal* 90 (1980) 247–293.

Wolcher, L., 'The Tragic Foundation of Human Rights,' *Wisconsin International Law Journal* 24 (2006) 523–556.

Wyschogrod, E., 'Doing Before Hearing: On the Primacy of Touch,' in F. Laruelle (ed.), *Textes pour Emmanuel Levinas* (Paris: Éditions Jean-Michel Place, 1980).

Yee Won v. White, 256 U.S. (1921) 399–400, 402.

Yeo, S. 'Rethinking Proximity: A Paper Tiger?,' *Tort Law Review* 5 (1997) 174.

Young, I. M., 'Asymmetrical Reciprocity: On Moral Respect, Wonder and Enlarged Thought,' *Constellations: An International Journal of Critical and Democratic Theory* 3 (1997) 340–363.

Young, I. M., 'The Ideal of Community and the Politics of Difference,' *Social Theory and Practice* 12 (1986) 1–25.

Zuidervaart, L., *Social Philosophy After Adorno* (New York: Cambridge University Press, 2007).

Index